THERE IS NOTHING BUT

MIND AND

EXPERIENCES

R. Craig Hogan, PhD

Greater Reality Publications
http://greaterreality.com

Contents

Contents

Contents

Contents

Contents

The Four Books

This book is one of four in a series explaining what we know today about the nature of reality, our purpose in this life, and what happens when we leave this life. The books contain explanations of these six important truths:

1. Your Mind is not produced by or contained in your brain. Your Mind doesn't need a body or a brain.

2. Your Mind is an individual manifestation of the Universal Intelligence all people are part of—we are all one Mind.

3. Our one Universal Intelligence creates the world we live in.

4. Our individual Minds continue to live after the body ceases to function.

5. There is nothing but Mind and experiences. We experience the world, but the world does not exist outside of our Minds and experiences.

6. We have a purpose in Earth School and can live in love, joy, and peace while we fulfill our purpose.

The first four truths are explained in the book *Your Eternal Self: Science Discovers the Afterlife*, developed and updated from the book *Your Eternal Self*. This contains the evidence that your mind is not in your brain, we are one mind, and you continue to live after the body dies.

The second book, *Earth School: Answers and Evidence*, explains what happens to a person through the major stages of life: deciding to enter Earth School; learning to succeed in Earth School; growing in love, compassion, and understanding; graduating; and living in the life after the Earth School life.

The third book, *There Is Nothing but Mind and Experiences,* explains that the Universal Intelligence is the basis of reality and we are individual manifestations of it. In it you will learn why we know this is true and what it means for your life in Earth School.

The last book, *Earth School: Love, Learn, and Be Happy,* is an easy-to-read summary of the contents of the other three books, meant for people who want the perspectives but not the detailed explanations and evidence.

Preface

We are not human beings having a spiritual experience.
We are spiritual beings having a human experience.
~ Teilhard de Chardin

Anthropologists tell us a creature that could be called human has lived on Earth for 200,000 years. So why are we just today coming to know we are much more than soft rocks that evolved by accident in a meaningless universe? One reason is that we have developed knowledge through the sciences that tells us more about ourselves and life on Earth than we ever knew before. The amount of knowledge we have about all things doubled every century until 1900. Today our knowledge is doubling every 13 months. IBM estimates that soon knowledge will double every 12 hours.[1]

Another reason we are just now learning these truths is that communication has made it possible for people to describe experiences and breakthroughs in knowledge widely and quickly. We are sharing insights, findings from science, and reports about our personal experiences instantaneously. Before the communication revolution, knowledge could be shared locally among only a handful of people at a time. It took more than a week for news of Lincoln's assassination to reach Great Britain. In 1963, the whole world watched the assassination of John F. Kennedy as it unfolded.

The Internet has revolutionized humankind's ability to share knowledge and discoveries. A 2016 United Nations report estimated that 81 percent of the population in developed countries used the Internet.[2] In 2019, 87 percent of the U.S. adult population used the Internet.[3] The National Science Foundation predicts that 5 billion people will have access to the Internet in 2020.[4]

Humankind's knowledge of the universe and our place in it is expanding exponentially. The knowledge is being shared among people instantaneously around the world. New insights and discoveries are emerging continually. Discoveries about this life and the other planes of life are being made by ordinary people having extraordinary experiences and sharing them as they never could before the communication revolution.

As a result, we have learned vast amounts from a wide variety of sources about the nature of this life and what happens to people when they go on to the next life. We now know the truth. We are eternal beings having a temporary experience in Earth School; we will live on, happy and healthy, after we stop using the body. We are evolving to live lives in love, peace, and joy by abandoning the fear, unhappiness, discord, and hostility that have gripped our world. People are learning the truth, and the truth is setting us free.

A great teacher, Yeshua bar Yosef (Jesus), is reported in two sources to have said humankind can live in the heaven of love, peace, and joy among all people now if we can only realize we have the capability:

> The kingdom of God is not coming with things that can be observed; nor will they say, "Look, here it is!" or "There it is!" For in fact, the kingdom of God is among you. (Luke 12:20-21, NIV)

And the Gospel of Thomas has the same message:

> The kingdom of the father is spread out upon the earth, and people do not see it. (Gospel of Thomas, saying 113)

We must see it. We now have the knowledge about reality that can lead people to live together in love, peace, and joy. We can live in heaven on earth.

Love, peace, and joy,
Craig

Links to the Earth School Answers website

Additional readings and links containing valuable information about the subjects of the chapters are at www.earthschoolanswers.com.

Information about the Afterlife Research and Education Institute, Inc. (AREI)

Information about the Afterlife Research and Education Institute, Inc., is at www.afterlifeinstitute.org.

1

You Must Change Your Perspective

We are accustomed to phrases that show we've changed our Mind: "I thought better of it," "I came to realize," "It dawned on me," "I figured out," "I made up my Mind," "I used to think," "I came to believe." All these phrases mean the person has weighed the knowledge, beliefs, and assumptions in his or her Mind and has come to a perspective that feels OK. The person can say "Of course that's true" to it. When knowledge changes, the person shifts the balance to a new perspective. However, all the knowledge, beliefs, and assumptions are entirely in the person's Mind, not in other people or the world. The person is changing his or her reality.

This is an example. Look at this image.[5] Do you see the young woman and the old woman?

To see the young woman, you must shift your Mind into "young-woman" mode. Her nose is the little bump to the left and she is facing away from you and looking left. To see the old woman, you must shift your Mind into the "old-woman" mode. Her mouth is the almost horizontal line above the border of the dress at the neck. Stare at the mouth line and you will see the old woman. What was the young woman's nose is a wart on the old woman's nose. It will be even easier to see one or the other if you cover up the old woman's mouth with your finger to see the young woman, or cover the little bump and eyelashes that are on the young woman's face and stare at the mouth to see the old woman.

Researchers in Australia studied 393 participants, ages 18 to 68. Subjects were shown the image for half a second, then were asked the gender and age of the figure they saw first. Older subjects saw the older woman first. Younger subjects saw the young woman first.[6] All saw the same image. They saw it differently at first look.

You will be able to shift your perception with ease once you realize each of the two images. However, your Mind is not able to see both at once; you must choose one. You impose a whole picture on the drawing: either a young woman or an old woman. You give the image meaning and organization that is not in the blobs of ink on the page. That's happening entirely in your Mind, not in the image. The image doesn't change. When you settle on one perspective, you cannot see the other perspective at the same time.

What you will learn in this book will give you a new perspective. The archaic perspective that the universe is made of matter and energy independent of us, that our Minds are in our brains, and that when the brain dies we die is a primitive misconception, just as the view that the earth is the center of the universe is archaic and untrue. In these books, you will learn that your Mind will never cease to exist and that the Universal Intelligence our Minds are part of is continually creating what we experience as matter and energy, including our bodies and brains.

You will find yourself going back and forth in your perspective. You can't help it. In these books, you'll learn that the universe is created by the Universal Intelligence, but then you'll watch videos of materialist scientists describing a universe comprising stars, galaxies, black holes, dark energy, and dark matter that they assert will eventually be destroyed by either dissipating its energy or being squeezed into a point smaller than a pinhead in a fiery crunch. You'll question the perspectives you have learned from this book. Both perspectives can't be true.

In these books, you will learn that your Mind is not in your brain, doesn't need a brain, and can do remarkable things the brain could never do, even if it were the originator of the Mind. But then you'll hear neuroscientists asserting that they're only a few years away from understanding where the Mind is in the brain, how the brain creates the Mind, and where memories are stored in the brain. Both can't be true. Either the brain creates the Mind or the Mind creates the brain. You'll find your perspective shifting back and forth. When the materialist assertions shift your perspective, you must make a conscious effort to shift it back to reality by reviewing the evidence, just as you must shift between seeing the old woman or young woman.

When you reexamine the evidence, you will always shift back to knowing these truths: There is nothing but Mind and experiences, and you never die.

2

There Is Nothing but Mind and Experiences

You may have heard it said that the world is an illusion, but that is not true. We have real experiences—sunsets, lakes, mountains, people, the smell of a rose, a melodic birdsong, the taste of chocolate, and puppies. The world is real. But the basis of our reality is not what we have been taught it is. At the basis of this reality there is only Mind.

This chapter explains what that means and why we know it's true.

What saying "There is only Mind" means

Matter and energy do not create Mind. Mind creates matter and energy. When your Mind experiences a sight, sound, touch, taste, or smell, the experiences are coming from the Universal Intelligence we are all part of. There is no objective reality outside of your Mind that you perceive from energy entering tiny orifices in a material body.

When you look at this book, where are you having the experience of a book? Is the book somehow entering you and merging with a body or a brain? No. But you're having the experience of a book. When you look at the book, the experience of a book is entirely in your

Mind. When you close your eyes and recall the image of the book, you have the sight experience of the book in your Mind. Both the sight experience you have with your eyes open and the sight experience you have with your eyes closed are sight experiences entirely in your Mind. If you repeatedly look at the book, then close your eyes and recall the book, you will see that the experience of the book never happens outside of your Mind. The experiences of the book and memory of the book are both only in your Mind.

This is another way to realize the experiences are only in your Mind. Recall the room you lived in during your childhood. You are reexperiencing the experiences you had in your childhood. But the experiences you recall aren't your room; they are your experiences of your room. If two friends were with you experiencing your room at the same time, the three of you would each have had unique experiences of the room that were not the same. Your experiences would depend on your personal perspectives, needs, and preferences. You would experience a room you live in with a picture of your dog. Friend 1 might experience the interesting posters on your wall because of her interest in posters. Friend 2 might experience the antique dresser and lighting fixture because of his interest in antiques. Each is having a unique experience of the room in his or her Mind. None is experiencing the room in all its detail, like a photograph.

Today, when you and your two friends recall your room, you may have the image of your room with all the functional and decorative things you added, such as a photograph of your dog. Friend 1 would remember the posters, but not the antique dresser, light fixtures, or picture of your dog. Friend 2 would remember the antique dresser and light fixtures, but not the posters or picture of your dog. You each are re-experiencing your experience of the room, not the room. It's like there are three rooms. None of you has a photo-like image of the room in your mind. You each had an experience of your room, and you each recall the unique experience you had. We apprehend and remember only the experiences our Minds have.

It's like we're having a dream. When we dream, we experience different people, scenery, and events. We also create ourselves in the dream. The dream seems real. We act in it as though it were real. But the dream is just our Minds creating experiences. If I see a red chair in my dream, there is no chair there. There is only the experience of a red chair in my Mind. But I have the feeling in the dream that there really is a red chair outside of me. I might walk to it and touch it. I might sit on it and move it. I might invite other characters in my dream to sit on it. It's only the experience of a red chair. There's no red chair there, but I feel it fully. The experiences exist without objects we sense outside of us.

Later, when I remember my dream, I remember a red chair and one of my characters sitting in the red chair. But it's just like remembering your room. The red chair and characters from your dream are entirely in your mind in the same way the image of your room is entirely in your mind. There is nothing but your Mind and your experiences.

Now imagine the characters in my dream are two friends in Earth School having the same dream. We're still individuals, but experiencing the same dream. Our individual Minds see a red chair, walk to the chair, and sit in the chair because each of us is having the experience of a chair, but the experiences are only in our individual Minds. We're having individual dreams of things that are not "out there." There's no physical chair there outside of us. Friend 1 sees a chair, but it's a chair in her Mind. Friend 2 sees a chair, but it's a chair in her Mind. That's what our life in Earth School is like. Since we're all in the same Earth School dream now, the Universal Intelligence gives the experiences to each of us. We feel we're having the same experience because we all are experiencing the same dream together, but each of us is being given the experiences of Earth School. There is no Earth School outside of us.

When the three of us awaken, we each describe generally the same experience, with a red chair. But each of us has different details, depending on what was most important or relevant to each of us. One remembers the red chair with upholstery tacks holding down the fabric. The second remembers the Eastlake antique back, but nothing about the upholstery tacks. I remember sitting in the chair and feeling how comfortable it was, but nothing about the upholstery tacks or the antique back. We were all accessing the same scenery and the same chair, but in our individual Minds. We experienced only our individual experiences of the scene and chair. There was no chair in the dream, and we each had only the unique experience of the chair, not a photo in our Minds.

These experiences the Universal Intelligence makes available to us are our own repertoires of experiences. Three people standing in the room you grew up in and three people in the dream I shared had six sets of experiences. Those experiences became what we call memories. The memory experiences became part of our repertoire of experiences. However, our repertoire is unique to each of us. Ten people standing in the room you grew up in would have come away with ten unique sets of memory experiences. Each of our lives comprises a unique repertoire of experiences.

However, the Universal Intelligence contains all the characteristics of the room, from the wall treatments right down to the plaster that made up the walls, with all the sights, sounds, smells, and textures someone might experience in that room. From all those characteristics, we experience the small set of characteristics that had the most meaning, relevance, or importance to us at the moment we stood in the room. The selection of experiences is determined by what cognitive psychologist Donald Hoffman calls "fitness" to our lives:

> Snakes and trains, like the particles of physics, have no objective, observer-independent features. The snake I see is a description created by my sensory system to inform me of the fitness consequences of my actions. Evolution shapes acceptable solutions, not optimal ones. A snake is an acceptable solution to the problem of telling me how to act in a situation. My snakes and trains are my mental representations; your snakes and trains are your mental representations.[7]

You can view a video of Donald Hoffman explaining his view of the universe of consciousness at www.earthschoolanswers.com/hoffman/.

Those few unique experience details in the room are what we have selected because they are important or relevant to us at that moment—they have "fitness" for us. They then became the memory experience of the room we will re-experience later as a memory. But the memory is not the memory of a room; it is the memory of our experience of the room.

In this Earth School realm, we are experiencing individually as part of the same dream. When we make a change, the change becomes part of the shared realm that is available from the Universal Intelligence. If I replace the red chair with a blue chair, Lisa, who has never been in the room, will see a blue chair when she comes in tomorrow. However, I created that experience of the blue chair, its position in the room, its composition, and all the other characteristics of the chair. Lisa will have experiences of a blue chair because the Universal Intelligence has the new experience in our shared reality. The Universal Intelligence contains all the characteristics of a blue chair, even those no one who comes into the room is aware of. Lisa may notice the turned legs of the chair but miss entirely that it has a cane bottom. Her experience, the one she remembers, will be of a chair with turned legs.

You might be wondering, "If everyone has the opportunity to choose experiences of the blue chair from the same set of hundreds of characteristics, doesn't that mean there's a blue chair in existence outside of us somewhere?" The answer is that the components of the blue chair are all part of what have become accessible experiences with the blue chair over years of people's experiences. The experiences of the person who designed the red chair are in the Universal Intelligence, along with the experiences of the person who cut the wood, the person who glued the pieces, the person who attached the fabric, and all the people who were involved with getting the chair into the room. No experience is ever lost. All make up the total accessible experiences of the chair in the Universal Intelligence, even though each of those people had different sets of experiences they then carried in their repertoires of experiences with the chair.

Now when someone sees the chair, the totality of experiences with that chair are accessible. However, since the person looking at it is choosing her own unique experiences within her sphere of interests or fitness for her life, only those relevant to her become part of her experience and memory of the chair.

Psychics and people gifted in psychometry can retrieve the experiences of other people who have been associated with the chair. "Psychometry" is the ability to hold an object and know psychically about the people associated with it. All the experiences of all the people who ever had anything to do with the chair are accessible experiences of the chair. Those experiences are all in the Universal Intelligence.

This Earth School was created in the minds of countless people before us. The chair, the room, the building, the landscaping, and everything else associated with the room and building are experiences created by people in Earth Schools before us. Each change they made changed the experiences accessible in the Universal Intelligence. We are living in the experiences others have created, and we are changing the experiences for all others who are or will be in Earth School. We are creating new experiences. We are creating reality.

Some of what we're experiencing in Earth School is scenery provided by the Universal Intelligence. Sunsets, kittens, volcanos, oceans, snow, and all the other scenery are backdrops for our activities on Earth. But everything people have had a hand in creating has resulted in the reality we're experiencing now within the scenery given to us. If any experiences made by humans in this reality are violent, harsh, or cruel, it's because people created the experiences that way. No god created them independent of people. And if experiences continue to be violent, harsh, and cruel, it's because we are continuing to maintain and perpetuate those negative experiences.

If any experience made by people in this reality is kind, loving, and compassionate, it's because people created the experience that way. And when we are creating the experiences of being kind, loving, and compassionate, we are adding kindness, love, and compassion to the world's experiences. We are creating a kind, loving, compassionate world.

Now the question is, if my friends and I had experiences only in our Minds, and there is no room outside of us that we're experiencing, why do we believe there is a world outside of our Minds?

Why do we believe there is a world outside of our Minds?

We're influenced to believe from infancy, through experiences, teaching, and modelling, that there is a world outside of us that generates the experiences we have in our Minds. However, that is not true. There is only Mind and experiences.

Deepak Chopra, MD, founder of the Chopra Center for Wellbeing, describes the fact that we have been taught to give labels to things as though there were something outside of us; but there is nothing outside of us.

> Consciousness, defined as awareness, is ultimate reality. It's truth with a capital "T." Now, scientists give labels to their experiences: electromagnetism, gravity, strong and weak interactions. Some of them are perceptual experiences. Gravity is a perceptual experience. . . . Electromagnetism is a word to describe certain behaviors. So everything that we call the four forces of nature, all mental, mathematical activities in consciousness, they are words we have created, and now we hold these words to represent fundamental truth. But all they are is perceptual and conceptual experiences in consciousness. There's no reality to any of that. Okay, that's what science does. It creates a language; it creates a description of a conceptual or perceptual experience. It says this is what reality is. Reality is none of that. What's a particle? It's a space-time event in consciousness. It's a happening in consciousness. There's nothing outside of consciousness.[8]

View a video of Robert Lawrence Kuhn interviewing Deepak Chopra about consciousness and the nature of reality at www.earthschoolanswers.com/chopra/.

People learn to believe there is a world outside of us for four reasons:

- We have the experience of space.

- When we have different sensory experiences of objects at the same time, they all confirm our assumption something is out there.

- When we leave a room and come back later, everything in the room is still there.

- When someone else has the experience of entering a room, that person affirms that most of what he or she experiences in the room is what we experience.

I explain these four reasons in the pages that follow.

We have the experience of space

The experience of space gives us the impression there are things close to us and things far from us, so there must be a world outside of us in space. We learn in the first years of infancy that some objects seem to be close enough to touch and others seem to be distant and untouchable. The things we cannot touch that seem distant from us appear smaller and vaguer, so we have the impression of space. The perception of space is just a result of our learning. Having experiences that suggest objects are distinct from each other and from us gives us the feeling there must be space outside of our Minds, and in that space are lots of objects. However, in reality the perception of space is just an experience, and the objects in the perception of space are just experiences.

Like all experiences, the experiences of space are entirely in our Minds. The experiences are accessible in the Universal Intelligence; there is no need for an objective world to give rise to the experiences.

We watch a movie on a two-dimensional screen. We have the experiences of the actors speeding through the streets of Chicago after a bank robbery. Faraway objects seem smaller and vaguer. We have the perception of space. But it's all on a two-dimensional screen. We have the experience of space, but there is no need for Chicago to be transported into the theater to give us an objective world with space to believe the characters are speeding through Chicago in a getaway car.

The illusion of space is an experience that happens in the Mind. There is no space on the two-dimensional screen. Our Minds create the space.

When we have different sensory experiences of objects at the same time, they all confirm our assumption something is out there

We can have the experience of seeing a red chair, then moving to it seven feet in space, and finally touching it. Those are three experiences. They combine to give us the sense that there's a red chair seven feet from us that is solid in a world outside of us. We've had three sensory experiences that confirm there's a red chair there.

However, those are just three experiences in the Mind. There is no need for a red chair outside of us seven feet away that we touch for us to have the vivid experience of the chair from three sensory perspectives. The three experiences come into our Minds without an external world responsible for them. We have the experience of seeing a red chair, the experience that it is vaguer and smaller than the experiences of objects closer to us, and the experience of moving to it in space. However, they are all experiences. Experiences don't require a world outside of us. Experiences happen entirely in the Mind.

When we leave a room and come back later, everything in the room is still there

The consistency of our experiences gives us the sense that there must be permanent objects outside of us that will always be there unless they're moved. The chair will be there when we return from a visit to another country. It will be there if we are hit by a bus and leave this realm. It seems to be out there, independent of us. But the reason we experience it in the room when we have the experience of returning is that the Universal Intelligence provides continuity in the experiences we have in our Minds. Whatever we expect to be there because of past experience will be there every time we enter the room and expect to see it. If someone moves it, the scene has changed and the Universal Intelligence makes accessible all the experiences that fit whatever the change is. The fact that it seems to be in a world outside of us because the experiences remain the same is just because this realm has continuity to allow us to have predictable experiences.

These consistencies and the changes in the world we all experience result from the fact that we are all the Universal Intelligence accessing the experiences available now for the same room. The room has an uncountable number of experience details from the contractor building the house, the people putting up the drywall, the electricians, the various owners, us, our friends, and anyone else who has had experiences with that room. We are able to access the room experiences by intending to enter the room or intending to recall the experiences we have that are now in our repertoire of memory experiences.

When we return to the room, the array of experiences is again available to us from the Universal Reality and we may choose another set of experiences to become another set of memory experiences of the room. The fact that the selection of room experiences available to us is the same gives us the feeling there is a room outside of us.

When someone else has the experience of entering a room, that person affirms that most of what he or she experiences in the room is what we experience

Surely, it would seem, since any person having the experience of entering the room experiences a chair, the chair must be outside of us in the room. However, the experience of the chair is given to every individual Mind in Earth School when one of us has the room experience. We are one Mind, the Universal Intelligence. We are all attuned to this same realm available for access in the Universal Intelligence. We all have access to the same sensed experiences. All of Earth School is prepared for us based on who we are and our expectations that result in the creations by the Universal Intelligence. There is no world outside of us with a chair in it.

And so, I experience grasping the doorknob to open the door to the room and I experience the door opening. Those are entirely my experiences. My friend has the experience of entering behind me. That is entirely his experience. But we are both accessing the experiences everyone before us had about the room that makes the room experience—the lighting, room color, wood floor, wall treatments, and all other experiences built by those who were involved with the room before us. The experiences that we access and remember are those about the room, as it is now, that fit our needs and limited perceptions.

We're both experiencing the room and having the experience of seeing a chair, but the experiences that register with us and that we remember are individual experiences. The experiences are all in our Minds (plural) as part of the Universal Intelligence (singular).

What evidence is there that there is nothing but Mind and experiences?

We would expect that if it's true that there is only Mind and experiences, with no world external to our Mind, we should have some evidence of it. This section provides the evidence that there is only Mind and experiences with no external world.

Even materialist scientists agree we cannot know if there is a world outside of us

We know the Mind is not in the brain. (Read *Your Eternal Self: Science Discovers the Afterlife.*[9]) However, even philosophers and neuroscientists who believe the Mind is an epiphenomenon of the brain agree that we cannot know a world outside of us. Neuroscientists assert that when we see a tree, for example, photons cascade upon the tree from a light source, some of which are reflected toward our eyes; billions of photons enter the cornea; the photons strike the rod and cone photoreceptors on the retina and are transformed into electrical signals that are transmitted over the optic nerve to the visual cortex; the electrical signals stimulate neurotransmitters that result in neurons firing to give us a configuration of firing neurons.

But the configuration of firing neurons is not a tree. There is no tree in the brain. There is no photographic likeness of a tree in the brain. The brain will never experience the light of day or a tree. In their materialistic conception, there are just neurons firing in a configuration that someone has told us is a tree configuration, so when we have those neurons firing again in that configuration we will say, "That's a tree!"

We have no way of knowing if there is a thing called a "tree" outside of us. As even a materialist neuroscientist or philosopher insists, all we have is a configuration of neurons firing that is the tree configuration.

Daniel Dennett, a philosophy professor at Tufts University, summarizes this perception:

> What we think of as our consciousness is actually our brains pulling a number of tricks to conjure up the world as we experience it. But in reality, it's all smoke, mirrors, and rapidly firing neurons.[10]

The materialist scientists assert that what we experience is just a pack of neurons firing;[11] and we call a particular pack of neurons firing a tree each time we experience those neurons firing together. In their view, we can never know whether there's a thing we're calling a tree out there. We can never know whether there's really a world outside of our Minds, the neuroscientists assert.

That doesn't prove there is no world outside of us, but it does show that we can't be sure that there is, even in the materialists' view. So we're on the fence thus far. The other evidence presented here knocks us off the fence onto the firm ground of realizing there is only Mind and experiences.

The mind is not in the body

A second reason we know there is nothing but Mind and experiences is presented in the book *Your Eternal Self: Science Discovers the Afterlife*[12] containing the evidence that we know the Mind is not in the brain or body. As a result, the Mind needs no sensory apparatuses of the body to have experiences. The eyes, ears, nose, taste buds, and skin are unnecessary. Even when the brain and body are incapacitated so they no longer function in near-death experiences or after death, the Mind has perfectly lucid sensory experiences, demonstrating that the sensory experiences are in the Mind, independent of any source other than the Mind. There is only Mind and experiences.

In the following pages, I cite authors who refer to the Mind's being in the brain. Their information is relevant to this explanation of the Mind and experiences, but when they refer to the Mind as being in the brain, understand that they are explaining the Mind using their materialist paradigm. Their observations about Mind are important, however.

Quantum mechanics posits that everything not being experienced is in probabilities only; it does not "exist"

Quantum physics revolutionized scientists' view of the universe. Its predictions have been verified repeatedly with an extremely high degree of accuracy. One of the key conclusions of quantum physics is that the world we refer to as the real world is in waves of probabilities that are not material until someone observes or records them.

Amit Goswami, the theoretical nuclear physicist and member of the University of Oregon Institute for Theoretical Physics, explains,

> The universe exists as formless potential in myriad possible branches in the transcendent domain and becomes manifest only when observed by conscious beings.[13]

Werner Heisenberg, the German theoretical physicist who was one of the key pioneers of quantum mechanics, also wrote about this:

> The idea of an objective real world whose smallest parts exist objectively in the same sense as stones or trees exist, independently of whether or not we observe them . . . is impossible. . . . The transition from the "possible" to the "actual" takes place during the act of observation.[14]

> The atoms or elementary particles themselves are not real; they form a world of potentialities or possibilities rather than one of things or facts.[15]

John Wheeler, an American theoretical physicist and professor of physics at Princeton University, wrote the following:

> No elementary quantum phenomenon is a phenomenon until it is a registered ("observed," "indelibly recorded") phenomenon.[16]

Andrew Truscott, Australian National University professor of atomic and molecular physics, wrote the following:

At the quantum level, reality does not exist if you are not looking at it.[17]

The fact that there is nothing but Mind and experiences explains why the world doesn't exist until we have the experience of it. From moment to moment, the experience with the highest probability comes into the now point of Awareness, creating our reality. The experiences are potential experiences until we give them substance in Awareness. They don't "exist" until they are in someone's Awareness. Otherwise, they are simply accessible.

Blind people, whose Minds cannot process sight images, are able to see during near-death and out-of-body experiences

Blind people, including those blind from birth, can see clearly during near-death experiences (NDEs) and out-of-the-body experiences (OBEs), demonstrating that their Minds must be independent of their sight-impaired bodies.

Kenneth Ring, PhD, professor emeritus of psychology at the University of Connecticut, and Sharon Cooper interviewed 31 blind and sight-impaired persons who had NDEs and OBEs. Ring and Cooper found that 80 percent of the blind individuals reported visual experiences correctly, including colors and details in their surroundings. One patient who had been totally blind for 40 years had the experience of seeing the pattern and colors on a new tie during an out-of-body experience, even though everyone denied having ever described it to him. The results of the two-year research study are in the book *Mindsight*.[18]

Dr. Larry Dossey, former chief of staff of Medical City Dallas Hospital, describes this case of a woman who had been blind from birth seeing clearly during her near-death experience:

The surgery had gone smoothly until the late stages of the operation. Then something happened. As her physician was closing the incision, Sarah's heart stopped

beating. . . . [When she awoke, Sarah had] a clear,
detailed memory of the frantic conversation of the
surgeons and nurses during her cardiac arrest; the
[operating room] layout; the scribbles on the surgery
schedule board in the hall outside; the color of the sheets
covering the operating table; the hairstyle of the head
scrub nurse; the names of the surgeons in the doctors'
lounge down the corridor who were waiting for her case
to be concluded; and even the trivial fact that her
anesthesiologist that day was wearing unmatched socks.
All this she knew even though she had been fully
anesthetized and unconscious during the surgery and
the cardiac arrest.

But what made Sarah's vision even more momentous
was the fact that, since birth, she had been blind.[19]

Sarah's Mind was seeing when her body was unable to see
because she was unconscious and had been blind since birth.

These blind people had sensory experiences in their Minds
because while their bodies were unconscious, their Minds were
unimpeded by their bodies' blindness. When they were no longer
following the set of rules in their body experience, they had visual
experiences with great acuity.

What makes this even more remarkable is that decoding sight
and associating experiences with sight must be learned over a long
period of time. A newborn's eyes are physically capable of seeing just
fine at birth, but the infant's Mind hasn't developed the ability to
process visual information. An infant is first able to see only as far as
the face of the person holding him or her. At two months, the infant can
distinguish colors. At four months, the infant has developed depth
perception. Learning to interpret and derive meaning from what comes
into the eyes takes months to develop.

Even if somehow a person blind from birth could suddenly have
a clear experience of sight, the person seeing for the first time would
not understand what the shapes and colors are. They would be
meaningless. And yet patients blind from birth who have never seen

have perfect visual experiences, interpret the images correctly and remember the visual experiences when they awaken. Sarah was able to identify the scribbles on the surgery schedule board and understand the sight experiences of her anesthesiologist's unmatched socks.

The reason Sarah and other blind people have clear visual experiences in near-death experiences is that visual experiences exist independent of a world of things. These blind people are all part of the Universal Intelligence, so they share the experiences available to all of us, but are following the rules for their lives in this realm that have dictated that their visual experiences would be impeded. When they are released from the constraints during near-death experiences, they experience the same clear sensory experiences anyone without vision impairment experiences. However, sensory organs are not necessary for the experiences because the experiences are accessible without reference to things in a world outside of us.

You can view the video of a woman who was blind from birth but was able to see during her near-death experience: www.earthschoolanswers.com/vicki/.

People whose bodies have died still have sensory experiences

Today we have written, video, and audio records of people speaking from the life after this life. They no longer have bodies on Earth, but they have the same sensory experiences people in this Earth life have. We also have the reports by people having out-of-body experiences who journey to distant parts of this realm and have experiences without using their bodies.

These residents of the afterlife realm and out-of-body experiencers describe worlds in which the people who have left the Earth body behind have sensory experiences that are clearer and more exhilarating than the experiences they were having during their Earth School experience. They describe structures made of a solid material with a pearl-like luminescence. There are large buildings housing schools, art galleries, and museums in vast, beautiful, clean cities.

Houses have gardens around them, with natural soil, just as on Earth. People who enjoyed gardening tend the gardens, and beautiful flowers grow continually and profusely. No one picks the flowers, however. They are left to grow naturally. The flowers have heavenly aromas and exude music.

Music and art are integral, vital components of the other planes. There is continual music, although a person doesn't have to listen to it. There are vast orchestras comprising thousands of people playing instruments, some of which are like those on the Earth plane while others are unique. As an orchestra plays, beautiful colors appear around the orchestra in keeping with the music.

The individuals living in the next realm of life left the Earth body experience behind. They have new body experiences with sensory experiences just as people having a body experience in Earth School have. Their Minds are part of the same Universal Intelligence our Minds are part of. They are able to have sensory experiences because the Universal Intelligence gives the sights, sounds, smells, touches, tastes, bodily sensations, and emotions to the residents of the life after this life just as we are given the experiences we are having in Earth School. No physical worlds outside of our Minds are necessary for these sensory experiences.

In dreams, we have experiences

Another indication there is only Mind and experiences is that we can have experiences in ways that clearly don't come from sensory organs. We have dreams in which all the senses are active. We witness scenes of people we don't know doing things we don't anticipate, saying things we don't remember anyone saying in our lifetime. Our Minds are off in the same place our memories, imagination, and thoughts are, where entirely new creations evolve in ways different from what we experience during our awake periods in Earth School.

We are individual manifestations of the Universal Intelligence. Our Minds are ceaselessly creating, just as the Universal Intelligence continually creates the Earth School experiences. In dreams, our Minds select experiences from our life and build on the experiences in marvelous scenes, with colorful characters and masterful scripts. In other words, the Mind in sleep goes into the same state in which memories are accessed and imagination creates. But since the Mind has a universe of resources to draw from, it sets about creating an entirely novel life for itself, like another Earth School realm, using our life experiences as the basis for the dreams.

There is no outside world when we are dreaming. All the experiences come to the Mind and we see, hear, feel, smell, and taste; all the senses are active. Mind and experiences are sufficient. There is no need for an outside world.

In Guided Afterlife Communication and Self-Guided Afterlife connections, people have experiences

Two methods of helping people have communication with loved ones living in the life after this life bring the individual into a state of Mind in which the communication can occur. In both methods, the individual closes his or her eyes and has vivid communications. In these communication experiences, experiencers speak with their loved ones, walk with them through landscapes, touch them, hug them, and even kiss them. All the sensory experiences are part of the event. But they all happen in the Mind.

Rochelle Wright, a Washington state licensed psychotherapist, originated a psychotherapy method named Repair & Reattachment Grief Therapy in which the psychotherapist helps clients enter a state of Mind where they have afterlife communications with loved ones who have left Earth School (www.repairandreattachment.com). The procedure is 98 percent successful and reduces grief by 86 percent or more in a single session. This is the transcript of a portion of the recording of a client describing the sensory experiences when she had contact with her daughter who had transitioned in a car accident:

> My eyes were closed and the visual right away was on the left side of my Mind. Kate appeared coming down a sidewalk. There was a wall, and it was beautiful. There was ivy growing out of it and a big old tree. Kate started walking toward me. It was amazing. I was sitting there with my eyes closed and Kate was walking to me. As she walked toward me, she put her hand out and I put my

hand out and I could feel hers on mine. I was able to feel
her fingers, to hug her, and to stroke her hair. She was
wearing a T-shirt and shorts and flip-flops just like she
did when she was here on Earth. She led me down the
sidewalk and we walked, and she was talking.[20]

You can view the woman giving her account of her Repair &
Reattachment Grief Therapy session at
www.earthschoolanswers.com/carole/.

Another method that helps people enter a state of Mind in
which they experience afterlife communication is called Self-Guided
Afterlife Connections. The person enters a state of self-hypnosis and
initiates the afterlife communication. The method is 86 percent
successful. The free, online training in how to have Self-Guided
Afterlife Connections is at www.selfguided.spiritualunderstanding.org.

In this excerpt, a participant describes the sensed experiences
she had:

It all came together for me just now. I found the room in
my parents' house where my husband, his mother and
my parents and sons would gather for holidays, to be the
warm, loved-filled room where my loved ones who had
passed were gathered. I hugged each one and smiled a
lot. Then I opened the screen door and sat on the
concrete steps with my husband, holding his hand and
putting it up to my face. He did not say anything, and no
one else did. I did all the talking, but I felt a tremendous
love and warmth. This was extremely healing, simply
because thoughts of my husband now can make me
smile, and I can go there on my own now.[21]

These procedures bring people into the state of Mind in which
they have afterlife communication connections with all the sensory
experiences people have in the Earth School environment. They are not
memories, so the sensory experiences are not recalled. They are all the
real people living in the life after this life who have intended to have the

experiences that are then created by the Universal Intelligence for the individual having the afterlife communication.

Asking for the connection is all that is necessary. No outer world is required for them to have the experiences.

Remote viewers have experiences of distant objects without contact or light

Remote viewers are able to close their eyes, calm their Minds, and describe sights, sounds, textures, smells, and tastes associated with objects and scenes that may be thousands or millions of miles away. The remote viewer has all the sensory experiences we associate with events in Earth School. The viewer sees scenes and objects, hears sounds, smells, feels textures, and senses emotions. The remote viewer is having the sensory experiences in the Mind while the body is sitting quietly with its eyes closed. There is no outside world experience occurring for the viewer.

Remote viewers are able to view photographs in sealed envelopes, shipwrecks at the bottom of dark oceans, objects in rooms at night with the room lights off, and other things in circumstances that preclude what we assume is normal vision. You can see a demonstration of master remote viewer Glenn Wheaton doing a remote viewing of a picture in a sealed envelope at www.earthschoolanswers.com/glenn/.

You can see a demonstration of my remote viewing objects on a table 700 miles away from me at www.earthschoolanswers.com/remote/.

For several decades at the end of the twentieth century, the CIA had a remote viewing program named Operation Stargate that used remote viewers to spy on the Soviet Union. The program had remarkable results. In 1974, a remote viewer named Pat Price was to view a mysterious, unidentified research center at Semipalatinsk, USSR, to see what was there. He sat with his eyes closed and focused on the area. Below is a sketch he made of what he saw through his remote viewing. It had all the distinguishing marks of a gantry crane.[22]

Later, the CIA obtained satellite photos of the site. A CIA artist created the following sketch of part of the Semipalatinsk site based on the photos. It was a grantry crane:

Pat Price had the experience of a gantry crane without using his eyes because the Universal Intelligence gave the sight experiences to him when he requested them.

Remote viewing is being used to discover archaeological sites buried beneath tons of soil. The experiences of the sites are available without the senses being involved in accessing them. You can see a description of remote viewing's use in discovering archaeological sites at www.earthschoolanswers.com/joe/.

The sensory organs couldn't have experiences even if the person were somehow transported to the scene. The experiences come to the Mind from the shared experiences in the Universal Intelligence. No visual organs are necessary.

You can read more about remote viewing in the book *Your Eternal Self: Science Discovers the Afterlife.*[23]

Many scientists are asserting today that Mind is the basis of reality

Many scientists are now asserting that what we experience is a creation of the Universal Intelligence. They refer to Mind as "consciousness."

A 2018 article by investigative reporter Olivia Goldhill explains the increasingly accepted view among scientists that Mind is the basis of reality:

> Consciousness permeates reality. Rather than being just a unique feature of human subjective experience, it's the foundation of the universe, present in every particle and all physical matter. This sounds like easily dismissible bunkum, but as traditional attempts to explain consciousness continue to fail, the "panpsychist" view is increasingly being taken seriously by credible philosophers, neuroscientists, and physicists, including figures such as neuroscientist Christof Koch and physicist Roger Penrose.[24]

Max Planck, the theoretical physicist who originated quantum theory, for which he won the Nobel Prize in Physics in 1918, expressed it this way:

> I regard consciousness as fundamental. I regard matter as derivative from consciousness. We cannot get behind consciousness. Everything that we talk about, everything that we regard as existing, postulates consciousness.[25]

An article in the *HuffPost* blog by the following four scientists explains their conclusion that Mind is the basis of reality.

- Deepak Chopra, MD, board certified physician in internal medicine, endocrinology, and metabolism

- Menas Kafatos, PhD, Fletcher Jones endowed professor of computational physics at Chapman University, a quantum physicist and cosmologist

- Bernardo Kastrup, PhD, specialist in computer engineering, artificial intelligence, and reconfigurable computing

- Rudolph Tanzi, PhD, Joseph P. and Rose F. Kennedy professor of neurology at Harvard University and vice chair of neurology at Mass. General Hospital, included in *Time* magazine's 100 most influential people in the world

These scientists summarize their conclusion about Mind's being the basis of reality:

> Indeed, to say that the universe is mental does not mean that it exists only within the limited minds of humans. Instead, the universe is the expression of a universal mind that transcends personal Awareness. This is what we call fundamental conscious awareness. Our seemingly separate human minds are dissociated personalities of this universal mind, akin to the multiple personalities of a person with Dissociative Identity Disorder. The ideas and emotions experienced by the universal mind—within which we are all immersed—are presented to us in the form of the empirical world we see, hear, touch, taste and smell.[26]

In *The Quantum Enigma*, Bruce Rosenblum and Fred Kuttner, both physics professors at UC Santa Cruz, describe the fact that objects don't exist in the traditional sense until we experience them:

> The waviness in a region is the probability of finding the object in a particular place. We must be careful: The waviness is not the probability of the object being in a particular place. There is a crucial difference here! The object was not there before you found it there.[27]

Pioneering physicist and mathematician Sir James Jeans, professor at the University of Cambridge and Princeton University, wrote his conclusions after studying the basis of reality from a physicist's perspective:

The stream of knowledge is heading toward a non-mechanical reality; the universe begins to look more like a great thought than like a great machine. Mind no longer appears to be an accidental intruder into the realm of matter, we ought rather hail it as the creator and governor of the realm of matter. Get over it, and accept the inarguable conclusion. The universe is immaterial-mental and spiritual.[28]

R. C. Henry, professor of physics and astronomy at Johns Hopkins University, wrote the following:

A fundamental conclusion of the new physics also acknowledges that the observer creates the reality. As observers, we are personally involved with the creation of our own reality. Physicists are being forced to admit that the universe is a "mental" construction.[29]

John Archibald Wheeler was an American theoretical physicist who worked with Niels Bohr in explaining the basic principles behind nuclear fission. This is how he assessed the nature of reality based on quantum physics:

Useful as it is under ordinary circumstances to say that the world exists "out there" independent of us, that view can no longer be upheld.[30]

Peter Russell, theoretical physicist, experimental psychologist, and computer scientist wrote the following:

All our experiences—all our perceptions, sensations, dreams, thoughts and feelings—are forms appearing in consciousness. . . . Everything we know, perceive, and imagine, every color, sound, sensation, every thought and every feeling, is a form appearing in the mind. It is all an in-forming of consciousness.[31]

Richard Conn Henry, PhD, professor in physics at The John Hopkins University, wrote about this in the journal *Nature:*

Physicists shy from the truth because the truth is so alien
to everyday physics. . . . The Universe is entirely
mental.[32]

Amit Goswami – Conservation of matter and energy

An approach to reality called the dualist approach suggests that
Mind is separate from matter and influences our brains and the world
of matter that is outside of us. However, Amit Goswami, the quantum
physicist, explains that Mind apart from matter cannot influence matter
because that would add energy from outside the system. The law of the
conservation of energy states that the amount of energy in the system
will always be the same. If immaterial consciousness influenced matter,
the action would add energy, which is not possible.

The idea of matter-mind duality seemed to violate a
sacrosanct scientific law that was discovered in the
nineteenth century, the law of conservation of energy—
energy of the physical universe alone always remains a
constant, in all transactions. The thinking went like this:
if the nonmaterial psyche interacted with matter, such
interactions must involve signals that carry energy, and
so energy would escape and enter the physical universe
contrary to the energy conservation law.[33]

We know Mind is not created by the brain. In the dualist
explanation, Mind is independent of the material realm, so it contains
no matter or energy from a physical realm. However, if Mind is to use a
material body to navigate a physical world, it must add energy to the
physical realm in every body activity. If Mind adds energy in any way,
since the energy isn't in the totality of matter and energy that exists in a
world the materialists believe exists independent of the mind, it must
be adding energy.

There are nearly 8 billion people on the planet influencing the
matter in their lives. That means a tremendous amount of energy would
be added to the system as people act in their daily lives to influence
matter.

The conclusion must be that since Mind is active in Earth School and Mind is not created by matter. Matter and energy must be Mind stuff.

Luminaries have asserted that the basis of reality is Mind

Many luminaries from the past have asserted that the basis of reality is Mind. Reality is like a dream our Minds are having.

Chögyal Namkhai Norbu: "In a real sense, all the visions that we see in our lifetime are like a big dream."

Swami Vivekananda: "To every one of us there must come a time when the whole universe will be found to have been a mere dream."

Swami Krishnananda: ". . . you will see that all the objects of the world are your own universal self."

Chuang-tzu: "There is the great awaking after which we shall know that this life was a great dream. All the while the stupid think they are awake."

Vajracchedika Sutra of Mahayana Buddhism: "Know that the world has no self-nature, no substance of its own, and has never been born. It is like a cloud, a ring produced by a firebrand, a vision, a mirage, the moon as reflected in the ocean, and a dream."

Jalal al-Din Rumi: "This world, which is only a dream, seems to the sleeper as a thing enduring forever. But when the morn of the last day shall dawn, the sleeper will escape from the cloud of illusion; laughter will overpower him at his own fancied griefs when he beholds his abiding home and place."

Meher Baba: "All your pleasures and difficulties, your feelings of happiness and misery, your presence here and your listening to these explanations, are all nothing but a vacant dream on your part and mine. There is this one difference: I also consciously know the dream to be a dream, while you feel that you are awake."

Tripura Rahasya: "This world is a mere figment of imagination . . . an image on the screen of the Mind . . . an image on the mirror of consciousness . . . a mental image."

Sankara: "The apparent world is caused by our imagination, in its ignorance. It is not real. It is like seeing the snake in the rope. It is like a passing dream."

Could there be a world of matter and energy created by consciousness outside of us

Everything in the physical world is made out of atoms. Atoms are made out of energy. And energy is made out of consciousness.

Author unknown

Since consciousness is fundamental, meaning there is nothing but consciousness, could it be that the Universal Intelligence is creating a world of matter and energy that has consciousness as its base and we are using our sensory organs to access it? This world would be like the physical realm the materialists believe exists independent of our Minds, but instead of being reducible to energy that exists independent of us, a world of consciousness would have as its basis consciousness.

That would create a sort of dualism of consciousness. Dualism is the suggestion that there is a material world of matter and energy and Mind is separate from it. Those who subscribe to the notion of dualism believe that somehow Mind outside of a matter and energy world is able to send signals to a physical brain that the brain uses to navigate in a material, physical realm. This view of reality is not valid. It holds onto the proposition that there is a material world, and Mind outside of it influences it. However, the previous pages have demonstrated that there is only Mind. There is no material world.

In a dualism of a world that has consciousness as its base, with our Minds apprehending this consciousness-created world outside of us, we would have all the experiences of the world we are having, but the experiences would be conveyed to us through consciousness-created sensory organs in a conscious-created physical body.

Such a dualism is not tenable. For one thing, since our Minds are having the experiences, a world for us to apprehend is unnecessary. We are the Mind having experiences. A world between us and the experiences is unnecessary.

We also could never know whether there is a conscious-created world because all we can know is the experiences we have. That is the same dilemma the materialists express. For the materialists, since they assert we know only the patterns of neurons firing, they all agree we can never know whether there is a world outside of us.

There is nothing but Mind and experiences. The evidence of atoms is an experience. The evidence of subatomic particles is an experience. The mathematics implying strings are just experiences. When we peer into the depths of the cosmos, we have the experiences of a background radiation and distant galaxies. However, they are all simply experiences. There is no world outside of our Minds, regardless of how deeply we look into matter and energy and regardless of how far we look into the vast abyss of space.

There is nothing but Mind and experiences. A conscious-created world outside of us to apprehend would be superfluous.

What about the indications the brain controls thought and movement

To understand why it seems the brain is controlling thought and movement and why the body chemistry changes with Mind activities, suggesting body chemistry affects the Mind, it is necessary to understand what we have learned from individuals living in the next realm of life.

In Earth School, everything has a reason. Earth is a world of cause, effect, space, and time. We need warmth and light, so there is a Sun to give us warmth and light. We need to support the body's functioning, so we eat things to give us nutrition. We must replenish excreted liquids, so we drink. We experience space, so we must move from one location to another. Organs are necessary to support the body's functioning. The body must die so people can justify to the remaining residents of Earth School that the person has left.

The life after this life has all the experiences of the Earth School realm, with solid mountains, animals, streams, buildings, and bodies. However, there is no need for cause, effect, space, or time. There is no Sun for warmth or light; there is always a pleasant, ambient temperature and comfortable temperature without cause. There is no diurnal measure of time and no clocks. People do not need to eat or drink to sustain their bodies, although they may do so if they want to. The people living in the life after this life remark that they don't believe they have organs; they don't need them. Space is optional. People can travel by intending to be at a location; they are instantly there. Their bodies never die. However, they can evolve into higher dimensional beings that don't need a body.

In Earth School, everything has cause, effect, space, and time, so the Mind must have a place where it seems to be located and generated in the body experience. As a result, the Mind has been assumed to be in the brain. We seem to have the experience of three pounds of protein and fat called a "brain," with neurons, areas of the brain that light up when functions are performed, and brain waves. However, the brain performs no services that affect the individual Mind's functioning in Earth School. Read the explanation in the book *Your Eternal Self: Science Discovers the Afterlife*.[34]

The brain shows signs of activity, but the signs are just part of the cause and effect of the Earth realm. The signs of activity in the brain are much like the whirling blue circle on a Windows screen when the computer is computing. No one would assume the whirling blue circle is where the computing is going on. The circle is just a prop. The brain shows activity when a person is having experiences, but the brain is just a prop.

The Mind is not in a brain. The brain is in the Mind. So we must understand an entirely different reality.

3

You Must Understand an Entirely Different Reality

The soul can never be cut into pieces by any weapon, nor burned by fire, nor moistened by water, nor withered by the wind.

Bhagavad Gita 2.23

There is only Mind and experiences. You are Mind, entirely. You are not **created by** the Universal Intelligence. You **are a manifestation** of the Universal Intelligence. The Universal Intelligence assumes individual personalities to have experiences in Earth School. We are having the same dream because who we are in the Universal Intelligence is tuned into the same reality. While you are in Earth School, you are wholly an individual member of the Universal Intelligence living in a world of experiences provided by the Universal Intelligence. And when we decide to stop playing these roles, we will still be the individuals we are as we take on other roles in other realms available for access in the Universal Intelligence.

If you were to relax, calm your mind, and close your eyes, you could imagine what your ideal island in the tropics would be like. As you allow your Mind to drift, you can see yourself walking on a sandy beach with the expanse of ocean beside you. You hear waves, feel the sand between your toes, feel the warmth of the sun on your body, and smell the ocean breezes.

When you imagine that experience, you have enabled yourself to be a personality in a world you materialized in your Mind. That person is 100 percent you. The feelings and all other sensations materialized as you intended to experience them: you saw, heard, and felt, but there was no world outside of that personality. There was no boundary between you and your imagined self. That person would not have to look outside to find the creator. That person was you taking on a role in a realm within you. It was all you.

In the same way, you and I are the Universal Intelligence being individual Minds. We were born, are growing, and will transition from Earth School to another completely real world as the people we are, with all our attitudes, memories, loves, dislikes, and everything else that makes us who we are.

The Universal Intelligence has no beginning and will have no end. Our individual Minds can never be cut into pieces by any weapon, nor burned by fire, nor moistened by water, nor withered by the wind. When the experience of the body stops being useful for us, we will end our focus on this experience and go on to focus on other experiences in other solid, real bodies in solid, real worlds. But we will never be harmed by the change.

When we graduate from Earth School, we will not dissolve into the Universal Intelligence. We will always be the individuals we are. Mediums have communicated with individuals from the sixteenth century, soldiers from the Roman Empire, citizens of ancient Egypt, Confucius from the sixth century BCE, and many other individuals living blissfully in the other realms of the Universal Intelligence.

Matter and energy are real. They just originate in a way that is different from what we've been taught. Tables and chairs are solid, mountains are made of hard stone, streams have wet water, and bodies have hard bones and soft flesh. Matter is made up of atoms. Atoms are made up of energy. Energy is made up of Mind.

So you must have a new understanding of who you are, the nature of the universe, where you came from, why you are here, what happens when the body experience stops, and the condition you will be in when you decide not to have body experiences anymore.

This understanding is based in the uplifting knowledge that our eternal lives can be filled with love, joy, peace, and wonderful adventures, even though we go through periods of distress, sadness, and unhappiness as we learn lessons in Earth School, and even though some will go through tragedies and suffering. Knowing these truths will relieve you of your worries about events in this life and your graduation from Earth School. You can live life abundantly, without concerns about what tomorrow will bring. You will look forward to all the tomorrows.

You just have to know the truth. There is nothing but your Mind and your experiences. You co-create the experiences because you are part of the Universal Intelligence that creates the Earth School realm every instant. The Universal Intelligence has unconditional love for you and envelops you. You just have to experience that love and live in peace and joy.

The chapters that follow explain this reality we live in.

4

The Point of Now Awareness

There is nothing but Mind and experiences. How then does the Mind have experiences?

Experiences come and go in our Awareness in the point of our lives we call "now." The now point is rather like the needle point of the reading head on a DVD player that plays whatever is at that point on the DVD. It may seem that our experiences last a long time, but that is an illusion, like the illusion of seeing a continuous stream of movement in a projected movie on the DVD. In a movie, we are actually looking at two-dimensional pictures appearing at 24 to 72 still pictures a second. Our Mind converts them into smoothly running actions.

Some researchers have suggested our lives are made up of now points that similarly animate life in discrete moments of consciousness. Stuart Hameroff, MD, the consciousness researcher at the University of Arizona, and Sir Roger Penrose, a theoretical physicist at the University of Oxford, suggest that we have 40 conscious moments a second, meaning our consciousness goes into a quantum state where it gathers information, then collapses into consciousness for the brain to use that information at 40 times a second.[35]

Julian Barbour, a British physicist specializing in quantum gravity and the history of science, describes our conscious moments as a succession of pictures, like snapshots in an album that change continually. He explains,

> In fact, many people who have written about time have conceived of instants of time in a somewhat similar way, and have called them 'nows.' Since I make the concept more precise and put it at the heart of my theory of time, I shall call them Nows. The world is made of Nows.[36]

"Now" has no duration. A geometric point has no dimensions. A line is made up of an infinite number of points, regardless of how long the line is. A one-inch line and a one-mile line each have infinite numbers of points. The points are seamless, from one to the next without a dimension. Our conscious experiences are made up of an infinite number of now points. "Now" has no duration.

Dr. Sean Carroll, a theoretical physicist in the California Institute of Technology Department of Physics specializing in quantum mechanics, gravity, and cosmology, explained time this way:

> . . . it's very tempting to wonder whether or not, like a filmstrip, moments of time are discrete. As far as we know, nothing in physics tells us that time is discrete. As far as we can tell, time is perfectly smooth and continuous.[37]

You can view Dr. Sean Carroll's full explanation of time at www.earthschoolanswers.com/time/.

Each now point of Awareness is being filled with experiences rapidly entering and being replaced. This is an example. A man is driving a car. It seems the entire event is one seamless experience, but it is not. Instead, the event is a churn of experiences in the point of now. Awareness is continually being reformed with new experiences. Now the man is seeing a stop light, hears a violin on the radio, smells the restaurant nearby, is seeing a woman walking on the sidewalk, is recalling that he needs to buy bread on the way home. All these experiences may have come in a second of time. Even when it seems a thought comes to mind and occupies the mind for ten seconds, the point of now awareness is continually being interrupted in nanoseconds by a flurry of experiences. The experiences in the point of now Awareness never remain the same. It may seem that we are having a single experience, but the animation of the now point of Awareness is a flow of an infinite number of point of now experiences.

If the now point of Awareness were not continuously refilled with experiences, the person would not be conscious. I have asked groups to try to stop their consciousness until I tell them to come back into consciousness. The meditators go into their characteristic mindset with their eyes closed and when I ask everyone to come back, they open their eyes and insist they've stopped their consciousness. However, I tell them that if they had stopped their consciousness, they wouldn't have heard me tell them to come back. They would still be sitting there as unconscious as a toaster. As long as an experience comes into Awareness, the person is conscious. Even in sleep, we are conscious. That's why alarm clocks work so effectively.

These experiences include everything the person registers, consciously or subconsciously: sounds, sights, smells, touches, tastes, body conditions, pain, pleasure, thoughts, words, skills, events, speaking, and all the other experiences we have in our daily lives. They include dream states and dreamless sleep, when we're told we venture off into other realms but don't recall the adventure.

Our Awareness is always present, unaffected, calm, and peaceful

The stable, unchanging component in all of these point of now experiences is our Awareness. Awareness is continually filled and refilled by an unceasing flow of transient experiences. However, our Awareness always remains. It is our soul.

In meditation, the meditator stems the flow of experiences into the point of now Awareness. What remains is a feeling of peace through experiencing only the underlying Awareness that is always nonjudgmental, loving, boundless, and peaceful. The basis of our Mind is the love and peace of our Awareness, the soul. We interrupt the natural state of being loving and peaceful by filling Awareness with experiences that naturally give rise to fear, sadness, excitement, anxiety, joy, and all the other emotions.

However, our goal in Earth School is not to be in a continual state of meditation, with no experiences that interrupt the natural love and peace of pure Awareness. Our goal is to use the power of our free will to understand and change the interpretations of experiences so we have the love, peace, and joy of pure Awareness even in the presence of experiences that could result in feelings of sadness, fear, and frustration. The experiences are not who we are. We are the Awareness having the experiences.

There is much more about that in the book, *Earth School: Love, Learn, Be Happy.*[38]

Conscious and subconscious Awareness

There are two areas of Awareness: conscious Awareness and subconscious Awareness.

The first of these areas of Awareness is conscious Awareness. Conscious Awareness is experiencing the sight of a bird, remembering a person's face, experiencing the smell of a rose, tasting chocolate, and any other single experience we are conscious of.

The now point of conscious Awareness is very limited and slow. It seems like we're looking at a panorama when we look ahead, but we are seeing only a small segment of the visual field. If you hold your arm out straight and put your thumb up, your field of vision is about the size of your thumbnail. While reading, readers will fail to recognize a word unless they are fixating within three to four character spaces of the word.[39] You can notice vaguely the area close to your thumbnail-size vision. However, everything outside of that area is filled in by your Mind. You can see it indistinctly, but you're not focusing on it. You assume it's there.

You move your eyes and stop to see, then move your eyes and stop to see, repeating the movement and stopping to see in discrete actions. You cannot see when your eyes are moving.

You can test that for yourself. Stand with your face around eight inches from a mirror. Look at your left eye. Then look at your right eye. See whether you can see your eyes move. Do that several times. You don't see your eyes moving. The move-stop-see movements your eyes experience are called "saccades." The fact that you can't see when your eyes are moving is called "saccadic suppression." You would live your life in a blur if you were seeing as your eyes were moving.

Each time your eyes stop, you see a small area. You aren't seeing a significant distance to the left, right, away from you, or toward you. It may seem that you're scanning in a smooth movement, but you are taking in only a thumbnail-size area at a time. If you were looking for a tiny pill that was a foot to the right or left, you likely would not see it in a single focus.

This focus on one sight area results in what is called "change blindness." In well-known demonstrations of change blindness, you can be looking at a picture that has a change made on it as you're looking at it and miss the change. You can see a video demonstrating change blindness at www.earthschoolanswers.com/blindness/.

In the same way, your attention to a sound, touch, smell, or body sensation is narrowly focused. Think about what is going on with your left foot. What does it feel like now? Think of your right hand. What does it feel like now? Think of the feeling in your left foot and right hand at the same time. You can't do it. Accessing the sensation of one body part occupies your point of now Awareness. You can focus on only one experience at a time.

Now think of your mother's name. That is filling the point of now Awareness with a new experience. Where was your mother's name before you brought it to Mind? Your mother's name is something you easily bring to Mind, so it is accessible, but is not the focus of Awareness at any moment unless you make it the focus or your Awareness is triggered by another experience in your Awareness, such as seeing your mother's picture. The intention and focus of your conscious Awareness on one thing precludes all other experiences.

This conscious Awareness, with its narrow focus on one experience at a time, has been estimated to process information at 40 bits of information per second by biologist Bruce Lipton,[40] 60 bits of information per second by MIT,[41] and 120 bits per second by Bell Labs.[42]

Daniel Levitin, professor emeritus of psychology and music at McGill University, describes the limitations of processing at these slow speeds:

> In order to understand one person speaking to us, we need to process 60 bits of information per second. With a processing limit of 120 bits per second, this means you can barely understand two people talking to you at the same time.[43]

I suggest that the confusion we feel when two people are talking at once indicates our processing speed is closer to the 40 or 60 bits of information per second. Our conscious Awareness is very limited in what it can attend to—usually one experience or one speaker at a time.

You can watch a video demonstrating that your Awareness is focused on the very small area of experiences at the point of now Awareness at www.earthschoolanswers.com/change/.

Subconscious Awareness in the point of now

The second area of Awareness in the point of now is subconscious Awareness. Subconscious Awareness is estimated to process 11 million bits of information per second in one source[44] and 20 million bits of information per second in another.[45] What is important is that subconscious Awareness is 100,000 to 300,000 times the speed of conscious Awareness.

Subconscious Awareness has access to all the experiences in the Universal Intelligence, from any place and any time, including thoughts, traumatic experiences, creative thinking, knowledge, and skill experiences such as being able play a piano or play tennis. While all experiences are accessible, we are able to access only those in our sphere or contacts and our focus of attention. For that reason, it seems that our repertoire of accessible experiences is small, but we have the capability of accessing any experiences.

A great variety of experiences come into our subconscious Awareness from this vast storehouse that don't rise to the level of conscious Awareness, so we don't know we have accessed them. This portion of the chapter explains this treasure trove of experiences that come into subconscious Awareness unbidden.

In the explanations of subconscious Awareness that follow, some writers I cite refer to the "unconscious," but generally references to the "unconscious" are for repressed memories. In this book, I refer to subconscious experiences and subconscious Awareness.

Bruce Lipton, PhD, a cell biologist in the University of Wisconsin Medical School, estimates that 95 percent of what fills our point of now Awareness is subconscious.[46] These are experiences, interpretations of experiences, and emotions that arise unbidden, usually because of triggers from other experiences passing through our Awareness. Subconscious Awareness is what allows us to perform skills such as speaking, driving a car, walking, and other common activities we participate in without having to bring into conscious Awareness every muscle movement, recollection of a word, review of how to construct a sentence, muscle action in hitting a tennis ball, or other activity that requires speed in processing. These experiences from the subconscious fly into the point of now Awareness and are replaced instantly. Someone can very quickly have a thought, create a sentence, form the words using language syntax, and speak the words in a sequence. All of that is coming from subconscious Awareness.

Researchers at the Brain and Mind Institute at the University of Western Ontario conducted a study of the amount of information a person processes. They discovered that while the conscious mind is perceiving the world, unconscious processes are ceaselessly operating. The lead researcher of the study, Jennifer Milne, PhD, wrote, "It's as though we have a semi-autonomous robot in our brain that plans and executes actions on our behalf with only the broadest of instructions from us."[47] "Us" refers to conscious Awareness.

Subconscious experiences flood into Awareness continually, changing from instant to instant. They may "pop into" our conscious Awareness, where we may be surprised at their appearance. We consider and articulate at very slow speeds in conscious Awareness what has already been decided at the subconscious Awareness level.

When we're looking for our car keys, we can go through a mental tour of our house very quickly, with notions interspersing our visual recall experiences. While looking for our car keys, conscious Awareness adds language that slows down the process: "Now what in the world did I do with those keys? Maybe they're in the bedroom." However, at the same time, subconscious Awareness is flooding the Mind with notions, worries, insights, intuitions, recollections, and a host of other unbidden experiences. Subconscious Awareness is fearing being late for work, sensing our spouse moved the keys, feeling irritated with ourselves, seeing the shirt on the floor and wanting to clean up the room, worrying the keys are lost. All these subconscious Awareness experiences are triggered by the experiences involving the keys; they flood Awareness with experiences that dart in and are replaced immediately.

The speed with which a concert pianist strikes the correct keys in sequence illustrates the speed of the subconscious. When a pianist is playing, there is no conscious Awareness involved at all. The activity is entirely subconscious Awareness providing the correct movements and correct sequences at a speed far faster than the pianist's conscious Awareness could ever keep up with. Pianists play between 13 and 14 notes per second. Such is the speed of the subconscious when the pianist has practiced repeatedly so the experience of each note, with each nuance of volume and duration, has come into the subconscious and is assembled into an entire piano concerto.

Ukrainian pianist Lubomyr Melnyk plays piano at 19.5 notes per second using a technique he calls "continuous music." He describes how the subconscious takes over his playing:

> In continuous music you can't make a mistake because you are living the music with the piano. My fingers disappear.

> All I hear and experience when I'm playing is the actual music, the sound, the piano. I barely feel anything. I'm barely aware, my mind is racing and I'm just flying through this landscape. It's beyond nirvana.[48]

However, every movement of the pianist's hands and feet is activated by an experience brought into subconscious Awareness. There is only Mind and experiences. No neurons are involved.

The mix of experiences in the point of now Awareness

Experiences in the point of now Awareness are not simply one sight or one sound or one smell. They are not like one note played on a piano.

The instruments in an orchestra are a fine illustration of what conscious Awareness and subconscious Awareness are. The point of now Awareness is like a piano concerto, such as Tchaikovsky's Piano Concerto No. 1 in B Flat Minor. To listen to a short sample, link to www.earthschoolanswers.com/piano/. The concerto is scored for a solo piano and an orchestra comprising 2 flutes, 2 oboes, 2 clarinets (in B-flat), 2 bassoons, 4 French horns, 2 trumpets (in F), 3 trombones, timpani, and over 28 stringed instruments: violins, violas, cellos, and double basses. When the needle point of now experiences the concerto for the listener, all these nearly 40 instruments flow into a single experience of "music." They are a unified experience in Awareness. However, the single experience comprises many component experiences.

When the concerto opens, there are four emphatic horn chords, leading into a passionate theme by the full orchestra, merging into the introduction of the magnificent piano alternating between high and low registers. At each point when the horns and the piano are prominent, the three dozen other instruments are contributing to the experience, but we don't distinguish the individual strings, woodwinds, brass, and percussions. They are blended into the one experience, so the identities of the subtler instruments are not prominent. But all contribute to the experience in now Awareness. You will hear the horns dominate, then the strings, then the piano. Your conscious Awareness is attending to one primary sound, with the other instruments less prominent, but contributing to the wonderful sound in the point of now Awareness. We don't distinguish the one violin played by Simon or the oboe played by Christine, but the sounds of their instruments are contributing to the experience.

Our experience of life from instant to instant in the now point is similar. There is a dominant experience that is usually our experience of the Earth School environment through which we are navigating. That seems to us to be the primary occupant of our now point, much like the horns, strings, or piano that dominate at different points, even though the full orchestra is behind them.

In our point of now Awareness, two, five, or more experiences and interpretations of experiences are in subconscious Awareness as we focus on the narrow, dominant experience in conscious Awareness. They are all affecting our Mind and the body experience, as all the instruments in the orchestra affect the performance at each point of now.

Someone may go through the motions of driving a car using subconscious experiences while the conscious Awareness is thinking about what to say to her boss to get a raise. As she thinks about what to say to get the raise, subconscious experiences and interpretations are playing in the background: the actions of driving the car, noticing lights controlling traffic, fear she will be rejected by her boss, the pain of a toothache, worry the tooth must be pulled, loving thoughts from her husband that register subconsciously, and a guide encouraging her to slow down because the roads ahead are dangerous. Many experiences are playing at once, coming to the person as a single event in the point of now Awareness.

How much of our day is spent being led by the experiences coming from the subconscious

During every instant of the day, our Awareness is being filled with experiences and interpretations from the subconscious that come unbidden when triggered by a previous experience that has come from the Earth School events or from memory experiences. The following authors explain the influence of the subconscious on our daily lives. Substitute "Mind" for "brain" or "neural networks" in their explanations.

Elizabeth Loftus, cognitive psychologist and professor at the University of California at Irvine, is a researcher on memories and memory modification. When asked how much subconscious memories affect us in our daily lives, this is what she said:

> We are aware of stimuli that we are not even aware have influenced us. . . . We are responding automatically based on these subconscious or unconscious details or aspects of our environment.[49]

View her interview at www.earthschoolanswers.com/control/.

David Eagleman is a neuroscientist who heads the Laboratory for Perception and Action at Baylor College of Medicine and is the founding Director of the Initiative on Neuroscience and Law. He is the author and presenter of the PBS series *The Brain*. He explained the influence of the subconscious on our daily lives:

> Brains are in the business of gathering information and steering behavior appropriately. It doesn't matter whether consciousness is involved in the decision making. And most of the time, it's not. Whether we're talking about dilated eyes, jealousy, attraction, the love of fatty foods, or the great idea you had last week, consciousness is the smallest player in the operations of the brain. Our brains run mostly on autopilot, and the conscious mind has little access to the giant and mysterious factory that runs below it [the subconscious].[50]

View the interview at www.earthschoolanswers.com/influence/.

Thalia Wheatley, associate professor in the Department of Psychological and Brain Sciences at Dartmouth College, explains what influences our normal behavior:

> Most of the time, we're just doing what we're doing, without thinking about what we're doing.[51]

Rupert Sheldrake, PhD, British biologist and researcher at Cambridge University, explains the phenomenon:

Consciousness is not, of course, all there is to the mind. Most of your activities and most of mine are unconscious; they're habitual. The vast majority of what we do is unconscious habit. So consciousness is concerned with only a tiny part of our psychic life. It's largely concerned with making choices. It's largely concerned with considering alternative possibilities.[52]

The subconscious can do its work on solving problems with no conscious Awareness involved

It is commonly known that brilliant discoveries and insights come spontaneously into the Mind. Most neuroscientists assume these eureka moments come from subconscious processing, as expressed by Neuroscientist David Eagleman:

> . . . you're an odd kind of newspaper reader, reading the headline and taking credit for the idea as though you thought of it first. You gleefully say, "I just thought of something!", when in fact your brain performed an enormous amount of work before your moment of genius struck. When an idea is served up from behind the scenes, your neural circuitry has been working on it for hours or days or years, consolidating information and trying out new combinations. But you take credit without further wonderment at the vast, hidden machinery behind the scenes.[53]

We live our daily lives being prompted by the subconscious

When we have a thought, it comes from the subconscious, becomes in part or whole a conscious experience, then is explained by the conscious Mind. What we regard as wholly rational, carefully thought-out statements are at their base the automatic upwellings from the subconscious. If we relied on the glacially slow conscious Mind to take us through the day, we would never get past our morning coffee. At every instance, we act quickly and automatically because we are relying on the subconscious to give us the knowledge experiences we need to make decisions and navigate through the day, then take over all the motor processing to put the decisions into action.

Speaking is the prime example. We don't speak using conscious Awareness. We speak from the subconscious. We have a concept we want to explain that may have come from conscious Awareness, but the totality of the explanation is in the subconscious. If we dragged the explanation into conscious Awareness to assemble it, we would dither for hours to voice a simple concept. Instead, we have a concept we access from our memory experiences and rely on the subconscious to give us words and syntax to match the message we want to communicate. We begin sentences, assemble the words using language syntax, and voice the words adeptly.

In addition to the subconscious using its creative and computing power in speaking, the subconscious brings us solutions to problems. If we insisted on evaluating every thought before acting on it, we would never solve a problem. We run through experiences that rise from the subconscious at lightning speed, accepting or rejecting them based on our judgments about what arises, not conscious reasoning. When we begin to reason every thought, we slow down the process to one word followed by the next at 40 to 120 bits of information a second.

We spend most of our lives functioning from the subconscious in automatic reactions and activities. In these automatic reactions, we assess where we are in the experiences of life and decide where to go next.

Evidence psychic experiences come to us at the subconscious Awareness level

The subconscious Awareness in the point of now knows information before it's even available for conscious Awareness to consider and process it. Then conscious Awareness notices it belatedly. The experience is so commonly known that the English language has a variety of terms for it: intuition, sixth sense, hunch, instinct, feeling, inspiration, second sight, a knowing, inkling, instinct, suspicion, gut reaction, and funny feeling. Many words refer to subconscious Awareness's receiving experiences from the future: foreboding, forewarning, precognition, presage, presentiment, premonition, portent, prophesy, prescience, and uneasy feeling.

The following are descriptions of studies showing people receiving experiences in the point of now subconscious Awareness that are not available to conscious Awareness.

People react to pictures seconds before seeing them

Dr. Dean Radin, senior scientist at the Institute of Noetic Sciences, performed carefully controlled studies in which people seated before a computer monitor were shown calm pictures (pastoral scenes and neutral household objects) or emotional pictures (erotic and violent scenes). The pictures were selected at random by a computer. The people's skin conductance levels were measured continually during the entire test. The skin conductance test is like a lie detector that shows whether the person feels stress. As you might expect, people showed stress at seeing the disturbing pictures and calm when shown the calm pictures.

Remarkably, the tests consistently showed that some people reacted to the pictures with the appropriately matched calm or stress as early as six seconds before the pictures were shown, even though the computer hadn't selected them at random yet. The subjects were having body experience stress reactions to their subconscious Awareness of the coming experience. They had no idea in conscious Awareness of what was going to be shown.[54]

The studies were replicated by Dick Bierman, a psychologist at the University of Amsterdam and Utrecht University.[55]

What this means is that the person's subconscious Awareness receives sight experiences in the point of now from the Universal Intelligence, interprets the experiences as disturbing or calming, and displays the interpretation's emotional effects in body experiences before the experience even exists in the physical realm for conscious Awareness to become aware of it.

Researchers from around the world, from Edinburgh University to Cornell in the United States, began to perform experiments to see whether people's subconscious Awareness receives experiences before the experiences are available to conscious Awareness. They extended the experiments into other dimensions with the same results. Radin and Bierman describe the studies:

> It was soon discovered that gamblers began reacting subconsciously shortly before they won or lost. The same effect was seen in those who are terrified of animals moments before they were shown the creatures. The odds against all of these trials being wrong is literally millions to one against.[56]

Subconscious Awareness receives experiences from the Universal Intelligence and interprets them before conscious Awareness has access to the experiences. The studies also show that experiences are accessible from at least a few seconds in what we call "the future," meaning all experiences from all places and all times are accessible.

People successfully anticipate someone's call or visit

It seems that, since subconscious Awareness receives experiences before conscious Awareness has access to the experiences, the phenomenon most likely affects people's daily lives. That is the case. We've all had the experience of thinking of someone and a few minutes later that person calls or knocks on the door. It could be someone we haven't communicated with for days or weeks.

To find out whether there really is a premonition that the person will call or knock on the door, Rupert Sheldrake, a British biologist, performed experiments in which he gave subjects a list of four people and had the subjects sit quietly beside the phone. They were then asked to select which of the four people they believed was about to call. The caller among the four was selected at random by rolling a die, so no one would know who was going to call.

We would expect that the subjects would guess correctly 25 percent of the time just by chance (one out of four). However, Sheldrake had results of 45 percent accuracy, showing that people often did know before a person called who was going to call.[57] The subjects had no conscious Awareness of the experiences to draw upon for the guesses.

People influence others through subconscious Awareness

In another set of experiments, people were able to influence other people's Minds and body experience by focusing on them, even when they were separated from one another by considerable distances. These experiments have been replicated several times with the same results: Braud and Schlitz, 1989;[58] Braud, 1990;[59] Schlitz and Braud, 1985.[60]

In these studies, one person (the "receiver") sat in a comfortable room with electrodes attached to two fingers to measure skin conductance (showing tension or relaxation). A computer did the measurements, so there was no person involved. In a separate, distant room, another person (the "influencer") also had electrodes attached to two fingers to see when the influencer was under stress. Records were available second by second of how each person's body was reacting.

The influencer attempted to either make the receiver feel calm or feel agitated during ten 30-second periods. The times and whether the influence was calming or agitating were chosen at random so the receivers couldn't know when the influencers were trained on them and couldn't know the type of influence being applied.

During calming attempts, the influencer relaxed and gently wished for the receiver to become calm, while visualizing the receiver being in a relaxing, calming attitude. During agitation attempts, the influencers tensed their bodies and wished for the receiver to become more agitated, while visualizing the receiver in energizing or agitated situations.

During the time between the influencing attempts, the influencers worked at keeping their Minds off the receivers and the experiment, thinking about unrelated things or visualizing the entire experiment as being successful.

The researchers performed 15 of these experiments, with 10 to 40 pairs of influencers and receivers in each experiment. In all, there were 323 sessions with 271 different subjects, 62 influencers, and 4 experimenters. The result was that 57 percent of the individual sessions showed the receivers were influenced at the subconscious Awareness level at the moment the influencers were sending calming or agitating thoughts. The receivers had no conscious Awareness of their being influenced.

The researchers replicated the study with 32 new subjects and had similar results.[61] They concluded that "... an individual is indeed able to directly, remotely, and mentally influence the physiological activity of another person through means other than the usual sensorimotor channels."[62] The receivers' conscious Awareness had no inkling of being influenced.

People receive message experiences from other people at the subconscious Awareness level because we are one Universal Intelligence. The implication is that when we have feelings of love or feelings of disdain for someone, that person knows it at the subconscious Awareness level. It shows why we feel uncomfortable with some people and immediately comfortable with others.

When healers send healing messages to receivers, the receivers' bodies react from subconscious Awareness

Healers have been known to have a positive effect on ill people both when in the same room and when separated by great distances. Whether healers could connect with those who are the focus of the healing ("receivers") was studied by measuring whether the receivers had changes in brain MRIs at the moments the healers focused on them. Jean Achterberg, PhD, professor of psychology at Southwestern Medical School and the Saybrook Institute, studied 11 pairs of healers and receivers of the healing intentions. The healers were asked to try to connect with the receivers in any ways they used in their healing traditions: prayer, sending energy, sending good intentions, or wishing the highest good for the receiver.

The receivers were in MRI machines, completely isolated from the healers and experimenters, who were in other locations. The healers were asked to send their prayers, healing thoughts, or good wishes for two minutes at irregular times determined by tosses of a coin. The study was blind because the receivers in the MRI did not know when the distant intentions were being sent.

The results of the study were highly significant. MRI scans of the brains of 9 of the 11 receivers showed major significant changes in brain function each moment the healers began praying, sending healing, or sending good thoughts to them. The experiences were at the subconscious Awareness level; subjects said they did not know when they were receiving the attention at the conscious Awareness level. In spite of that, during the moments when they were being sent healing thoughts, their brains, according to Dr. Achterberg, "lit up like Christmas trees."[63]

Measures of brain waves show people in the same room synchronize their brain waves

People commonly describe a feeling of a group unity among people assembled for a meeting. That phenomenon was studied by Dr. Nitamo Montecucco, professor at the University of Milan Centro di Medicina Olistica e Psicosomatica. His research, with up to 12 subjects in a room, showed a synchronization of the brain waves of the entire group, a phenomenon happening entirely in subconscious Awareness.[64]

People know when someone is staring at them

Between 68 and 94 percent of the population report having experienced the sense of being stared at.[65] A significant number of studies have shown that people in fact sense when someone is looking at them. The sense results because the subjects' subconscious Awareness is receiving the experience of being stared at, although their conscious Awareness has no knowledge of it.

Rupert Sheldrake, a British biologist well known for his research on consciousness, studied the sense of being stared at. In a series of trials, he had "lookers" stare or not stare at subjects at random times determined by tossing a coin. At times they were asked to guess whether at that moment they were actually being stared at; at other times they were asked to guess whether they were not being stared at. The results showed the subjects correctly guessed when they were being stared at on average 56.9 percent of the time. We would expect 50 percent correct by chance. This positive effect was highly significant, with the odds of its being by chance of one in 3 million.

In one school in Germany in which students known to be sensitive to such impressions were tested repeatedly, 71.2 percent of the guesses were correct, and two of the students were right about 90 percent of the time. Sheldrake duplicated the study in more than 15,000 trials involving more than 700 subjects with the same results.[66]

In an effort to eliminate any possibility that the people being stared at might receive cues that the lookers were staring at them, Richard Wiseman, professor of public understanding of psychology at the University of Hertfordshire, and Marilyn Schlitz, PhD, vice president for research and education at the Institute of Noetic Sciences, had a looker in one room looking at a monitor, while the person being stared at (the "stare receiver") was in another room with a video camera trained at the back of his or her head.

The stare receiver had electrodes attached to the first and third fingers of the hand to measure skin conductance that would reveal subtle tension in the body. When people see someone staring at them, their tension increases. That tension would show up on the skin conductance test if the stare receiver received the subconscious feeling that someone was staring at him or her.

The stare receiver sat alone in a room with the door shut and had no possible contact with anyone outside of the room. The looker watched the person on the monitor only when told to do so. The times were recorded, along with the stare receiver's finger skin conductance changes. The result was that the stare receiver often reacted when being stared at from the other room, with the results beyond chance, just as Sheldrake's subjects had done with both people in the same room.[67]

The study was replicated by Dean Radin, senior scientist at the Institute of Noetic Sciences, Dick Bierman, PhD, a professor at the University of Amsterdam, and Robert Morris, PhD, at the University of Edinburgh with the same results. Many people's bodies reacted when they were stared at from another room.[68]

William Braud, PhD, a University of Houston psychology professor, co-director of the William James Center for Consciousness

Studies, and director of research at the Mind Science Foundation, replicated the studies in 1990 and 1993.[69]

This sense of being stared at is an experience that comes into the point of now subconscious Awareness, is interpreted at the subconscious level, and gives the person a bodily reaction at the subconscious level. Conscious Awareness has no knowledge of being stared at.

Siblings' minds are linked at the subconscious level

We would expect that the Minds of people who are closely related would be even more closely linked. We've all experienced a sense of knowing what's going on with a person we love or knowing what they're thinking or finishing their sentences.

To learn whether the Minds of people close to one another are actually linked in subconscious Awareness, studies have been performed with siblings. One test was performed under the intense scrutiny of television cameras in 1997 on a program titled *Carlton TV's Paranormal World of Paul McKenna*. The subjects were sisters Elaine and Evelyn Dove.

Elaine sat in the studio in front of a large pyramid. Evelyn was in a separate room sealed off from all noise and communication from outside the room. Evelyn had standard polygraph devices attached to her body to measure her stress. She went through some relaxation exercises and her polygraph showed she was nicely relaxed.

Meanwhile, in the other room, sealed away from Evelyn, Elaine was asked to watch the pyramid intently. As Elain focused on the pyramid, without warning the pyramid exploded in a burst of sparks, flashes, and colored smoke, startling Elaine and giving her a considerable shock. At exactly that moment, Evelyn's polygraph pen recorded a huge swing, with one pen running off the top of the paper. Without trying to communicate with her sister, Evelyn had experienced her distress in subconscious Awareness. When asked whether she felt or sensed anything, Evelyn said she experienced nothing out of the ordinary. Her conscious Awareness was not involved at all.[70]

Twins' minds are linked at the subconscious Awareness level

It is widely known that twins are often telepathic, and when something happens to a twin, the other very often feels the same emotions or pain in exactly the same way even though they are separated by thousands of miles. A well-known, extensive review of the studies of twins' mental connections was written by Guy Lyon Playfair.[71] The conclusion of the review of the studies was that there is powerful evidence that twins are joined psychically through shared emotions, thoughts, tactile sensations, and even physical manifestations such as bruising or burning. The experiences in the receiving twin are in the subconscious Awareness.

The journal *Science* published a study by two physiologists who reported finding significant correlations in brain waves between isolated identical twins. These sorts of studies came to be known as distant mental intention on living systems (DMILS). At the subconscious Awareness level, the twins' Minds share experiences.[72]

A demonstration of this link between twins was shown before a vast audience on January 10, 2003. Richard and Damien Powles, identical twins, were invited to a television studio to participate in a telepathy experiment to be shown later that day on a chat show named *Channel 4's Richard and Judy Show*.

Richard Powles was taken to a soundproof room in the television studio and was asked to sit before a bucket of ice-cold water. In another studio well out of sight and earshot, his identical twin brother Damien was sitting quietly, connected to a polygraph machine. Sitting beside Damien was a polygrapher, who was monitoring his respiration, abdominal muscle tension, pulse, and skin conductance. The polygrapher and Damien had no idea what Richard, in the other room, was about to do.

When told to do so, Richard plunged his arm into the bucket of near-freezing water, giving a gasp as he did so.

At the exact moment Richard's icy plunge caused him to gasp, there was a sudden blip on the line monitoring Damien's respiration rate. It was as though he too had gasped, but he actually hadn't. The effect was so obvious that the polygrapher pointed to it with his thumb to indicate that he knew something had happened to Richard.

The researchers continued the experiment with the twins on the same show. Richard was asked to open a cardboard box placed before him. He did, excitedly, expecting to find something nice (preferably edible) in it. Instead, a huge rubber snake shot out of it, giving him a fright. His twin Damien's pulse rate, indicated by the pen on the polygraph, shot up at the same moment.[73]

One twin feels the emotions and pain their twin feels at the level of their subconscious Awareness. However, their conscious Awareness has no knowledge of the experiences unless there is pain involved.

Unusually talented artists and musicians describe their abilities as coming from outside of their conscious Awareness

The ability to access experiences at a higher level of capability characterizes gifted people, such as mathematicians, musicians, and artists. During Earth School pre-birth planning, these people established that they would be able to have access to experiences such as the ability to perform mathematical calculations, compose music, or paint. They are known as geniuses, or if they have genius in one area and mental disabilities in other areas, they are known as savants. Their Awareness is receiving subconscious experiences that inspire their creations.

Akiane Kramarik, the renowned artist who began drawing at age 4 and was an accomplished artist by age 8, had profound visions of Heaven. She wrote that her main inspiration comes from the Heavenly Father, who gives her visions of Heaven:

A vision is like an oasis in a desert. You can't have it all the time, as you need to keep on continuing your journey through the desert of life experiences, full of trials. . . . I am not so concerned about waiting for a vision to appear because I know it will come to me when I least expect it."[74]

The inspirations came from her subconscious Awareness from a source outside of her Mind.

Minnie Evans, an African-American visionary artist had captivating spiritual experiences in the 1930s that led her to paint. *Art and Design Inspiration* wrote this about her:

> It was Good Friday when she claims to have heard God's command telling her to draw. Following this vision, she was inspired to paint for the next five decades."[75]

The inspirations came to her subconscious Awareness.

Alma Deutscher, composer of piano and violin sonatas, was described as a little Miss Mozart. Deutscher is brimming with charming melodies, which often arrive unbidden and fully formed:

> Even when I'm trying to do something else, when people are talking to me about something completely different, I get these beautiful melodies that play inside my Mind. Sometimes it might be a human voice singing, sometimes a piano, sometimes a violin.[76]

She describes how, in the middle of the night, an entire set of piano variations in E-flat announced itself to her subconscious Awareness:

> I woke up and I didn't want to lose the melodies so I took my notebook and wrote it all down, which took almost three hours. My parents didn't understand why I was so tired in the morning and didn't want to get up![77]

You can view a video of Alma Deutscher playing the piano variations in E-flat at www.earthschoolanswers.com/deutscher/.

Alonzo Clemons is an animal sculptor and savant. He suffered a brain injury as a child that left him with severe mental disability, but he creates accurate animal sculptures of clay from a single viewing of an animal's picture in as little as 20 minutes.

When asked how he could keep a picture of a horse in his mind and create the horse sculpture, Alonzo replied, "I remember. God in Heaven." Dr. Darryl Clifford, a psychiatrist who reviewed Alonzo's abilities, explained,

That's a very characteristic response. When you ask any
of the savants, "How do you do it?" they say they
remember or it's their mind . . . it just comes naturally to
them.. . . He does . . . see a picture in his head. It's there,
and it's much more detailed and has a retention much
more than the rest of us do. We would have to go back
and keep reinforcing that in our mind, especially with
respect to detail.[78]

Remarkably, Alonzo can look at a picture of an animal such as a
horse and sculpt even the details he can't see in the picture, such as the
bottoms of the horse's hooves with the horseshoes. He does not need to
refer back to a picture. He has access to the image in his subconscious
Awareness to create the sculpture.

The most parsimonious explanation is that Alonzo, with his
limited conscious Awareness function, is open to the subconscious
Awareness experiences, where he has access to the image of the animal
from the Universal Intelligence as he sculpts.

Blind people are able to perform sighted activities, even though they insist they see nothing

The book *Your Eternal Self: Science Discovers the Afterlife*[79]
describes abilities blind people have that show they are receiving
experiences in subconscious Awareness that enable them to perform
actions they should not be able to perform. However, while performing
them, they insist their conscious Awareness is unable to see or identify
what they are responding to. The ability is called "blindsight."

Sight experiences come into Awareness from the Universal
Intelligence. A body with eyes is not necessary for the person to have
the sight experiences. The sight experiences come into subconscious
Awareness. The blind person must then accept the sight experiences to
be able to use them in normal functioning. Even after learning to do so,
the blind person still may insist he or she is completely blind and
unable to have sight experiences.

In a study published in *The Journal of Neuroscience*, researchers
wanted to discover whether the phenomenon of blindsight is real. They

tested a patient with a destroyed visual cortex resulting in full cortical blindness. While in an fMRI machine, the subject's amygdala, the area of the brain that activates to evaluate whether something is a threat, activated each time someone looked at him at random points. The subject was receiving sight experiences in subconscious Awareness, even though he was completely blind.[80]

In studies when people were made blind temporarily, they were still able to locate things on a computer screen. However, they were not conscious of seeing a visual image. The perception was in their subconscious Awareness.[81]

A patient known as D. B. had brain surgery that accidentally damaged one side of his V1 visual cortex. He could no longer see anything to the left of his nose. However, D. B. would reach for things outside of his field of vision on the left side as though he could see them. Researchers shined a point of light at a location in his blind spot area. When asked where the point of light in his left blind area was, he said he couldn't tell because he was blind. When he was asked to guess where it might be, he was correct at rates far greater than chance. However, his conscious Awareness was not aware of the objects or lights.[82]

David Linden, professor of neuroscience at Johns Hopkins University, found that if the visual cortex is damaged, people will assert that they cannot see anything, but when asked to pick up an object in an unknown location within reach, many can do so on the first try. They also can judge an emotional expression on a face, especially anger, more often than chance would predict they would.[83] The experiences are coming from subconscious Awareness's accessing them from the Universal Intelligence.

Another phenomenon, called "echolocation," also demonstrates that blind people can have subconscious Awareness of objects in their environment even though their conscious Awareness registers nothing. Two examples of blind people able to use echolocation to navigate the world adeptly follow. In both cases, the explanation for their abilities is that sight experiences are accessible by subconscious Awareness, apart from the body. They use clicking sounds in what they believe is "echolocation," but these sounds are only devices that give their conscious Awareness confidence to accept what the subconscious reveals to them, much like scrying.

Ben Underwood, who lost his sight to cancer as a toddler, had two artificial eyes made of plastic. However, he walked without a cane or seeing-eye dog, played video games, and identified objects he passed by name: "That's a fire hydrant" or "That's a trash can." Ben made clicking sounds with his mouth that he claimed were like sonar, bouncing off objects and returning to his ears so he could identify them by sound. However, that claim was never tested, and he was able to name things distant from him, such as buildings, that his clicking would not be able to identify. He could play video games, and in a pillow fight, he could throw a pillow to hit a targeted person even when the person was moving silently.[84]

You can watch a video about Ben at www.earthschoolanswers.com/ben/.

Other blind people believe they are using echolocation to perform sighted activities. One example is Brian Bushway. Brian lost his sight when his optic nerves deteriorated as a child. He now is completely blind, but is able to identify objects in his surroundings with an accuracy far beyond the ability of a person using clicks in a sonar-like fashion. He can ride a bike while avoiding obstacles, distinguish a bush from a tree, and tell a footpath's direction. He can identify fine movements that the gross capabilities of sound echolocation could not account for. As he said, "It was more than just hearing. I was actually imaging the world around me."[85]

Melvyn Goodale is a Canadian neuroscientist and director of the Brain and Mind Institute at the University of Western Ontario, where he holds the Canada Research Chair in Visual Neuroscience. After working with Brian, he reported,

> When we tested Brian on his ability to detect changes in the position of an object, he was absolutely astounding. He could tell if we moved the object only a few inches, something that I never expected someone who is echo-locating would be able to do. He doesn't have super hearing or anything of that kind. He was tested by a

clinical audiologist, you know, someone who tests how good your hearing is. He's actually normal for his age. What he can do and what is quite amazing is he can attend to these very tiny echoes that we ignore.[86]

You can see a video about Brian's ability at this link: www.earthschoolanswers.com/brian/.

A blind autistic savant named Ellen Boudreaux is able to walk without running into obstacles using chirping sounds.

As she learnt to walk, her parents noticed that she had a spatial sense that was impressive for a blind child. She was able to pin-point the exact location of objects in front of her such as fences, walls and buildings that were at a distance of about 6 feet away from her. Throughout her childhood, she developed and used a form of radar that consisted of little chirping sounds that enabled her to get a very good sense of direction and navigate her way through life.[87]

The possibility that she is able to detect the sound waves bouncing back from objects was never demonstrated to be possible, and she is able to avoid soft obstacles such as stuffed chairs and couches that would not reflect sounds. She is accessing subconscious experiences that enable her to avoid obstacles. The chirping sounds give her mind permission to accept in conscious Awareness what is coming through her subconscious.

In another case of blindsight, a patient named T.N. had his visual centers damaged from two strokes that left him completely blind. Nurses noticed he seemed to have visual responses, so researchers curious to know more about his condition asked him to walk down a hallway he thought was empty, but which was cluttered with boxes, chairs, and a filing cabinet. He walked down the hallway avoiding all the obstacles perfectly.[88] However, T.N. had no conscious Awareness of anything in the hallway. His sight experiences of the obstacles were coming from the Universal Intelligence in the Mind.

To view a video explaining these examples of blindsight, go to this link: www.earthschoolanswers.com/20/.

Blindsight in monkeys

The fact that the Mind receives experiences without having what we normally would call visual ability demonstrates that there is only Mind and experiences. Mind extends to animals. They are conscious in the same way we are conscious, but with different abilities. That means they have conscious Awareness and subconscious Awareness.

Professor Nicholas Humphrey studied a monkey named Helen that had the visual cortex of her brain removed so she was completely blind. However, he discovered that Helen was able to navigate her environment and locate objects just as though she had sight. When she was anxious, she lost the ability.[89]

This ability in monkeys indicates that monkeys also have a sixth sense, allowing experiences coming from the subconscious to influence behavior.

Watch a video of Dr. Humphrey describing blindsight in monkeys at www.earthschoolanswers.com/humphrey/. Watch a video of Helen the monkey navigating through obstacles at www.earthschoolanswers.com/helen/.

People are able to have sight experiences with blindfolded or bandaged eyes

The same phenomenon as the ability to have sight experiences in echolocation is apparent in the practice of having people identify objects and avoid obstacles when their eyes are blindfolded or bandaged.

Richard Hodgson was a professor of philosophy at Cambridge University and a researcher with the British Society for Psychical Research.[90] To demonstrate Hodgson's abilities to have sight experiences with closed and sealed eyes, researchers emulated experiments that has been previously performed with a man known only as "Dick." Dick could describe objects held in front of him or name any card drawn at random from a deck of cards when his eyes were sealed and bandaged. The researchers went to great lengths to ensure Hodgson could not see:

> I covered each eye with a piece of gummed paper, cut as nearly as I could remember of the same shape as the plaster put over "Dick's" eyes on Saturday and Sunday last. This was stuck both over the eyelid and down to the check. Mr. Hodgson finds it essential to success to have it stuck to the cheek. [N.B.—So does "Dick."] Over each eye a penny was placed, and held there with a strip of gummed paper right across from temple to temple, and over this a handkerchief was bound. . . .

> Mr. Hodgson could distinguish objects and read cards. Form was more easy to see than colour. He was generally right about the suit in the small number of trials we made, but the number of pips gave him more trouble, especially when the number was large.

Since then, individuals have demonstrated their abilities to have sight experiences without using their eyes, including the renowned psychic Dr. Richard Ireland.[91] Ireland first realized he could see without using his eyes when he was five years old. He had corrective operations on both eyes and was fully bandaged so he could see nothing. The nurses were surprised to see little Richard sitting on the floor bouncing a ball off a wall repeatedly and catching it without missing.[92]

View a video of Dr. Ireland's demonstration at www.earthschoolanswers.com/ireland/.

Today, organizations are teaching people how to have sight experiences while blindfolded. One company called Vibravision® trains people how to identify objects and navigate around obstacles while fully blindfolded. Participants hold their hands out to register "vibrations" from obstacles to avoid them.[93] The company's website is at www.mp-usa.org/vibravision/. As far as I know, the company's methods have not been rigorously tested. However, the demonstrations and testimonials seem quite convincing that the subjects are able to have sight experiences without using their eyes. The sight experiences are accessible from the Universal Intelligence.

You can see a video of Vibravision® practitioners and students navigating around obstacles at www.earthschoolanswers.com/vibravision/.

A woman in the UK named Nicola Farmer has established the Inspiring Children University (ICU) that teaches children how to see, read, and play without using their eyes—fully blindfolded. She explains that children between the ages of 6 and 12 are still at the stage when they are able to access their psychic abilities so they can use their Minds to access the experiences of sight when their eyes are not functioning. The children's abilities have not been rigorously tested, but the testimonials from parents all agree that the children are able to have sight experiences while fully blindfolded.

You can view a demonstration of the children's abilities at www.earthschoolanswers.com/icu/.

If 95 percent of our thinking is from the subconscious, where is free will?

We must remember that we are not the experiences coming into the point of now Awareness. We are not the interpretations or emotions. We are the soul that is Aware. We chose this Earth School experience and planned it before we entered. We are the Awareness that is always present when the experiences continually enter Awareness and are instantly replaced. And when we graduate from Earth School, we will return to our identity as our individual eternal soul, with the freedom to go on with our growth in the life after this life in any realm we choose.

We also have free will in our conscious Awareness. Through our conscious Awareness, we are free to evaluate what is arising from our subconscious and reject it at once or modify it through examining it and altering it over time. We are freely able to reject the natural inclinations we were taught in our early years in Earth School that might be self-absorbed, materialistic, and insensitive so the subconscious experiences and interpretations that arise as we have experiences in Earth School are more loving, compassionate, and other-centered. It just takes time and effort.

Conversely, if we decide through our free will not to challenge those interpretations and strategies coming from the subconscious, then we will continue to allow them to determine the life we live and the person we are. But we are making that free will choice to live bound by the chains that were forged in our childhoods.

Cognitive dissonance in interpretations

People don't organize the interpretations in the subconscious. They're just thrown into the box as the experiences come to us, like the contents of that disorganized catch-all drawer we all have. As a result, the person may be surprised to find interpretations she holds that contradict other interpretations. She doesn't realize the problem until the two interpretations are juxtaposed by some event. The result is cognitive dissonance.

For example, the person who proclaims that she supports the role of her church to care for the poor is asked what she has done to help the poor in her city. She realizes she has done nothing and remembers she has a "No panhandlers" sign on her door because she has been bothered by panhandlers. How can she reconcile the belief that society must take care of the poor with her own activities?

The cognitive dissonance makes her uncomfortable. Like the other negative emotions, discomfort indicates that something is amiss or threatening. To remove the discomfort, she scans the thoughts in her subconscious to reassemble her interpretations until she comes to a combination that results in her feeling comfortable. She is creating a rationalization. A rationalization is a conscious attempt to reconcile two interpretations at odds with one another to feel comfortable. But the reconciliation is entirely in the person's mind. A rationalization is much like rearranging furniture in a living room so the arrangement feels good. No arrangement is right or wrong; the feeling is entirely personal.

And so, the woman concerned about the cognitive dissonance between what she professes about the poor and what she is doing may scan her subconscious interpretations and rearrange the furniture into this configuration: "I have looked for agencies that help the poor in my city and couldn't find any. I've done as much as I can do until someone tells me where I can help the poor. I'll take down the 'No panhandlers' sign." As a result, she feels she's doing a noble deed by taking down the sign, and feels satisfied she has given it her best effort to find an agency to help the poor. With the interpretations rearranged, she feels comfortable. All's right with the world.

However, all that has happened is that she has rearranged her interpretations. We spend much of our lives moving the furniture in our minds to feel good about ourselves. Whether the resulting rearrangement is true or logical or valid makes no difference. What matters to the person is that he or she creates an arrangement that removes the discomfort and results in an OK feeling.

Ordinary life rewards the automatic subconscious responses that are most satisfying to our culture. The self-assured manager, the empathetic mother, the hard-working teenager all are acting from the spontaneous activities of the subconscious. They are good at performing well so they receive rewards.

At times, out of the subconscious comes fear, defensiveness, anxiety, and other negative emotions. These automatic responses from the subconscious arise from what neuroscientists call the "reptilian brain." The interpretations of experiences are those the culture has taught, which include generous amounts of fear, insensitivity, and even violence.

Changes in the subconscious interpretations normally occur through the experiences of reward or punishment following actions, without conscious effort. However, people can change to have more empathetic, other-centered, loving, compassionate interpretations by using the conscious mind to rethink interpretations. The book *Earth School: Love, Learn, Be Happy* explains how to make those changes.

Subconscious experiences affect our interactions

Subconscious experiences continually come into Awareness during all interactions with others. While we are speaking in a normal conversation, the subconscious experiences and interpretations are flooding our Awareness at the level below conscious Awareness. We are not aware of them, but they affect us.

For example, Marge is meeting with Frank and Lucy about the project the three of them are working on. Frank looks at Lucy with a knowing look, then at Marge. He says, "Marge, I know you're very busy right now. It might be a good idea if you don't spend time keeping the finance records for the project. Lucy has time on her hands and can do that. So give her the books this afternoon." Lucy is nodding her head, "yes."

What experiences is Marge having during the meeting? If you think she is learning from Frank that Lucy will take care of the books, you've identified only five percent of the experiences Marge has had flowing into her Awareness. Those are the words Frank said, with the sight experiences of Lucy and Frank. However, Marge is receiving a constant flow of experiences and interpretations in her subconscious awareness:

- Marge experiences Frank glancing at Lucy with a knowing look. The interpretation comes into her subconscious Awareness that Frank and Lucy have something bad to say. That triggers the interpretation that she's being judged. The emotional response is anxiety. She doesn't process any of that consciously. It all flows into her subconscious so the interpretations affect her.

- Marge experiences Frank saying something she knows isn't true. Contrary to Frank's statement, Marge has lots of time, so she interprets the experience as Frank's manipulating or deceiving her. She feels fear, anxiety, and a little anger.

- The experiences of the knowing look and manipulative statement trigger the interpretation that Frank and Lucy have been talking about her behind her back. She interprets the experience as her being rejected by them, judged negatively, and being unloved. She feels fear, anxiety, and anger.

- The experience of hearing Frank say "Give her the books this afternoon" triggers the interpretation she is being commanded by a colleague, followed by the interpretations she is being patronized and is not valued, that her views and feelings are of no consequence. She feels greater fear, anxiety, and anger.

- The experience of seeing Lucy nod her head is interpreted as reinforcing that Marge is not valued, is not esteemed, is not welcome as a part of the group, and is not loved. Marge feels fear and anxiety that give rise to anger.

This is just a sampling of the experiences Marge is having in her subconscious Awareness that are affecting her but are not being processed in conscious Awareness, where logic and reason could think them through. In the subconscious Awareness, the experiences and interpretations are triggering emotions. Her behavior is going to be determined by the subconscious experiences, regardless of what the conscious experiences may seem to be.

Frank and Lucy are also thinking and acting using the 95 percent of the experiences in their subconscious Awareness. The result is that Marge, Frank, and Lucy are all having a heated interaction dominated by subconscious interpretations that give rise to negative emotions. The five percent of thoughtful conscious Awareness that is involved will be buried in the subconscious interpretations that drive the interaction.

Through her subconscious Awareness, Marge has learned much more than the fact that Frank wants Lucy to handle the books:

- Frank and Lucy talk about her when she isn't present.

- Frank and Lucy are aligned; Marge is not accepted in this social group.

- Frank and Lucy don't believe she is competent as a bookkeeper.

- Frank will tell her half-truths or untruths to manipulate her.

- Frank believes he can command Marge, so she is viewed as an underling, not a partner.

- Frank is in charge. Lucy and Marge are peons.

Marge now has new experiences that will come to subconscious Awareness when she has encounters with Frank and Lucy. The new experiences will have the same interpretations and the same emotions as the experiences she had with Frank and Marge in the meeting. She will be easily "set off" by Frank.

Marge can break the cycle of having the negative interpretations and negative emotions come into subconscious Awareness during interactions with Frank if she draws the experiences and interpretations out of her subconscious and examines them to see whether she wants to continue having the interpretations that result in her negative emotions. At the time the dialogue is taking place, she has little control over the immediate subconscious experiences triggered to come into conscious and subconscious Awareness. To change them, she must take time to work on them at some other, calmer time.

The 95 percent of the learning Marge has experienced is coming from subconscious experiences. Most of our day is spent living out of the experiences we are not consciously aware of. We then explain the experiences and interpretations that have already determined our conclusions using the most rational conscious explanations that fit the situation, whether they are coming from the subconscious experiences or not. The interpretations were set before the first word of the explanations was uttered.

Subconscious messages and inspirations come from guides and people who love us living in the next life

We are continually receiving messages and inspirations from guides, helpers, loved ones, and people living in the next realm of life who are interested in us. All of their inspirations are intended to help us. We just have to allow them to come into our conscious Awareness so we can act on them. We have much evidence that we are receiving inspirations all day.

In Rob Schwartz's *Your Soul's Plan*, medium Staci Wells' spirit guide describes how a man's classmates were inspired by their guides at the subconscious level to say things to the man for his benefit:

> "I'm told that John's classmates were not soul mates in the sense of having made a soul-level agreement with him," [Staci] replied, echoing the words of her guide. "But they were impressed by their guides to say things. Their guides were working in concert with John's. They were given phrases, things to blurt out. I just asked if that was every time it happened, and I was told, 'Yes, that was every time, and they would likely have no recollection of this.'"
>
> [Rob adds this note.] I was surprised by this information. I had not yet heard that spirit guides influenced people in their speech. Nevertheless, it was consistent with other sessions in which I learned that our guides work diligently to ensure we have the experiences we planned before birth, even when those experiences are painful. Though perhaps unpleasant or difficult to comprehend when viewed from the perspective of the personality, this idea takes on an entirely different meaning when considered from the viewpoint of the soul. As souls, we know that life is a drama on the earth stage and that we can be permanently harmed no more than an actor can be by another actor's lines.[94]

Madame Curie, the Polish-French physicist and chemist who was a pioneer in the study of radioactivity and the first two-time Nobel laureate in two different sciences, transitioned from Earth School in 1934. She came through in a direct-voice session with Leslie Flint on November 3, 1988, to describe her learning after her transition. She had been inspired in her discoveries to a much greater extent than she realized. You can listen to the recording of her speaking from the life after this life at www.earthschoolanswers.com/curie/. This is a portion of the transcript of her speaking:

I don't know, I think to myself as I look back on my life, I realize now that what I had to do I did. It was not just by myself, you know. A lot of things you know, we call inspiration, you know, which in a way is so. I did not know then that I was to some extent induced by people from this side of life. A lot of the things that we sometimes think come from ourselves do not necessarily come that way. But we are inspired, inspiration, you know, guidance from people on this side of life who help us, you know. I was I suppose in a way a medium. I never thought it was like that. I did not understand this Spiritualism. I had some experience of it, yes, but not much.

But now I know that many of the things that have been done and the things that I did, you know, were things that were given to me from people on this side, people that I have now met, you know. I have met many souls here who are deeply involved, you know, in the work, to heal the sick and the suffering, to find ways of curing diseases. And I now know that some of the things that happened with me which I thought at the time I was aware were truths of my own invention, I was inspired, you know, impressed what to do and how to go about it. You know, we are all children. We don't understand perhaps sometimes. In a way, we are being impressed, we are given guidance, we are helped. We are children and we need guidance and help, but we don't always understand or accept, you know.[95]

Our subconscious Awareness is being filled by messages and inspirations from guides, helpers, loved ones, and people living in the next realm of life who are interested in us. We can benefit from them by being open to the messages and inspirations and allowing them to rise into conscious Awareness.

Methods to bring subconscious knowledge into conscious Awareness

A variety of experiences and interpretations are always in subconscious Awareness but do not come into conscious awareness because of the Mind's focus on everyday life activities that fill conscious Awareness, like the concert piano that rises above the other instruments. At any moment, insights and messages are entering and being replaced in subconscious Awareness. They're just not registering in conscious Awareness.

This information is experiences coming from sources in the Universal Intelligence. We are individual manifestations of the Universal Intelligence, so we receive experience information continually about people and objects that is not accessible to conscious Awareness. We are all psychic at the subconscious Awareness level.

When someone is doing mindless work, such as walking, taking a shower, knitting, or other activity that lulls the conscious Mind into a relaxed state, subconscious knowledge and experiences can come into the unoccupied conscious Awareness. During these times, people may receive messages from loved ones living in the life after this life, answers to problems, insights into issues, and other experiences that normally would not be realized because of the intensity of conscious Awareness's navigating through the day.

In a hypnogogic state, between sleeping and waking, conscious Awareness is less preoccupied with experiences in the Earth School environment, so knowledge and experiences from the subconscious may enter conscious Awareness. People often describe messages from loved ones and insights into problems as they awaken. The messages were always there, and the insights were always available, but they couldn't come into conscious awareness as long as conscious awareness was filled with Earth School experiences.

In dreams, the Mind accesses subconscious experiences because the conscious Awareness is anesthetized. However, control by conscious awareness isn't operating, so the dream can access a wide range of experiences and knowledge knitted together into a drama that has organization, but doesn't fit real life. At other times, the content of the dreams can be dramatic insights, dream visitations from loved ones, exciting adventures, and surprising events. They are all bubbling up from the subconscious when conscious Awareness is quieted.

Experiences from subconscious Awareness can also come into conscious Awareness through a process very similar to a magician's sleight of hand. A magician relies on the viewer's acceptance of a reality that confirms what the viewer expects subconsciously to be happening. In the simplest example, Grandpa has a quarter in his hand concealed from view. He reaches behind his grandchild's ear and pulls out the quarter, to his grandchild's amazement and delight. The child accepts the assumption from the subconscious Mind that Grandpa's action of reaching behind the child's ear and pulling out a coin is actually what it appears to be: ears have quarters behind them and Grandpa has the ability to pull them out.

Psychics know the Mind can be manipulated so knowledge in subconscious Awareness can be brought into conscious Awareness through a similar sleight of hand. Psychics have the unique ability to access experiences from the Universal Intelligence that pertain to an individual or situation the psychic has no personal knowledge of. The information comes to the psychic in subconscious Awareness. Many psychics have a talent that allows the knowledge to come from subconscious Awareness directly into conscious Awareness. However, others use a sleight of hand to allow the information to come from subconscious Awareness into conscious Awareness so the psychic can describe it. They use scrying.

Scrying is a method of using a visual surface to allow the subconscious images to enter conscious Awareness. In scrying, the psychic looks at a pool of water, blackened mirror, polished metal, crystal ball, or other surface that distorts light. The psychic relaxes his or her conscious Awareness to allow the indistinct shapes on the shimmering surface to seem to take on form. When the psychic asks a question about a person being read or a situation such as a crime, experiences come from the Universal Intelligence into the scryer's subconscious Awareness. The psychic then allows the indistinct shapes in the scrying medium to seem to form images.

The answers are not in the play of lights on the surface, however. That is the sleight of hand. Conscious Awareness believes it sees images, but what it is seeing is the images and stories subconscious Awareness has received psychically about the life of the person or the situation.

The same is true of Tarot cards. Each Tarot card has images with symbolism. The cards have stories attached to them, but the stories behind the cards are less important than the stories the psychic allows to emerge from the psychic's subconscious Awareness into conscious Awareness. The knowledge of the person being read emerges naturally from the psychic's subconscious Awareness where the knowledge is accessed from the Universal Intelligence. The stories the Tarot reader sees in the cards contains the experiences pertaining to the person being read that emerge from the subconscious into conscious Awareness.

Another way the conscious Mind can be manipulated into allowing subconscious Awareness to come into conscious Awareness is through using bodily sensations. Psychometry is the ability to hold an object and access knowledge about the owner. One method of learning whether a person has psychometry ability is to use playing cards to see whether the person is able to identify the color of a card without looking at it by sensing a feeling in the body. It is another sleight of hand that fools conscious Awareness into letting experiences from subconscious Awareness to emerge.

You can try this yourself. Put 10 black and 10 red playing cards in a shuffled pile face down. Take the top card without looking at it and hold it face down on the palm of one hand. If the card feels mildly cold, it is black. If it feels mildly warm, it is red. Without looking at the card, put the card into a pile for the warm red cards or another pile for the cold black cards. After doing this with all 20 cards, turn the piles over. If the warm red pile contains more than 5 red and the cold black pile contains more than 5 black, it could mean you have psychometry ability or other psychic ability. In my own case, when I first performed this procedure I didn't count out 10 red and 10 black cards; I just took cards from the deck as they came. I did about 23 cards. When I turned the piles over, all the cards in the cold black pile were black. All but one of the cards in the warm red pile were red. I had fooled my conscious

Awareness into thinking the cards were warm or cold so the information about the color of the cards could come to my conscious Awareness from my subconscious Awareness.

The same phenomenon seems to be at work in a company called Vibravision® that trains people how to identify objects and navigate around obstacles while fully blindfolded. I explained Vibravision® earlier. Participants hold their hands out to register "vibrations" from obstacles to avoid them. The founder describes feeling the temperatures of objects he holds while blindfolded to identify their colors. These sensations allow the experiences to come from subconscious Awareness into conscious Awareness as signals about temperature that are not in the objects. The knowledge about objects in space and colors are correctly accessed from the Universal Intelligence into subconscious Awareness, but the blindfolded person holding the object or walking around obstacles must allow the information to come from subconscious Awareness into conscious Awareness.

I previously provided the following link to a video of Vibravision® practitioners and students navigating around obstacles and identifying things while blindfolded: www.earthschoolanswers.com/vibravision/.

Another method of allowing experiences to come from subconscious Awareness into conscious Awareness is through the use of hypnosis. Hypnosis puts the conscious Awareness into a relaxed state that allows the subconscious messages to come into conscious Awareness. Some of these subconscious experiences are messages from loved ones living in the life after this life. The Self-Guided Afterlife Connections self-hypnosis training (described at www.selfguided.spiritualunderstanding.org) teaches the participant self-hypnosis to allow the connections with loved ones in the life after this life to come from subconscious Awareness into conscious Awareness. The method has an 86 percent connection rate.[96]

Other bodily sensations can help someone make a decision. Some people are able to "feel" good decisions and bad decisions. When considering a decision, if an alternative seems to have life in it and feel good, it could be a good decision. If it seems cold and lifeless or even anxiety producing, it could be a poor decision.

These and other methods are like sleights of hand that allow experiences to emerge from subconscious Awareness into conscious Awareness so the person can experience and understand them.

Unaccepted subconscious experiences and doubt

Scrying, blindsight, and echolocation give the person the conviction the experiences coming into subconscious Awareness are actionable reality. Subconscious experiences register continually at a subtle level in everyone's Awareness, but people don't notice them, or they receive subtle intuitions and ignore them. When the person uses a sleight of hand technique such as scrying, blindsight, and echolocation, the subconscious experiences become actionable: the person acts assuming the intuitions or notions are reality. As Brian Bushway said of his senses when using echolocation, "It was more than just hearing. I was actually imaging the world around me."[97]

When we drive a car, walk, climb stairs, or otherwise act, we do so using subconscious Awareness. We take for granted the realities of our environment and act without doubt or reservation. We lift our feet to the next level on stairs confident the next level is there. We walk through a living space avoiding obstacles without thinking about the obstacles. Our walking is automatic. The senses of objects are in subconscious Awareness. We don't have to recheck the sight or knowledge realities involved in walking through the room before acting.

The subconscious Awareness a sighted person has about objects that enables him or her to navigate a room comes from experiences given by the Universal Intelligence. The blind person also has experiences from the Universal Intelligence, but the experiences are different from the experiences of the five senses; they are a sixth sense. The blind person has subconscious sensed experiences akin to sight, accepts them as reality, and navigates around obstacles using those experiences in the same way a sighted person uses the subconscious experiences of sight in peripheral vision to navigate without consideration of the experiences.

A blind person believes making clicks or chirps creates a sonar effect that allows him or her to identify objects, so the sixth sense impressions from the Universal Intelligence that are coming into subconscious Awareness are accepted as actionable. The result is that for both the sighted and blind person, the person believes without doubt that what is coming from subconscious Awareness about the environment is actionable reality, so the person is successful in acting without conscious consideration, even though the subconscious experiences do not rise to the level of conscious Awareness.

Doubt blocks the experiences from becoming actionable. The doubt about the reality of the sixth sense experiences keeps the experiences from becoming actionable because there is a vast array of five-sense experiences waiting to fill the point of now conscious Awareness, including experiences in the Earth School environment, memories, imagination, and competing experiences in subconscious Awareness. When the person doubts the validity of the subtle subconscious experience, one of the many other experiences occupies the space; the subtle subconscious experience is not acted upon. The normal blind person feels he or she has no senses to navigate a room, so the ability doesn't manifest itself. Echolocation gives the blind person confidence in the sixth sense; it eliminates doubt, so the sixth sense experiences become actionable.

The interference resulting from involving conscious Awareness in attempting to receive the subtle experiences from subconscious Awareness has been demonstrated in studies by Dr. Dean Radin, senior scientist at the Institute of Noetic Sciences described earlier in this book. Dr. Radin had a computer randomly select and show calm pictures (pastoral scenes and neutral household objects) and disturbing pictures (erotic and violent scenes) to see how long it would take for viewers to react to the pictures. The tests consistently showed that some people reacted to the pictures with the appropriately matched calm or stress as early as six seconds before the pictures were shown, even though the computer hadn't selected them at random yet.

However, when the subjects were asked to guess whether a disturbing or calming picture was to be shown next, the guesses were no better than would be expected by chance guessing. More important for this discussion, when subjects were asked to guess which pictures would appear next, their skin conductance showed the effort to guess eliminated the impact of the upcoming picture on their feelings of stress or calm in their bodies. The subconscious experiences were no longer accepted at even the subconscious Awareness level. The effort to involve conscious Awareness had effectively supplanted the subconscious Awareness experience so it no longer had any effect.[98]

Doubt and conscious analysis will interfere with receiving subconscious messages such as intuitions, psychic knowledge, inspirations, and communication coming from loved ones living in the life after this life.

Therapies bring the subconscious experiences and interpretations into conscious Awareness

Subconscious experiences and interpretations of the experiences can cause a person to experience anxiety, hostility, depression, and other negative emotions. The standard psychological therapies are intended to allow the person to examine the subconscious experiences and interpretations using conscious Awareness to evaluate and change them so the person feels better.

Repressed memories and traumas can also be harbored in the subconscious. The Mind's defenses keep the memories and traumas from rising to conscious Awareness so the disturbing interpretations don't trigger negative emotions. Psychotherapy can help clients bring the repressed memories and interpretations into conscious Awareness so the clients can understand them and reinterpret them to reduce their impact.

In talk therapy, the psychotherapist asks the client leading questions and guides the client into reexamining the interpretations that come from the answers. The psychotherapist looks for opportunities to create cognitive dissonance so the person must reexamine the interpretations to reconcile them. Especially important is the psychotherapist's effort to have the adult client reexamine the child's interpretations that are no longer suitable for an adult.

Self-talks in cognitive therapy let the person bring the subconscious experiences and interpretations to conscious awareness. A self-talk is words a person says in his or her Mind that reveal the subconscious interpretations the person holds that automatically come to mind when the client faces experiences. The client may be saying to herself, "I'm so stupid. I can't learn anything." These self-talks voice what the client has as interpretations for experiences gained from childhood. The psychotherapist helps her examine her interpretations by guiding her through evaluating her statements rationally and challenging her interpretations. "Why do you believe you're stupid?" "My dad told me that, because I didn't do well in algebra." "Does what your dad said create truth in the world?" "No." "Then could your dad be wrong?" "Yes." "Then what is true? What have you done that shows you are capable?" "I'm getting Bs and As in my coursework now." "Does that show you're not stupid, that you're very capable?" "Yes." "Then was your dad wrong?" "Yes."

Eventually, the client may change the interpretation to, "My dad had his own set of problems. He was wrong about a lot of things. I have trouble with math, but I'm great with remembering facts about people" and "I won't be Einstein in math, but I can learn enough to finish my degree." These reinterpretations help the person feel OK and comfortable. The interpretations will give the person confidence and feelings of self-worth and wellbeing. The talk-therapy process helps the person bring subconscious interpretations into conscious Awareness so the adult can change the child's experiences to fit his or her adult world.

Eye movement desensitization and reprocessing (EMDR) enables the person to reevaluate experience memories and interpretations that enter subconscious Awareness during experiences. In EMDR, the psychotherapist asks a client who is having emotional problems because of traumatic and disturbing experiences to recall the experiences and rate each on a scale of 1 to 10, with 1 being little disturbance and 10 being great disturbance. The psychotherapist then asks the client to visualize or think about the most disturbing memory experience while the psychotherapist stimulates the left and right sides of the body using eye movements, headphones that play alternate clicks or louder and softer volumes, objects that vibrate alternately between the left and right hands, or tapping alternately the left and right knees. This procedure is called "bilateral stimulation."

The bilateral stimulation seems to bring the Mind out of its normal broken record repetition mode so the disturbing memory experiences and interpretations can be examined from an objective point of view. The objective point of view draws out subconscious issues and helps the client view them from another perspective. The result is often dramatic healing of traumatic and disturbing memory experiences.

These methods used by psychotherapists have as their primary goal drawing subconscious memory experience and interpretations into conscious Awareness so the person can examine them and decide whether they align with reality now. The result is that the subconscious interpretations can be replaced by healthier, more comfortable interpretations. The person feels better.

We exist in the point of now experiences

Every moment of our conscious functioning is composed of conscious and subconscious experiences and interpretations of the experiences in the point of time called "now." Our lives are composed of the stream of experiences and interpretations occupying the seamless now points. If we were not having an experience and interpretation, we would cease to be. We live our lives in the point of now Awareness.

5

What Are the Experiences?

Everything that comes into the point of now Awareness is an experience. That includes sensory impressions, bodily experiences, memories, skills, knowledge, intuitions, and other experiences from all manner of sources. All of the various types of experiences come into conscious Awareness or subconscious Awareness so, at that instant, the experience dominates Awareness. The experiences are of different types: sight experiences, sound experiences, smell experiences, a backhand tennis stroke experience, a guitar riff experience, a piano note experience. The procedural experiences such as a piano note experience aren't the sound; the experience is the unique set of muscular actions that will cause the sound on the piano. Each of them comes into Awareness and has an effect on us. The experiences come into the Mind before the actions occur.

We have the smell experience of fresh baked bread. We have the sight experience of a friend. We allow the experience of a guitar riff or piano note to engage our muscles to create the sounds. They are all experiences in our repertoire that we are able to bring into conscious and subconscious Awareness. We then have reactions or responses to the experiences.

Some experiences are coming into conscious Awareness from current activities in Earth School. However, the great repertoire of experiences we bring into our conscious and subconscious Awareness comes from what we generally call "memories" or "skills." We can't think of the memory or skill experiences as existing somewhere, like in a library or on a massive hard drive. They don't have form until we experience them. They are simply accessible. That's a difficult concept to understand, but one introduced by quantum physicists who assert that, at the quantum level, things don't exist until someone observes or measures them. A group of Australian scientists tested the assertion and concluded, "At the quantum level, reality does not exist if you are not looking at it."[99]

Everything that ever was or ever will be is accessible in the Universal Intelligence. Everything is a potential experience we can have. When a person is not aware of the experience, it doesn't exist, but is accessible. For experiences that are accessible to exist, they must come into Awareness.

Our individual Minds are not able to access all the experiences in the universe. Instead, we have a personal repertoire of experiences we can intend to come into conscious Awareness or that come into subconscious Awareness unbidden because they are associated with something in the now point of Awareness. They are part of what we call our Mind. They are not in the Mind before being accessed. They are potentials for being in the Mind's point of now Awareness available for us to access.

This repertoire of experiences the person is able to access is what gives us the primary sense of who we are. We feel we are a person with certain beliefs, skills, personality characteristics, attitudes, knowledge, experiences, and the body experience. However, these are simply potential experiences that could come into the point of now Awareness. We are not the experiences. We are the Aware soul that is allowing the Mind to have the transient experiences.

Experiences are brought into our Awareness by the Universal Intelligence when

- We navigate through the Earth School environment and experiences come to us as our circumstances change.

- Our intention summons an experience into Awareness from memory.

- An experience in Awareness cues another experience that comes spontaneously into conscious or subconscious Awareness.

- Some source such as guides, helpers, and loved ones living in the life after this life bring messages into subconscious Awareness.

Aphantasia

The explanations in this book often refer to experiences that are mental images. Being able to visualize images in the Mind's eye is a common ability, but not common to all people. People have a cognitive style of mental processing on a continuum from being a visualizer to being a verbalizer. A visualizer spends more time visualizing and is able to bring visual images into Awareness. A strong visualizer can experience colored, detailed images. A verbalizer processes verbal information and experiences indistinct images in the Mind. Most people are somewhere on a continuum between the two extremes of the cognitive styles, seeing various degrees of distinct, indistinct, and gray images.

People with aphantasia have no experiences of mental images at all. For more about aphantasia, view this video: www.earthschoolanswers.org/aphantasia/. That page has the link to a network for people with aphantasia.

You will be somewhere on the continuum of visualizer to verbalizer style and may have aphantasia. When the explanations refer to images, if you are a verbalizer or have aphantasia, interpret the explanation to refer to the impressions you have about an experience.

People Without an Inner Monologue

The explanations also refer to having inner monologues in conscious Awareness. You may be a person without an inner monologue. You will have lists and impressions that don't involve a dialogue of words. Dr. Russell Hurlburt, psychology professor at the University of Nevada, Las Vegas, suggests that inner speech is not as common as people believe it to be, and having no inner monologue is common.[100]

If you have little inner monologue, substitute references to voicing words in conscious Awareness with visual imagery or impressions you have in your conscious Awareness. You can view a video about not having an inner monologue: www.earthschoolanswers.com/monologue/. Read about not having an inner monologue in a *Psychology Today* blog at the link on the same page.

You can also see an informal talk by someone who has both aphantasia and no inner monologue at www.earthschoolanswers.com/neither/.

The 17 Categories of Experiences

The point of now Awareness can be filled with at least 17 categories of experiences:

1. Vivid experiences we have during Earth School events

2. Memory experiences

3. Dream experiences

4. Body sensation experiences

5. Pain and pleasure experiences

6. Imaginative and creative experiences

7. Knowledge experiences

8. Rote-memory experiences

9. Emotion experiences

10. Experiences in performing a skill

11. Experiences in the act of speaking

12. Experiences in performing intellectual skills such as mathematics

13. Experiences in art and performance

14. Out-of-body and NDE experiences

15. Experiences by the knower

16. Experiences inspired or guided by entities

17. Psychic or intuition experiences

These 17 categories of experiences are explained below.

Vivid experiences we have during Earth School events

The experiences we have in Earth School come to us spontaneously when we intend to experience them or the conditions in Earth School bring the experiences to us. We intend to have a relaxing evening listening to the Mystic Moods Orchestra with a glass of our favorite wine. As a result of our intention, we turn on the music and have pleasant auditory experiences. We lift the glass of wine to our lips and have the experience of a pleasant taste of the wine.

However, in Earth School, we also have experiences brought to us that we didn't intend. We experience the sound of a phone ringing as we're having our glass of wine. Then we experience the sound of our beagle barking insistently because she wants the experience of going on a walk.

The experiences we intend and those that occur spontaneously all happen in Awareness. They are not in a world outside of us.

The Universal Intelligence provides experiences. The human-made realm of experiences has been built up by people living their lives in Earth School for millennia. For example, we stand in a room that is a complex set of experiences in the Universal Intelligence that we experience as a room. We have the experiences of seeing and touching a wall, seeing the furniture, hearing the floorboards creak as we walk, and seeing curtains blowing in an open window. I have the same experience of a wall you have because we are each having the experiences of this room presented by the Universal Intelligence. There is no room outside of us.

This room is experiences made accessible by the experiences of settlers in the territory who cleared and plotted the land, builders who built the building, drywall hangers, painters, real estate salespersons, previous owners, and us. All had individual experiences that added to the experiences of the room that became accessible in the Universal Intelligence. The most prominent for us are the experiences of the room as it is now because they have fitness for our lives now. These experiences are in our sphere of connections. We intended to enter the room, so that is our connection. If we want to bring a room experience into Awareness from memory, we must have had the experience of the room in the past to give us the connection. Embodied in that room are the potentials of accessing all the experiences of all the individual Minds that had a part in developing the room as it is. We just don't have connections to all of them and are unable to access the broader range of experiences that are accessible.

The experiences are always changing as we navigate through Earth School. We can manipulate the environment in Earth School to create new experiences. And as we participate in the Earth School experiences, the environmental experiences we are all having collectively result in the Earth School experience.

Memory experiences

Memory experiences come to us in the same way as experiences in Earth School. Instead of saying they exist, we can say only that they are accessible.

Experiences do not disappear. Every experience that ever was, ever will be, in any time and any place, whether an Earth School event or a thought in an individual's Mind, is accessible. We access them in the Universal Intelligence when we request them or they come into Awareness when cued by other experiences. However, we are able to access only those experiences within our sphere of connections.

Event memories are experiences we have had in Earth School that are now accessible as memory experiences. They are not facsimiles of a single Earth School experience outside of us, like a photograph of a single scene; they are the experiences we had in our Minds. That is why two people can be in an event but recall different experiences, interpretations, and emotions. And when we reexperience an experience, we are going through the experiencing process as a completely new experience. We are not accessing an exact duplicate of the experience we are reexperiencing; we are not accessing an image from a hard drive. As with the experience of an Earth School event, when we reexperience we are selecting details that then become a new experience.

New experiences are created every time we relive an experience. Later, we can retrieve the old experience and the new experience. That's why someone may say, "I recalled gathering peaches at the old house today and thought we ought to go get some. Then I remembered we cut down the peach tree." Both memories are accessible. The memory of the house with no peach tree did not replace the new memory of the tree's being cut down. However, over time, as the experiences of the house without the peach tree are accessed repeatedly, the old memory of the house with the peach tree will be less prominent. It will then be accessible only if the person wants to recall that memory.

Experience memories are not forgotten. They become less prominent because other memories come to the fore when the person intends to recall a memory experience associated with the event. However, something may cue a memory experience that had not been brought into conscious Awareness for decades.

Memory experiences come to Mind because we ask for them or something in an experience cues another memory experience. When we ask for the memory experience, the memory experience may come to conscious Awareness, but if the memory experience is now buried by other memories, it may be difficult to have it come to conscious

Awareness. That doesn't mean the memory experience is gone. All memories are accessible. It just means we have lost the cues to bring it into conscious Awareness.

Dream experiences

Dream experiences are unique because they have the same vivid, real quality as experiences in Earth School events, but with the creative, unimpeded additions of imagination and creativity. The Mind and the Universal Intelligence are always creating. In normal daily life, the creativity results in our co-creation of the environment available for access in the Universal Intelligence and our conscious efforts to use our creativity to navigate Earth School successfully. In sleep, the creative Mind has no constraints. The result is that the point of now Awareness accepts some memory experience from daily life and, without the cause and effect requirements of conscious Awareness, creates its own cause and effect world. The result is the unique experiences we have when we are dreaming.

Those who study dreams have developed a variety of explanations for dreams. The most valid is the "continual activation theory." It suggests that people dream so consciousness does not turn off—another way of saying we dream because consciousness never ceases to be active. Fragments of experience memories come into Awareness and the continuously creating Mind and Universal Intelligence create stories around them.

Body sensation experiences

We tend to think of ourselves as the body. We look at ourselves in a mirror or a photograph and say, "That's me." But we're much greater than the body. We are functioning, individual manifestations of the Universal Intelligence.

We have senses we associate with a body during Earth School events that are body experiences: touch, sense of movement, sense of balance, sense of body parts, pain, itch, burning, pleasure, heartbeat, nausea, hunger, sickness, fever, dizziness, pressure, electric shock, tension, chemical substance ingestion, and other such senses. We were reared to believe these senses are in a body in a physical world that exists by itself. That is not true. We have body experiences, but they are all experiences in the Mind, available for access in the Universal Intelligence. There is no body outside of our Minds.

We agree to have body experiences for a period of time while in Earth School, then stop accepting the body experiences when the experience of the current body is no longer useful and we've changed the focus of our attention to the next realm of our lives. After we abandon the body experiences, we continue on as eternal beings with other body experiences in other realms of experiences.

Our body experiences have characteristics that are part of the planning we did before entering Earth School. The experiences may be with us at birth or develop as part of the process of growing and navigating through Earth School. For example, we might have planned to be born with a mental disability that will affect our experiences in Earth School. A person with Down syndrome has less ability to access experiences than people without the condition. That condition was part of the person's pre-birth planning. The planning could have been for the person's growth or to assist in another person's learning.

Or we might have planned to have an accident that impairs our mental functioning. Materialists would say we have loss of function because the brain is injured, but that's not what happens. There is no brain outside of our Mind that can be injured. Instead, our situation in Earth School has undergone a change in the capabilities to access experiences in Earth School because we're following the rules of our Earth School experience. As with a character in a play, we have agreed to play the part of an individual with a brain malfunction so we don't access and process experiences as well. That is entirely in the body experience, not in the eternal soul we really are.

An article in the *HuffPost* blog written by a board-certified physician, a quantum physicist, a specialist in computer engineering, and a professor of neurology at Harvard University describes the body experience:

> When we say that the universe is mental, many people interpret this to mean that reality is in our heads. Precisely the opposite is

the case: if *all* reality is mental, then our heads and bodies, as parts of reality, are in the mind. This may sound surprising at first, but it is entirely consistent with everyday experience. There is nothing to our bodies but our felt perceptions of them. A body is what a particular swirl in a transpersonal flow of experiences looks like, just like a whirlpool is what a particular swirl in a stream of water looks like.[101]

The sense of experiencing a rose, for example, includes the experience of redness, experience of a position in space, experience of the feel of the silky smoothness of the petal, and experience of the smell of the rose. However, there is no rose in a physical world we are experiencing. The experiences that are meaningful to us as a rose are available for access in the Universal Intelligence when our Minds intend to have the experiences of seeing, touching, and smelling a rose. We associate the bodily sight, feel, and smell with the bodily experience of a rose, but the experiences are solely experiences our Minds have, accessible to us from the Universal Intelligence.

Pain and pleasure experiences

Pain is experiences in the Mind, not in a body. The Mind feels pain and attributes it to something happening in the body, but the pain is only in the Mind. Pain, like emotions, is irreducible, meaning we cannot dissect it to tell what it is made of. We can only say, "I feel pain" or "That hurts." Pain is an experience.

The use of hypnosis to eliminate pain demonstrates that pain is an experience in the Mind, not a sensation in a body. An analysis of 18 published studies on the use of hypnosis to manage pain by psychologists Guy Montgomery, PhD, Katherine DuHamel, PhD, and William Redd, PhD, showed that 75 percent of clinical and experimental participants with different types of pain obtained substantial pain relief from hypnotic techniques.[102] Affecting the Mind's experience of pain reduces pain.

The Arthritis Foundation reports, "Studies show that more than 75% of people with arthritis and related diseases experience significant pain relief using hypnosis."[103]

Professional hypnotherapist and psychotherapist Alex Lenkei, 61, hypnotized himself before an 83-minute procedure in which the base of his thumb was removed and some joints were fused to alleviate his suffering from arthritis in the hand. The doctors used a chisel, a hammer, and a medical saw to break his bone, remove the arthritic joint, and attach a tendon to the thumb. Lenkei remarked, "I didn't feel anything at all. There was no pain, just very deep relaxation. I was aware of everything that was going on in the (surgical) theater. I was aware of the consultant tugging and pulling during the operation. But there was no pain."[104]

Lenkei had altered his Mind's acceptance of the pain experience. If pain were in a body, it could not be controlled through hypnosis. The pain experience is in the Mind.

Pleasure also is not in a body, even though testing reveals elevated chemicals such as endorphins and serotonin when someone is feeling pleasure. The experiences of chemical changes result from the Mind's experiences, not the reverse. Pleasure is in the Mind, not in a body in a realm outside of us.

Imaginative and creative experiences

We have the remarkable ability given to us by the Universal Intelligence to create experiences from the raw material of our past experiences. We call these abilities imagination or creativity. The creations begin with the raw materials the person has in his or her repertoire of experiences, but then some qualities are added that result in a creation so unique that it seems to the originator to have been provided in an inspiration by some outside influence.

Knowledge experiences

We are able to bring knowledge experiences into Awareness by intending to recall the knowledge based on some cue. We are asked by someone, "Who was president of the United States during World War II?" We set about scanning our knowledge experiences to remember who was president of the United States during WWII. We bring into conscious Awareness experiences concerning the war: the bombing of

Hiroshima and Nagasaki, signing the surrender documents, presidents before Eisenhower. We scan the experiences in our repertoire, accessing one after another to see whether one of them will cue access to the knowledge experience that is the answer. The experiences come automatically and quickly into Awareness from the subconscious each time an experience cues a related experience. We recall the knowledge experience that Truman gave the order to use the atomic bomb. Yes, Truman was president. That gives us a satisfaction that validates the conclusion.

But that cues the experience memory that Truman wasn't president during the entire war. Our Minds scan the knowledge experiences related to a president before Truman. We can't get it, so we scan knowledge experiences connected to the beginning of the war. That cues Pearl Harbor. Immediately the cued knowledge experience of "a date which will live in infamy" comes into conscious Awareness. That cues the knowledge experience of "Roosevelt."

Scanning knowledge experiences takes place at great speed. When we're attempting to recall knowledge experiences, we go through a succession of experiences to try to cue the correct experience to come into Awareness. We can get some parts of the experience: "It's on the tip of my tongue. I know he decided to drop the atomic bombs." When we finally trigger the right experience, other knowledge experiences validate it: "Right, Truman was just before Eisenhower." That results in a satisfaction feeling. The feeling lets us know we have cued up the correct knowledge experience.

Knowledge experiences are learned by linking them with other knowledge experiences. It's much easier to bring the knowledge experiences to a high level of probability of recall when there are many links the Mind can scan to bring the experience into Awareness. Learning and accessing knowledge experiences follow the same procedures learning and accessing other experiences follow, including recalling sight experiences, stringing words to make speech, and stringing piano key strikes to make a concerto. All these activities result from bringing experiences into conscious and subconscious Awareness.

Rote-memory experiences

Rote-memory experiences such as memorizing numbers or facts are called declarative memories. When we have an experience in Earth School that has senses associated with it, the memory immediately takes its place in the repertoire of experiences with a higher probability that we can bring the experience to mind later. We see a dog and can remember it easily later. We hear a melody and can recall it in a few hours or days. These experiences have high probabilities of our being able to reexperience them.

However, experiences that involve symbols such as numbers and words are not so easily remembered because they are not sensory experiences. As a result, we must make them into experiences. We do so by repeatedly bringing them into the point of now Awareness until they become experiences we can easily bring into Awareness through our intention. The memories of strings of numbers or words are experienced in a sequence. The recall of a number or word cues the recall of the next memory or word. When we are asked to begin the string in the middle or say every other number or word, we have difficulty doing so. We have created experiences of the numbers or words in strings that cue in turn the next numbers or words.

Emotion experiences

We also have emotion experiences. Emotions such as fear, happiness, and sadness are pure experiences that have no component parts. We cannot dissect them. They are subjective experiences. We can say "I feel afraid" or "I feel happy," but we cannot sketch afraid or happy or figure out what afraid or happy are made of. The experiences of emotions result from interpretations of experiences. When we interpret an experience as a fearful experience, we feel afraid. When we interpret an experience as a welcome experience, we feel happy. We cannot make ourselves feel an emotion without the trigger of the interpretation.

Experiences in performing a skill

We also have experiences we call skills, such as walking, speaking, playing a piano, welding, driving, and all the many other skills people learn. These skills comprise complex series of experiences. They come to the individual Mind after we have practiced them so we have increasingly sophisticated experiences that come into subconscious Awareness resulting in adept motor performance. What comes to Awareness is a complicated, intricate latticework of experiences. The person uses the experiences to act.

These experiences are called procedural memories, meaning they are memories of the sequences required to perform procedures. The abilities are not in the muscles. They are accessible from the Universal Intelligence by the Mind. The recalled experiences come into subconscious Awareness at the point of now and result in rapidly performed series of actions. The skill experiences are like memory experiences, but they are memory experiences of manipulating the keys on a piano in a particular way or memories of swinging the racket in a variety of ways in tennis.

In learning these skill experiences, new experiences of performing adeptly don't replace old experiences; they become more prominent. The new experiences have a higher probability of being accessed, so they come to Mind more readily. In learning a skill such as playing a piano, the inexperienced novice has experiences with the piano that are crude. Note after note is a separate experience being streamed together. As the person plays the piano over and over, the experiences that come into subconscious Awareness become more sophisticated. The experiences in Awareness result in more sophisticated piano playing, with notes being played at the rate of 13 to 14 per second.

The later-performed experiences have a higher probability of coming to mind than the previous crude experiences. The increasingly sophisticated new experiences that come to Mind enable the fingers, arms, and feet to work in the sequences of remarkably intricate patterns of experiences that result in a concert performance. The concert pianist sits at the piano and the experiences that come into subconscious

Awareness are the latest ones the person can access; they are the most sophisticated. So the piano playing is accomplished.

When we have the body experiences of performing the activities, the activities are experiences being accessed by the Mind. If an individual with no knowledge of how to play a piano could access the experiences that come into the concert pianist's mind, the individual would instantly be a concert pianist. That's why people can have a sudden physical capability, such as being able to play the piano adeptly after being hit on the head. We in fact have instances of spontaneous savants who suddenly are able to bring to Mind the sequences of experiences that result in their arms and fingers playing piano proficiently. (See pages 134 to 136.)

Experiences in the act of speaking

Speaking is a complex set of experiences that became accessible to us as we developed our ability to speak. In early efforts to speak, our speaking was rudimentary and fragmented. As we brought to Mind the experiences of speaking each word to express an experience of a thought, we received feedback about our success. That resulted in a new experience's increasing probability of being brought into subconscious Awareness. Speaking is just a string of these memory experiences that are continually coming to mind combined with experiences of syntax to fluently produce vocalizations.

The more sophisticated the experiences, the more they involve whole phrases and sentences brought to subconscious Awareness as quickly as we need them. However, every word and phrase is an experience that has taken the fore in strength so one connects to the next to express the thought experience we have in Mind. An experience of one word that comes to Mind cues another word brought together with the correct syntax that has come through experiences. Whole phrases are one experience, so the act of speaking flows effortlessly. During the speaking process, the words and phrases are continually being referenced to the experience concept being explained.

When the speaker pauses or stumbles, seeking a specific word or phrase, the speaker is scanning the word experiences to find one that fits the conception in Awareness. Finally, a word experience feels right and is vocalized.

We know speaking ability results from accessing experiences because some people have suddenly been capable of speaking a language that is not their native tongue or have suddenly taken on the accent characteristic of a language that is not their native language. They were able to access the experiences that enabled them to speak another language without having to develop their own repertoire of these experiences. (See pages 136 to 140 for examples.)

Experiences in performing intellectual skills such as mathematics

Intellectual skills such as mathematics result from bringing experiences into Awareness that enable the individual to perform activities and solve problems.

Being able to manipulate mathematical concepts is a prime example. Performing mathematical calculations is the result of bringing into subconscious and conscious Awareness strings of experiences the mathematician has made accessible in his or her repertoire of accessible experiences over decades of refining the experiences. The latest experiences that come to mind acquired through years of experiences with mathematics enable the mathematician to perform sophisticated mathematical processes.

As with skills, the process of bringing the intellectual experiences into Awareness happens primarily in subconscious Awareness, where the speed of processing enables the person to perform complicated calculations adeptly.

Here also, we know mathematical abilities result from the accumulation of experiences because there are cases of people having suddenly acquired the ability to perform complex mathematical calculations by accessing experiences that weren't developed over time in their repertoire. (See page 141 for examples of spontaneously being able to perform mathematics.)

Experiences in art and performance

Art is a skill that is also a series of experiences the artist brings to Mind as needed. The experiences have been acquired over a long period of artistic practice. However, in some cases an individual with no artistic ability can suddenly acquire art talent. The condition is known as "sudden artistic output." This is another indication that the abilities are in experiences, and all experiences can be accessed. (See pages 141 to 144 for examples.)

Out-of-body and NDE experiences

All experiences that ever were and ever will be at any place in any time are accessible. In an out-of-body experience, the person has the sensory experiences of locations in our shared reality experience that are apart from the body experiences. The experiences are not actually "out of body" because there is no "in body." We always have body experiences that fit with our Mind's expectations for experiences in an environment given to us by the Universal Intelligence. We walk into a room and have the body experiences of being in the room. In an out-of-body or near-death experience, the experiencer has body experiences of places other than those pertaining to where the person believes he or she is at that moment in the world. But the world is just shared experiences.

What changes in an out-of-body experience is the array of experiences the person has. They seem to be "out of sync" with where the person is having normal body experiences in Awareness. However, the out-of-body experience and near-death experience are happening in the Mind and are given to us by the Universal Intelligence.

Experiences by the knower

People describe being able to ask for knowledge and receiving it from some greater, knowledgeable source. The knower is sometimes called the Nous or Higher self. Anthony Peak refers to the Daemon as a guiding spirit that travels with the Earth School self, giving guidance and knowledge.[105] The conscious mind has experiences that are attributed to the knower, who can be queried. The result of the queries is the experience of an answer that comes into Awareness from "out of the blue." The knowledge experience "just popped into my mind." The source is whatever constitutes the knower.

Experiences inspired or guided by entities

We also receive experiences from guides, helpers, loved ones living in the life after this life, and others. These people and beings are all integral parts of the Universal Intelligence with us, so they bring experiences to our individual Minds just as we recall memory experiences. The experiences coming into our subconscious Awareness may not come into conscious Awareness because our conscious Awareness is preoccupied with life experiences. However, these experiences that are messages can be brought into conscious Awareness by entering a state of mind in which conscious Awareness's focus on life events is diminished. Then experiences from subconscious Awareness can enter.

In Self-Guided Afterlife Connections and Repair & Reattachment Grief Therapy, the participants report vivid sights, senses of touch, smells, and sounds inspired by the people living in the life after this life. The experiences happen when the person sits with eyes closed and enters the state of mind in which the experiences can come into conscious Awareness. The experiences have the same sensory impressions and feelings that conscious Awareness has in Earth School events. They are just not so vivid.

Learn more about Self-Guided Afterlife Connections at www.afterlifeconnections.org/newentries.htm.

The Self-Guided Afterlife Connections training is at www.selfguided.spiritualunderstanding.org/.

Learn more about Repair & Reattachment Grief Therapy at www.earthschoolanswers.com/repair/.

We are in continual contact with unseen entities and people intent upon helping us as we live our lives in Earth School. They bring experiences to us that will help us as we go through our Earth School experiences. We just have to learn to allow them to come from subconscious Awareness into conscious Awareness.

Psychic or intuition experiences

Remote viewers, psychics, and intuitive people can have experiences of things not in their spheres of contact. Psychics describe their knowledge as "memories of things I have not experienced." The experiences are accessible as all experiences are accessible, from the Universal Intelligence.

However, for the most part, even remote viewers, psychics, and intuitive people must have a connection to experiences they are accessing. They must have a person in mind or a place they are asking about.

All of these experiences are accessible

All experiences that ever were or ever will be, in thought or in activities, are accessible by our Minds because we are individual manifestations of the Universal Intelligence. We just have to have a connection to the experiences, the ability to access the experiences, and the state of Mind that allows the experiences to come from subconscious Awareness into conscious Awareness.

6

Every Experience That Ever Was or Ever Will Be Is Accessible

"I'm sure [my memory] only works one way," Alice remarked. "I can't remember things before they happen."

"It's a poor sort of memory that only works backwards," the Queen remarked.

Lewis Carroll –
Alice through the Looking Glass

One of Carl Jung's favorite quotes on synchronicity

The Universal Intelligence is constantly filling the now point of Awareness with experiences that may come from anyone, anywhere, anytime, in any place. We are one with everything because there is nothing but the Universal Intelligence, and we are integral parts of it. We are what Donald Hoffman, the cognitive scientist, calls "conscious agents"[106] and Tom Campbell calls "individuated units of consciousness," with the Universal Intelligence as the "greater consciousness."[107] We are individual manifestations of the Universal Intelligence.

The Universal Intelligence retains everything that ever was and ever will be in space or time, including thoughts, statements, and all sensory experiences. Because we are all individual manifestations of the Universal Intelligence, anything that ever was or ever will be, anywhere, at any time, is accessible to us. We can "re-member" or "re-mind" ourselves of anything that ever was or ever will be.

> The knower and the known are one. Simple people imagine that they should see God as if he stood there and they here. This is not so. God and I, we are one in knowledge.

> Meister Eckhart

Every experience is accessible. The experience does not "exist," because existence implies an objective reality with matter and energy independent of Mind. Instead, experiences are simply accessible. These experiences include experiences people have had as they have lived in Earth School or on any of the other millions of planes and spheres. All of them are accessible by the Mind from the Universal Intelligence.

However, we are normally able to access only experiences in our sphere of connections. We can access our own memories of events in Earth School and may be able to experience things happening to people close to us, such as our twin, sibling, or other loved one. Psychics are able to access experiences of people they intend to learn about because of something that has brought the person into the psychic's sphere of connections. Mediums are similarly able to experience communication from people living in other realms after leaving Earth School because of a connection to someone's loved one or the intention to connect with an individual.

Every experience that ever was, ever will be, anywhere in space or time, in any realm, is accessible in the Universal Intelligence. That doesn't mean the experiences are in a vast library or a hard drive apart from us. Every experience is as much a part of us as the image of our mothers we bring to mind or memories of exciting events in our lives we can bring into conscious Awareness. We can access those experiences and could as easily access the experience of George Washington's thoughts as he crossed the Delaware River. But Washington is not in our sphere of connections so there is zero probability we will get to know what Washington was thinking.

You can have experiences come to you now that you have not accessed in years. I'm going to give you instructions to bring something to mind. If you are a visualizer, you most likely will bring images to conscious Awareness. If you have the style called a "verbalizer" or have aphantasia, you may get few or no images, but you will bring into conscious Awareness impressions. Stay with whatever you get.

After you read these instructions, close your eyes and relax for a few minutes. Concentrate on feeling your breathing only. Say "Breathing in. Breathing out" repeatedly. After a few minutes, when you are relaxed, bring to mind the kitchen in your childhood home if it is filled with OK or good memories. If not, bring to mind another room or another house that is OK. I want you to spend a few minutes in the kitchen, looking carefully. Walk around the kitchen. Look at each wall in turn. Look at the ceiling. Look at the floor. Look at the counters and appliances. Listen to hear what you can hear. Focus on smelling smells. Touch things. Take your time. Do that for a few minutes now.

As you were there in your kitchen, you most likely experienced things you haven't thought about since childhood. You noticed things on the wall or the light fixtures or the floor or the contents of the countertops. Those experiences are all accessible. Every experience in every place you have ever been to is accessible. You will be able to bring experiences to mind if you take a tour of any location you have ever been to. But even experiences that don't come to you easily are accessible.

When we "re-member" or "re-call" or "re-mind," we are accessing experiences. The only limitation to our accessing memories is that they are buried under days, weeks, or years of other experiences so we can't recall them easily, or they are someone else's memories and thus are not in our sphere of connections.

When we believe our Minds are limited to what we have experienced and are experiencing in Earth School, we see ourselves as tiny, limited beings, hardly the significance of a grain of sand on the vast beaches of all the oceans. We believe ourselves to be one eight-billionth of humanity, so insignificant we are hardly more than a bit of dust being swept around by the breeze.

However, we are the Awareness having the experiences, an individual manifestation of the Universal Intelligence. We chose some of what we would experience in our pre-birth planning, and we now choose experiences based on our sphere of connections, activities in Earth School, and state of mind. However, the fact that we are limiting our experience choices doesn't diminish the capability of our Awareness to experience much more.

Herman Minkowski space-time

Mathematical physicist Herman Minkowski was Albert Einstein's teacher. When Minkowski saw Einstein's paper on special relativity, he suggested that space and time as Einstein was describing them are not separate; they must be referred to as "space-time," a four-dimensional block made of our three dimensions plus time as a fourth dimension. While time has traditionally been seen as an arrow traveling from past to present to future, in Minkowski space-time, all events that ever were or ever will be are somewhere in the infinite block of space-time right now. We are having experiences at this instant, so we are accessing experiences we're calling "now," but we could as easily be accessing any experiences in Minkowski space-time. We need continuity, causes and effects, and the accumulation of a repertoire of experiences, so during this Earth School period we have a sense of time, meaning one thing happens after another and we can recall a past.

Massachusetts Institute of Technology physicist Max Tegmark describes it this way:

> We can portray our reality as either a three-dimensional place where stuff happens over time or as a four-dimensional place where nothing happens ["block universe"]—and if it really is the second picture, then change really is an illusion, because there's nothing that's changing; it's all just there—past, present, future.

So life is like a movie, and space-time is like the DVD. There's nothing about the DVD itself that is changing in any way, even though there's all this drama unfolding in the movie. We have the illusion, at any given moment, that the past already happened and the future doesn't yet exist, and that things are changing. But all I'm ever aware of is my brain state right now. The only reason I feel like I have a past is that my brain contains memories.[108]

You can watch Dr. Tegmark explain this conception of time and reality at www.earthschoolanswers.com/max/.

Brian Greene, professor of physics and mathematics at Columbia University and co-founder of the World Science Festival, explains it like this:

Just as we think of all of space as being "out there," we should think of all of time as being "out there" too. Everything that has ever happened or will happen . . . it all exists![109]

You can watch Dr. Greene explain why that's true at www.earthschoolanswers.com/greene/.

Quantum Physics and the Plane of Possibility

Quantum physicists describe a "plane of possibility." In this plane of possibility are all the potential objects and actions, but none can be said to exist. Daniel Siegel, a clinical professor of psychiatry at the UCLA School of Medicine and executive director of the Mindsight Institute explains:

Before anything arises, [the plane of possibility] is a source of potential energy, but there's no energy in the plane, but energy arises from it. . . . the formless source of all form.[110]

It is a mathematical concept that is also called the "sea of potential," the "quantum vacuum," or "cosmic field of potentiality."

Lothar Schäfer, Distinguished Professor of Physical Chemistry at the University of Arkansas, describes the cosmic field of potentiality:

> Everything that exists in the visible world has first
> existed as a state in the cosmic field of potentiality.
> Nothing comes out of the blue; everything emerges out
> of the cosmic potentiality.[111]

The Vedic Ocean of Pure Consciousness

Maharishi Mahesh Yogi describes the Vedic view of this ocean of consciousness:

> The infinite diversity and dynamism of the creation is
> just the expression of the eternally silent, self-referral,
> self-sufficient, unbounded field of consciousness. All life
> emerges from and is sustained in consciousness. The
> whole universe is the expression of consciousness. The
> reality of the universe is one unbounded ocean of
> consciousness in motion.[112]

Mystics and seers describe a Book of Life

Mystics and seers have long referred to what they call the Akashic Records, Book of Life, and Book of Lives. It is traceable at least as far back as the ancient Assyrians, Phoenicians, and Babylonians. Their conceptions show their intuitive understanding that every experience that ever was or ever will be is accessible.

The Hebrew Scriptures

In Psalm 139, David is purported to have said that God has written down everything about him and all the details of his life—even that which is imperfect and those deeds which have yet to be performed.

The Christian New Testament

In Revelation, the writer described what the first-century readers would have understood as commonly held knowledge:

> And I saw the dead, great and small, standing before the throne, and books were opened. Another book was opened, which is the book of life. The dead were judged according to what they had done as recorded in the books. (Revelation 20:12, NIV)

Paul, the likely author of the letter to the Philippians, wrote the following:

> Yes, and I ask you, my true companion, help these women since they have contended at my side in the cause of the gospel, along with Clement and the rest of my co-workers, whose names are in the book of life. (Philippians 4:3, NIV)

Edgar Cayce

Edgar Cayce said that he accessed information from the Book of Life or Akashic Records:

> Upon time and space is written the thoughts, the deeds, the activities of an entity—as in relationships to its environs, its hereditary influence; as directed—or judgment drawn by or according to what the entity's ideal is. Hence, as it has been oft called, the record is God's book of remembrance; and each entity, each soul—as the activities of a single day of an entity in the material world—either makes same good or bad or indifferent, depending upon the entity's application of self towards that which is the ideal manner for the use of time, opportunity and the expression of that for which each soul enters a material manifestation. The interpretation then as drawn here is with the desire and

hope that, in opening this for the entity, the experience may be one of helpfulness and hopefulness.[113]

Theosophists

H.P. Blavatsky, founder of the Theosophical Society, wrote that the Akashic Chronicle is

> A vast memory that stores all events that occur throughout time . . . which the paranormally gifted can tap into in order to know past and future events.[114]

Emanuel Swedenborg

Emanuel Swedenborg, the theologian, scientist, philosopher, and mystic, described the life review each person experiences after leaving Earth School. The life review is not a punishment; there is no hell or other retribution. It is an opportunity for people to learn from their lives by reliving what they were thinking and feeling and knowing what others involved were thinking and feeling. Swedenborg describes the detailed records of people's lives:

> I should like to add to this something noteworthy about the memory that we keep after death, something that convinced me that not just the general contents but even the smallest details that have entered our memory do last and are never erased. I saw some books with writing in them like earthly writing, and was told that they had come from the memories of the people who had written them, that not a single word was missing that had been in the book they had written in the world. I was also told that all the least details could be retrieved from the memory of someone else, even things the person had forgotten in the world. The reason for this was explained as well; namely, that we have an outer and an inner memory, the outer proper to our natural person and the inner proper to our spiritual person. The details of what we have thought, intended, said, and done, even what

we have heard and seen, are inscribed on our inner or spiritual memory.

There is no way to erase anything there, since everything is written at once on our spirit itself and on the members of our body, as noted above. This means that our spirit is formed in accord with what we have thought and what we have done intentionally. I know these things seem paradoxical and hard to believe, but they are true nevertheless.[115]

Notable examples of the fact that all experiences are accessible

There are especially notable examples of the fact that all experiences are accessible: savant performance, hyperthysmesia, psychic knowledge, past-life regressions, precognition, remote viewing, mental medium communication, and experiencing the author's intentions in the life after this life.

A remarkable range of experiences is accessed by someone whose conscious Awareness is weak: Savants

Savants normally are autistic in most areas of their mental development, meaning they are withdrawn, don't react normally to their environments, don't communicate well, and have mental deficits. However, savants have abilities called "splinter skills," meaning they are focused in a highly specialized area such as recalling facts, numbers, license plates, maps, books, and extensive lists of statistics after being exposed to them only once. It is likely that because their conscious Awareness is weak, they have greater access to experiences in their subconscious Awareness, where all experiences are accessible and the processing speed is between 11 million and 20 million bits per second.

George Finn and his twin brother are calendrical savants. George can state with perfect accuracy the day of the week any date will fall on, within a second or two of being given the date. He is also able to describe accurately the weather on every day of his life.[116] The experiences of the calendrical calculations are accessible for him most likely because his conscious Mind is not so well developed. View a video about George Finn at www.earthschoolanswers.com/finn/.

Kim Peek, whose life inspired the movie *Rain Man* with Dustin Hoffman and Tom Cruise, had macrocephaly resulting in damage to the cerebellum. He didn't learn to walk until age four and walked in a sidelong manner throughout his life. He could not button his shirt and had difficulty with other motor activities. His IQ score was well below average.

However, in spite of his deficiencies, he could recall books in their entirety, from memory. He had photographic recall of about 98 percent of what he read one time. He was able to recall every page of 7,600 books.[117]

A materialist might suggest that the brain simply has greater capabilities in a highly focused area when the other parts of the brain that should have developed are reallocated to that focused area. However, there is no research to indicate that other parts of the brain somehow become so dramatically converted to the focused skills or how that is even materially possible; in fact, damage to the brain means parts of the brain simply don't work.

The most reasonable explanation for the savant's unexplainable ability is that the savant's point of now Awareness is not filled by experiences from the environment or experiences people generally have access to, such as conversing or tying a shoe. As a result, the savant has access to a great variety of other abilities and memories that come into the subconscious Awareness from the Universal Intellect.

Another objection to the suggestion that the savant's brain is able to hold the vast banks of data is the fact that the brain is not capable of holding much information. American computer science expert Simon Berkovich and Dutch brain researcher Herms Romijn, working independently of one another, came to the same conclusion: it is impossible for even an ordinary person's brain to store everything we think and experience in our lifetimes. Simply watching an hour of television would already be too much for the normal brain.[118]

Another proof that this ability doesn't develop gradually as unused parts of the brain are dedicated to the unusual abilities is that the abilities can appear suddenly, without a period of time to develop. The person is called an "acquired savant."

That was the case with savant Orlando L. Serrell. Orlando was an ordinary boy until, at age 10, he was struck by a baseball on the left side of his head. He fell to the ground but didn't report it to his parents or receive medical attention, although he suffered from a headache for a long time. However, he found that he was suddenly able to perform calendrical calculations of incredible complexity. If you ask Orlando what day of the week a date will fall on, from anytime in the past or future, he will state the day instantly, without calculating and with perfect accuracy.

This ability to perform calendrical calculations results from being able to access calendrical experiences from the subconscious, which has access to all experiences and great processing speed. Watch a video about Orlando at www.earthschoolanswers.com/orlando/.

Spontaneous artistic savants are able to have an experience of seeing something for a very short time and reproduce what they have seen in great detail. They continue to access the sight experience as they reproduce the complex details of what they are seeing.

Steven Wiltshire, a British artistic savant, has been called the artistic camera. He can look at a building for 10 minutes and sketch it from memory in less than an hour. He sketches the exact number of windows and floors, accurate position, and other details, without error. In a test of Steven's ability, he was taken on a 15-minute helicopter ride above London. From that one experience of the city, he was able to sketch every building in the city in perfect location and detail. Someone who watched Steven work remarked, "He goes into another world. Absolute stillness is the word I would use to describe Steven as he becomes the artist. He's just responding to something greater, beyond himself."[119] That other world is the world of experiences where he is able to access the experience of seeing the city of London. Then he refers to that experience as needed to make his drawings. You can see a video of Steven drawing the cities of London and Singapore at www.earthschoolanswers.com/wiltshire/.

Alonzo Clemons is the animal sculptor and savant described earlier in this book.[120] He suffered a severe brain injury as a child that left him with developmental disability, but he can create very accurate animal sculptures of clay from a single viewing of an animal's picture in as little as 20 minutes.[121] View a video about Alonzo at www.earthschoolanswers.com/alonzo/.

These savants are drawing their experiences from the Universal Intelligence's limitless resources that are accessible, though few people are able to access details as the savants are. All experiences are accessible.

Experiences from an entire lifetime are accessible: Hyperthymesia

Another demonstration that all experiences are accessible is an ability called hyperthymesia. Some people, like actress, producer, and author Marilu Henner, have highly superior autobiographical memories. Marilu and at least 10 other identified people can bring into conscious Awareness most of the memories of every day of her life. It isn't that they're stored in a brain. They are accessible, and she has the ability to access a wider range of memory experiences than other people can. She is bringing into conscious Awareness the experiences the Universal Intelligence has available to anyone. She was just given the ability to access a great number of the ones in her sphere of contact.[122] You can see a video of Marilu Henner and others demonstrating their ability at www.earthschoolanswers.com/henner/.

As with the sudden appearance of calendrical calculation abilities, hyperthymesia can develop suddenly. In 2015, a woman explained how she had developed hyperthymesia after a ski accident in which she hit the ground hard. Two days later, she was having symptoms of a head problem, so she saw a neurologist who determined she had a mild concussion.

As she was recovering, she noticed odd occurrences in her Mind: "I kept telling my neurologist that I could remember too much. It wasn't right. . . . I could remember everywhere, like flicking through the pages of a book. Every place I had ever been, but specifically the buildings."

As a result of her new ability to access experiences, the woman was able to draw incredibly accurate sketches of every building she had ever seen. After more than a year and hundreds of tests, she was diagnosed with acquired savant syndrome, meaning she had acquired her hyperthymesia quickly, without developing it over a long period of time.[123]

Experiences outside of a person's sphere of contact are accessible: Psychic knowledge

Psychics are able to access experiences outside of their spheres of contact. They can focus on a person and have impressions about the person come into subconscious Awareness. They have the ability to then allow the experiences to rise into conscious Awareness so they can explain to the person what they have learned. That ability illustrates that all experiences are accessible.

Psychic Michelle Whitedove, in a televised demonstration, located a stuntman buried alive (with an oxygen tank) somewhere in a 10-acre area in the California desert. She had no clues about where the person was buried and the ground surface offered no signs of the burial. She walked into the empty area and within 30 minutes stood over the spot where the man was buried. She was correct.[124] You can watch the video at www.earthschoolanswers.com/whitedove/.

Some psychics do not need to meet with a person. They can focus their attention on a situation and access experiences about the situation. Psychic detectives receive specific details about cases knowing nothing about the people involved or visiting the town where the crime took place. Their actions are corroborated by statements from credible witnesses, including the police officers involved in the cases. Psychic detectives are able to access the experiences of other people's lives because they focus their attention on the case or person, drawing the case into their sphere of contacts. There, all experiences are accessible.

Katherine Ramsland, of Court TV's *Crime Library*, summarizes what we know about police use of psychic detectives:

Although skeptics galore decry the use of psychics for anything but entertainment, police departments around the country call on certain psychics when all else fails. They've been doing that for more than a century, and when forbidden to do so, they sometimes use unofficial means.[125]

One such case was recorded in an Australian series on psychic detectives entitled *Sensing Murder*, which aired in 2002. In this case, the television producers and skeptics witnessed psychics Debbie Malone and Scott Russell Hill's attempt to provide details about a case, knowing only that it was a murder, nothing else. The psychics focused their intentions on accessing experiences having to do with the crime that are accessible in the Universal Intelligence. These are the details they identified. Every one was found to be correct:

- The victim was female.

- Her name was Sarah.

- She was in her early twenties.

- Her body was still missing.

- The victim had been dead around 13 years (it was actually 15 years).

- She was coming home from playing tennis.

- A car involved was a cream-colored early '80s Holden Commodore.

- The victim was attacked getting into her little red car.

- Frankston was the area.

- Kananook was the specific place of the murder.

- She was killed with a knife.

- The incident was at night.

- The killer was with a group.

- There was a female in the group.

- One member was nicknamed "Dwarfie."
- The group leader was nicknamed "Rat-head."
- They identified the attacker by name.
- They identified the exact parking space used by the victim.
- They identified where there had been blood on the ground.
- They identified where a witness who hadn't come forward had stood.
- Scott drew a map which was identical to the area concerned.[126]

The experiences the psychics were receiving were accessible. Psychics can bring experiences into their spheres of connections by intending to acquire experiences connected to a person.

In another case, a psychic detective named Phil Jordan and detectives involved in a case appeared on a television show titled *Nancy Grace* on December 30, 2005.[127] Jordan had been brought in on a case because two men had apparently drowned in a fast-moving stream in the Finger Lakes region of New York, but their bodies could not be found. He said that he accessed the experience of a red flower floating down the stream where the body of the larger of the two men would be found, but it was late winter, so it didn't seem possible to have flowers. He sat before a map and pinpointed a pool of water where he said the larger man's body would be found.

The detectives went to the pool of water and found the larger man's body. There they also found red flowers floating down the stream. Friends of the deceased had dropped flowers into the water upstream where the man most likely fell in, as a memorial, with no knowledge of the psychic's words. The flowers had floated downstream to where the body actually was. That experience was accessible, even though access seemed unlikely.

During the same *Nancy Grace* show, Jordan, the psychic, described what he told detectives when he was brought in on the case of a police officer killed in Akron, Ohio. He focused on the case and was able to access experiences. He described it as a robbery gone bad, felt there were five individuals involved, said that the murdered officer knew the killer through his drug-unit police work, experienced the sight of a basketball hoop near the body, and felt the killer had the tip of his trigger finger missing.

Jordan hadn't seen the crime scene, but there was, in fact, a basketball court there. As a result of these statements by Jordan, detectives pulled photos of suspects known to the drug unit the murdered officer had worked in, narrowing them down to 35 or 40 suspects. They asked Jordan to see whether men in any of the photographs seemed to be among the murderers. He picked five of the photos as being the men most likely involved. The detectives interrogated all five. Three were eventually found guilty of the murder. The convicted shooter had the tip of his trigger finger missing.[128]

Psychic activity such as that reported in these documented cases happens commonly today. The psychics are accessing experiences in the Universal Intelligence that are available to all people, but few can bring experiences other than those in their sphere of contacts into conscious Awareness. When the psychic intends to access the experiences, they become available in the psychic's sphere of contacts, and the experiences come into the psychic's conscious Awareness.

Experiences from the past are accessible: Past-life regressions

Another demonstration that all experiences are accessible is that experiences from someone's past life are accessible through past-life regressions. The common assumption is that in past-life regressions, people describe experiences they have had during some other life. However, we only have evidence that people can access experiences other people have had in prior lives. Our understanding of reincarnation from statements by people now living in the life after this life is that individuals remain individuals in the life after this life. However, other individuals who are part of our Higher Self or oversoul do "incarnate." People who can access other people's lives from the past are accessing the experiences of another individual in the Higher Self probably linked to the person experiencing the past-life regression, resulting at times in body features connections.

The following individuals were able to access experiences from the past that people experienced, illustrating that experiences from all places and all times are accessible.

Dr. Damian Bertrand took a woman through the experiences of two past lives. The first person whose experiences she accessed was a woman who lived in Egypt in the 1500s and was barren; she described herself as being an outcast because of it. The woman having the past-life regression had no way of knowing that during that time in Egypt, women who couldn't have children were outcasts. She spoke in Arabic while under hypnosis and told the doctor details about life in Egypt during that time that she had no way of knowing. In accounts of this woman's life, she was able to access experiences revealing verified facts about life in Egypt during that time.[129]

In a famous case described in the book, *Looking for Carroll Beckwith*,[130] Captain Robert Snow was able to describe accurate details of the life experiences of a man named Carroll Beckwith who lived in the nineteenth century. Snow was in charge of the Department of Homicide and Robbery and the Department of Organized Crime in the Indianapolis Metropolitan Police Department. In a past-life regression, Captain Snow accessed very clear, detailed experiences about people who had lived in the past. Captain Snow said his perceptions of the past-life events were more clear than his perceptions during his waking consciousness. He accessed experiences from several different lifetimes, but the one that was most prominent was the life experiences of a portrait artist in what seemed to be the nineteenth century. Captain Snow accessed 30 specific experiences from this artist's lifetime.

The details were so specific and lifelike that he was determined to find out if there was an artist in the nineteenth century whose life details matched what he experienced. The most unusual detail was highly specific. This artist had painted a portrait of a hunchback woman. During a trip to New Orleans with his wife, Snow chanced upon an art gallery and saw, to his great astonishment, the portrait of the hunchback woman he had seen in his past-life regression. He learned the artist was an early twentieth century portrait artist named Carroll Beckwith. Snow located information about the artist and verified all the details about Carroll Beckwith he had stated during his past-life regression:

1. He painted a portrait of a hunchbacked woman.
2. He painted portraits to make money but hated painting portraits.
3. He went by the name "Jack."
4. He used a walking stick.
5. His wife and he spent time in France.
6. His wife could not have children.
7. They were desperate for money. He argued with his wife about money.
8. Despite their problems with money and inability to have children, their marriage was happy.
9. He had an art studio with a bank of skylights and a row of windows.
10. He once stayed at an estate with large gardens.
11. A female relative died of a blood clot.
12. He died in a large city with tall buildings in the fall of 1917.

You can view a video describing Captain Snow's experience at www.earthschoolanswers.com/snow/.

Experiences from people's pasts, including thoughts and sentiments, are accessible experiences in the Universal Intelligence that come into Awareness when the person requests them.

Experiences from the future are accessible: Precognition

All experiences from any time or place are accessible. Scientists have convincing data showing that people access experiences from the future.

Professor Dick J. Bierman of the University of Amsterdam and Utrecht University has been active in the field of parapsychology for over two decades, though he had been skeptical about the reality of psychic phenomena. After receiving his PhD in experimental physics, he became involved in research in artificial intelligence, specifically intelligent tutoring systems. His decades of research into how people gain knowledge led him to change his viewpoint about psychic phenomena. This is his description of the conclusion he came to about people's ability to access future experiences:

> We're satisfied that people can sense the future before it happens. . . . We'd now like to move on and see what kind of person is particularly good at it.[131]

Professor Brian Josephson, a Nobel Prize winning physicist from Cambridge University, drew similar conclusions:

> So far the evidence seems compelling. What seems to be happening is that information is coming from the future.[132]

A meta-analysis of all precognition experiments conducted at Stanford Research Institute from 1973 to 1988 was conducted by Edwin May, PhD, a researcher in low-energy, experimental nuclear physics, and his colleagues. The analysis was based on 154 experiments with more than 26,000 separate trials conducted over 16 years. They concluded that the studies showed that people are able to access experiences from the future, with the statistical results of this analysis showing odds against chance that were of more than a billion billion to one.[133]

Studies performed by Dr. Dean Radin and others showed that many people reacted to pictures about to be shown at random on a computer monitor six or seven seconds before the pictures were shown, even though the computer had not yet selected the pictures. The people insisted they didn't know in conscious Awareness what the pictures would be. If the pictures that were to appear in six or seven seconds were of disturbing images, the subjects' bodies would show tension. If the pictures to be shown were calming pictures, their bodies would show calm.[134] The subjects accessed the future experience at the subconscious Awareness level, even though the computer had not yet selected the image at random.

Experiences are accessible across space: Remote viewing

Many people are able to access experiences without having the environment of the experiences present through an ability called "remote viewing." This ability demonstrates that experiences from any location are accessible. The person sits quietly with his or her eyes closed and focuses on something that could be hundreds or thousands of miles away. The remote viewer is able to see it, hear it, smell it, feel its texture, sense movement, and sense emotions involved with it. In other words, the person is accessing sensory experiences given freely by the Universal Intelligence that are not within the person's current experiences of a location.

For several decades at the end of the twentieth century, the CIA had a remote viewing program named Operation Stargate that used remote viewers to spy on the Soviet Union. One of the most accomplished remote viewers was Joe McMoneagle. McMoneagle was tested by Edwin May, PhD in nuclear physics, president and founder of the Laboratories for Fundamental Research. McMoneagle was to remote view a team of CIA researchers as a test of his ability. The team was hundreds of miles from McMoneagle's location. He sat in his office, warmed down by meditating for a while, and closed his eyes, focusing his thought on where the team was. After a short time, he produced this sketch of where they were:

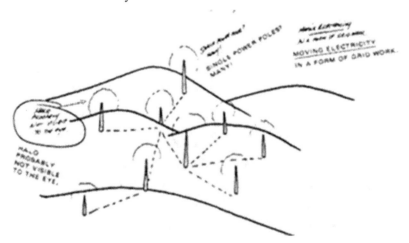

On the next page is a photograph of where the team actually was.

The writing on the sketch describes the windmills: "single power poles – many," "moving electricity in the form of grid work," "halo probably not visible to the eye." The sketches and descriptions exactly fit the location where the team was.[135] Joe McMoneagle was able to access the experiences of sight from hundreds of miles away.

The Princeton Engineering Anomalies Research (PEAR) Laboratory at Princeton University performed the same test of remote viewers by having a person travel to some distant location undisclosed to the remote viewer and having the remote viewer attempt to identify details about the location. The remote viewers in 334 trials were able to describe details about where the person was with odds against guessing the details of the location of 100 billion to one.[136]

Joe McMoneagle was also involved in a six-year remote viewing project to identify whether the shaman empress of ancient Japan named Himiko was mythical or real. She was the subject of many stories about ancient Japan and was mentioned briefly in one ancient Chinese document. He conducted his remote viewings of Japan from his home in Virginia. McMoneagle was able to access the experiences of the ruins of an ancient mountaintop castle, two temples, and a royal tomb, all previously undiscovered. The ruins were found where he stated they were, in the configurations he described. These discoveries were the subject of a best-selling book on the subject, published in Japanese.[137]

You can see a video of Joe McMoneagle describing his remote viewing of Himiko's archeological site at www.earthschoolanswers.com/joe/.

As an experiment while working with the CIA, the remote viewer Ingo Swann remote viewed Jupiter and had the sight experience of rings around the planet, a supposition no astronomer had suggested. Years later, a satellite flyby revealed that in fact Jupiter has rings around it. No human being had ever been close to Jupiter. However, Ingo Swann was able to access the sight experience of the rings from the Universal Intelligence.[138]

In an experimental project named The Caravel Project, remote viewers were tasked with finding sunken ships within a 4.35-square-mile search area. "The discovery of artifact and ship remains were made within the Remote Viewing predicted areas, and nowhere else, although substantial areas outside of the Remote Viewing locations were searched."[139] The experiences of the knowledge of the sunken ships were accessible, even though no human being had ever experienced them before.

A large number of studies have demonstrated that remote viewing is valid. The Stanford Research Institute (SRI) performed 154 experiments with 26,000 separate trials over 16 years. They concluded that the odds against someone merely guessing what remote viewers had described when focusing on a target at a distant location was more than a billion billion to one.[140]

Congress and the CIA commissioned a study by the Science Applications International Corporation (SAIC). The study resulted in the following conclusion of Jessica Utts, professor in the Division of Statistics at the University of California at Davis:

> It is clear to this author that anomalous cognition
> [remote viewing] is possible and has been demonstrated.
> This conclusion is not based on belief, but rather on
> commonly accepted scientific criteria. The phenomenon
> has been replicated in a number of forms across
> laboratories and cultures.[141]

Read more about remote viewing in *Your Eternal Self: Science Discovers the Afterlife.*[142]

Mental Mediums

All experiences are accessible, including communications from people now living in the next realm of life. The residents of the next realm of life are part of the Universal Intelligence as we are, and so are able to communicate with us Mind to Mind.

One of the most famous examples is of a housewife from St. Louis named Pearl Curran who began spontaneously communicating with a person living in the life after this life called Patience Worth. Patience was a seventeenth century English woman who had emigrated to America. Curran had dropped out of school when she was 14, had no knowledge of life in the seventeenth century, and had no literary ability.

Using automatic writing, Patience Worth produced through Pearl Curran's hand 2,500 poems, short stories, plays, allegories, and six full-length novels in five years. Four novels were published: *The Sorry Tale, Hope Trueblood, Light from Beyond,* and *The Pot upon the Wheel. Telka,* a lengthy play of 60,000-70,000 words, is considered by researcher Walter Franklin Prince to be superior to analogous works.[143] *The Sorry Tale* is considered by Dr Roland Usher, professor of history at Washington University, to be the greatest story penned of the life and times of Jesus since the biblical gospels were written.[144]

W. T. Allison, professor of English literature at the University of Manitoba, wrote that Patience Worth dictated words found only in Milton's time that sometimes had to be researched in old dictionaries and books to find their meanings. One evening when Allison was with Curran, she produced 15 poems at an average of five minutes per poem. Allison wrote that

> All were poured out with a speed that Tennyson or Browning could never have hoped to equal, and some of the 15 lyrics are so good that either of those great poets might be proud to have written them.[145]

The remarkable works by Patience Worth through Pearl Curran demonstrate that experiences such as authorship and language are transmitted to people from individuals living in the life after this life. Curran had no capability to produce the literary works she produced without Patience Worth's conveying to her the writing experiences.

The author's intentions in books are available to experience

All thought experiences are accessible in the same way event or sensory experiences are available. An example is the fact that an author's thoughts are available to people living in the life after this life. In the life after this life, all books that were ever written are available in vast libraries. However, the residents speaking through mediums tell us they don't need to read a book. They can close their eyes, focus on the book, and experience the book's reading itself to them. In fact, they can experience the author's original thoughts as he or she was writing the book, so readers can experience the book as the author intended it to be.

Leslie Flint was a direct voice medium in the twentieth century. People living in the life after this life came into sessions he led and spoke clearly about our Earth world and their world. In a session on December 18, 1967, a woman named Alice Green came through from the life after this life and explained that every book that was ever written is available and readers can access the author's thoughts and intentions. A transcript follows. You can listen to the recording at www.earthschoolanswers.com/alice/.

Transcript:

[Alice Green (AG) speaks] Oh, well, of course there they've got every book that's worth reading, any book that's of value, you know. It's there, and you can take it down and you can read it. But then again, you see, you don't have to read, really. It's funny, isn't it? There isn't much point in having books is there.

[Betty Greene (BG), a sitter, speaks] You don't have to read?

AG: Well, not in the same kind of way.

BG: Well, how do you assimilate what is in the books?

AG: Well, I don't know. It's as if the book speaks to you. They really don't, of course not really.

BG: Can you take the books out of the library if you want to?

AG: Oh, as far as you can take the books out, I should say, you know, but, oh yes, you can take things home, but it's really not necessary. That's the funny part about it, when you come to think about it. It's as if there's everything there that you expect, that you would want, but you soon begin to realize that many of the things are not really necessary in quite the same sort of way. If you mentally sort of tune in to a particular something or somebody that you want a communication, or telepathy. It isn't as if you have to borrow a book and read it as such. It's as if you want to know about the book, perhaps a very famous book, you can either read it, but when you begin to realize that this book can express itself to you. How it's done, I don't know. It's as if you can sit there and you can close your eyes and you can hold the book in your hands and all the happenings in the book can just sort of tell you. You know, yes it's funny, but I don't know. So instead of getting, you know, your own idea, which may not be quite what was intended, you can get the identical thought impressions of the author and publisher, you know.[146]

You can listen to Alice Green's entire session at www.leslieflint.com/alice-green-december-1967.

You can learn more about Leslie Flint at www.earthschoolanswers.com/flint/.

All experiences from anywhere, anytime are accessible

We are all individual manifestations of the Universal Intelligence. Anything that ever was or ever will be, anywhere, anytime, is accessible to us. We are normally able to access only experiences in our sphere of connections, but people with unusual abilities are able to access a wide range of experiences, illustrating that we have not found a limit to the experiences the human Mind is capable of accessing.

7

How Do We Have Experiences?

Experiences come into the point of now Awareness

New experiences continually occupy the point of our lives we call "now." The now point is like the reading head on a DVD player. A now experience plays and is immediately replaced by another now experience in a ceaseless string.

The experiences may seem to have a duration, but that is only because the experiences have continuity in the successive needle points of nows. Driving seems to be one seamless experience, but it is a series of experiences in the point of now Awareness. Even when it seems a thought comes to mind and occupies the mind for a few seconds, the thought is continually changing and being interrupted by other experiences. The experience in the point of now Awareness never remains the same.

What duration is the point of now?

A geometric point has no dimensions. A line is made up of an infinite number of points, regardless of how long the line is. A one-inch line and a one-mile line both have an infinite number of points. The points are seamless, from one to the next, without a duration.

A state-of-the-art camera is capable of recording one trillion frames per second.[147] That is like 1,000,000,000,000 nows a second. But there's an even smaller duration of time. Physics suggests that there is no measurement smaller than the Planck time unit. A unit of Planck time is an inconceivably small 10^{-43} seconds. That is so small that there are more units of Planck time in one second than all the seconds there have been since the Big Bang, 13.7 billion years ago. But the point of now is even smaller; it has no duration.

The "I" is always there

We are manifestations of the Universal Intelligence, individuated so we can have unique experiences in Earth School. But there is only Mind and experiences. Throughout all the experiences in all the nows, our Awareness is the same. Our awareness is our soul that is not changed by the wide range of experiences, interpretations, and emotions.

We have the experience of sitting down to eat. We have the visual experiences of the table, food, the room, and our companions. We feel joy. We have the sound experiences of silverware, people talking, noises from the street, and chairs moving. We have the olfactory experiences of the smell of food. We have the tactile experiences of the chair beneath us, the feel of the table, the feel of our clothing, and the temperature in the room. And we have the taste experiences when we put food into our mouths. From instant to instant, our Awareness contains the experiences that dominate. However, our Awareness, the I that we are, always remains the same.

The Universal Intelligence's creative power influences the experiences

Accessing the experiences is not mechanical, like accessing files from a hard drive. As experiences flood the mind from the subconscious, they are assisted by the creative power of the Universal Intelligence.

This is an example. You must do a little work to understand this concept, but only by having the experience can you understand the creative power of the Universal Intelligence. In a moment, I want you to close your eyes and relax for two or three minutes so your mind is calmed down. Then I want you to imagine you are in a new city you have never been in before. You might choose a country you haven't visited in which to place the city, but don't identify a city. Walk down a street in this new city. If you are a visualizer, you will see images. If you think more in words and impressions, you are a verbalizer. You will see few or no images. Instead, you will have the impression you are in the city. Most people have cognitive styles between the two extremes.

Give yourself a minute or two. If you're enjoying the process, let it go on longer. Stroll down the street of this imaginary city. Notice the buildings, street, storefronts, people, sounds, and smells. Interact with people or animals you come upon. Remember all the details of this city street and the events. Open your eyes after a few minutes and read on here.

Close your eyes and stroll down the street now.

You probably were able to envision or have the impression of the street, buildings, pavement, storefronts, and people. You may have heard sounds and smelled smells. You may have interacted with people. Where did all that come from? It didn't come from your conscious Mind. You couldn't create fast enough to make all those details. You would have had the snail's-pace slowness of creating a painting one brushstroke at a time. You had dozens of detailed memories created during your stroll that you now remember with all the details intact. You didn't think to yourself, "I'm going to create a brown building with large windows and displays. I'm going to have a woman with blonde hair walking past the window wearing a business suit." You didn't create all the details. Where did the scene and events come from?

They came from the creative power of the Universal Intelligence. It is the same creative power that creates the Earth School environment we take for granted, with all its detail and complexities.

When we intend to bring an experience into our conscious Awareness, such as a memory experience, it comes to us immediately. We are an individual manifestation of the Universal Intelligence, so we ask and are granted our request. However, we receive much more than we ask for. We receive a creation. When we want to imagine something unusual, we just ask the question differently. "I want to walk through a marvelous castle. Give me the interior of the castle with people in it." Our Universal Intelligence creates the castle, rooms, people, and events on the spot, without hesitation. We just allow it to come into conscious Awareness as we tour the castle.

As a result, when we intentionally bring experiences to Mind or when we have an experience come into Mind because of its affiliation with something in a current experience, our experiences are augmented by the creative power of the Universal Intelligence. In other words, we have godlike abilities to create what we want without the conscious mind's involvement in the creation.

And so, we may be puzzling over a problem we have, bringing to Mind experiences relevant to the problem, looking at all sides of the issue using the repertoire of experiences we can access. Then, suddenly, the solution pops into our Mind. It comes "out of the blue." We have other phrases for the phenomenon: "dawned on me," "realized," "came to me," "popped into my head," "occurred to me," "a notion," "it hit me," "a eureka moment," "an intuition," "a revelation," "an epiphany." We have phrases in the language referring to allowing this creation to occur: "I'll sleep on it," "we'll let it percolate." People commonly describe experiencing the sudden revelation: "It came to me in the shower," "I awoke the next morning and just knew what to do," "I solved the problems while I was going for a walk," "I was just driving along and it hit me."

In descriptions of the process of creating, the sequence most often referred to is preparation, incubation, illumination, and verification. The illumination stage is where a solution or an idea comes to Mind that was unanticipated or unusually suited to the situation. "Illumination" is described as a stage out of the person's control. It simply happens:

As this process of unconscious activity (sometimes also conscious) goes on, suddenly, the individual finds a right answer to his problems, doubts and questions. This sudden understanding or insight very often occurs when the person is sleeping or doing something totally different and far removed from the main problem or issue. Thus Archimedes found an answer to his question [about the displacement of water], in his bathtub, the "Eureka" experience.[148]

Great theoreticians, writers, painters, and composers describe the process in which their breakthroughs and works of art come to them spontaneously. In 1862, the Scottish mathematician James Clerk Maxwell developed a set of fundamental equations that unified electricity and magnetism. On his deathbed, he said that something within him discovered the famous equations, not he. He admitted he had no idea how ideas actually came to him—they simply came.[149]

William Blake related a similar experience about writing his long narrative poem, *Milton*: "I have written this poem from immediate dictation twelve or sometimes twenty lines at a time without premeditation and even against my will."[150]

Johann Wolfgang von Goethe claimed to have written his novella *The Sorrows of Young Werther* with practically no conscious input, as though he were holding a pen that moved on its own.[151]

We are all familiar with the synchronicity phenomenon. Someone is searching for a solution or an idea and can't discover it with the conscious mind. Out of the blue, a stranger makes a comment that perfectly fits the situation and solves the problem or provides the idea.

These perfect solutions can come from the Universal Intelligence's creative power, or from prompting by a guide, helper, or loved one in the next realm of life. Whatever the source, accessing experiences is not a mechanical process. The accessed experience is often a novel experience developed when needed by our Minds, the Universal Intelligence, guides, and others interested in helping us. They are adding their input to the raw material of our repertoire of experiences.

Deliberate approaches to allowing the power of the creative Universal Intelligence to solve problems and realize creative conclusions are through relaxation, meditation, and self-hypnosis. By shutting down the normal flow of experiences into conscious Awareness, experiences in subconscious Awareness can rise into the available space of conscious Awareness. Accessing these subconscious experiences requires being positive and open to the Universal Intelligence, guides, helpers, loved ones, and people in the life after this life to bring realizations to us that cannot penetrate when the Mind is dominated by the experiences coming to us from the focus on Earth School experiences.

Acting from the subconscious in performances

Relying on the subconscious for processing is especially important in complex skills such as speaking, sports, art, music, and other such performance activities. The person is acting from the subconscious, with agility and rapidity. The conscious Mind plays a minor role in the activity for accomplished performers. The subconscious takes over processing to bring the desired results. In extreme cases for sports or performance arts, the conscious mind is bypassed so the sports figure or performance artist can act entirely from the subconscious. The person is "in the zone," "on automatic pilot," or "in the groove." The experiences the person has access to are sophisticated and skilled. The highest quality experiences have been developed over time, with considerable practice. They are then executed with little intervention from the conscious Mind.

The performances are enhanced by the Universal Intelligence that gives us what we ask for. When we speak, play an instrument, perform in a presentation, or play a sport, we are acting from our subconscious with the Universal Intelligence assisting and guiding us through every thought, action, and reaction. That is what makes the fluid, adept performance possible.

The skill is entirely in the Mind, not in the muscles. All performances, regardless of how sophisticated or complex, are made up of strings of experiences brought into subconscious Awareness resulting in muscle activity. The experiences of striking the correct keys in the correct ways and correct sequences to play a piano concerto masterfully have been accumulated through practice over years that progressively creates new experiences the person then brings into subconscious Awareness to perform. Feedback through hearing the correct sound and responses from others help the pianist acquire the experiences that strike the piano keys in the way that results in the virtuoso performance. The most recent correct experiences come into subconscious Awareness to supersede the early, less accomplished experiences.

At the same time, the Universal Intelligence is giving the performer what he or she is asking for, in greater measure than the performer could accomplish without the assistance. Performing is a creative act. The repertoire of experiences accumulated through practice is the basis for the performance, but the result when the person surrenders to the performance is greater than the person could have accomplished through conscious Awareness alone.

We can have any experiences not in our repertoire come into Awareness

In Earth School, the rule is that we must develop our repertoire of experiences in playing the piano by experimenting over time. That takes practice. Normally people are able to access only the experiences in their own repertoire of experiences, not in other people's repertoires. Someone who stopped taking piano lessons after four weeks will not have developed the repertoire of experiences to play adeptly.

However, the experiences involved in activities such as playing a piano and speaking are accessible by anyone, even if the person has not acquired them through practice. There are validated cases of people suddenly accessing experiences that result in sophisticated performances, even though the experiences were not developed in their own repertoire through practice. The ability to access a wider range of experiences than the person previously had access to is called the "acquired savant syndrome."

Acquired savant syndrome in the ability to play a piano

Examples of the sudden acquisition of the ability to accesses experiences that result in proficient piano playing follow.

Derek Amato was 40 years old when he hit his head hard after diving in a shallow pool. Prior to the accident, Derek had absolutely no musical training or ability. When he woke up after his accident, he immediately had the ability to play music with the proficiency of a trained professional.

> As I shut my eyes, I found these black and white structures moving from left to right, which in fact would represent in my mind, a fluid and continuous stream of musical notation. . . . My fingers began to scale the piano keys as if I had played all of my life. I can't explain the feeling of awe that overcame my entire being, although I can tell you the expression on my friend's face was enough to put us both in tears.[152]

These sophisticated experiences became accessible to Derek's subconscious Awareness, from which piano playing comes. Their origin is not known, whether the experiences have a life of their own or whether they were the experiences of a master pianist. We just know that any experiences from anywhere, anytime, and any person are accessible. Derek's accident enabled him to access the experiences of playing the correct notes suddenly.

He said of his gift, "It's almost like the ghost of Beethoven jumped into my body, right, and took over and I just kind of went crazy."[153]

View a video of Derek describing his sudden abilities: www.earthschoolanswers.com/derek/.

In another case of a man developing the ability to play the piano spontaneously, a 28-year-old man from Israel known as K. A. reported that prior to his spontaneous change, he could play only simple popular songs from rote memory on a piano. He describes something unusual that happened one day when he came across a piano as he strolled through a mall:

> Suddenly at age 28 after what I can best describe as a
> 'just getting it moment,' it all seemed so simple. I
> suddenly was playing like a well-educated pianist. I
> suddenly realized what the major scale and minor scale
> were, what their chords were and where to put my
> fingers in order to play certain parts of the scale. I was
> instantly able to recognize harmonies of the scales in
> songs I knew as well as the ability to play melody by
> interval recognition.

He searched the Internet for information on music theory and read it with great interest. To his amazement "most of what they had to teach I already knew, which baffled me as to how could I know something I had never studied."[154]

K. A. had access to the experiences he needed to be able to play adeptly and to have the knowledge of music theory. All of it came from the Universal Intelligence that made the experiences he had not created in daily life available to him to access when he played the piano.

In another case of spontaneous knowledge of how to play the piano, a man named Lachlan Connors explained that he was so musically incapable that he couldn't even remember the melody and lyrics for nursery rhymes like "Twinkle, Twinkle, Little Star." His mother, Elsie Hamilton, corroborated this.

> He really had no talent. I would say 'Can't you hear
> what's next?' with something like 'Mary Had a Little
> Lamb' or 'Twinkle, Twinkle, Little Star' and he'd say
> 'No.'[155]

However, in sixth grade he suffered several injuries to his head while playing lacrosse. He began to experience serious epileptic seizures and hallucinations. The seizures and hallucinations eventually subsided, but he had spontaneously developed the ability to play musical instruments. Without lessons, he could effortlessly play 13 instruments, including piano, guitar, mandolin, ukulele, harmonica, African karimba, and bagpipes. Connors played music solely by ear. He couldn't read music. The ability to play came in experiences he accessed in subconscious Awareness from the Universal Intelligence.[156]

View a video about Lachlan Connors at www.earthschoolanswers.com/lachlan/.

Another savant who developed his piano-playing talent with no training or practice was Leslie Lemke. Leslie was profoundly mentally disabled, and yet he spontaneously, without training, was able to play piano concertos:

> At 16 years of age, Leslie Lemke bloomed. In the middle of one night, May [his adoptive mother] woke up to find Leslie playing Tchaikovsky's Piano Concerto No. 1. Leslie, who has no classical music training, was playing the piece flawlessly after hearing it just once earlier on the television.
>
> From then on, Leslie began playing all styles of music from ragtime to classical. Like the Tchaikovsky piece, he only has to hear the music once in order to play it again perfectly. He became famous after being portrayed in national television shows. Before his health started to deteriorate, Leslie gave many concerts around the world.
>
> Leslie would play the piano and sing perfectly, but had not learned how to speak.[157]

A video of Leslie Lemke is at www.earthschoolanswers.com/lemke/.

These examples demonstrate that the experiences of manipulating the keys on a piano to play adeptly are accessible as all experiences are accessible, whether they were developed in the repertoire of experiences or not. The person just has to be able to access them.

Sudden acquisition of the abilities to speak a language

Speaking a language also results from access by subconscious Awareness to a language's words, pronunciations, and syntax to adeptly speak or write a language. Strings of individual experiences with the language are accessed to form complex streams of recalled experiences with language that enable the person to perform the motor activities of speaking or writing the language. Being able to speak and write a language normally results from being brought up in an environment in which the person experiences use of the language and develops the abilities in his or her repertoire of experiences. However, the language abilities also can develop spontaneously; all experiences are accessible, including the complex experiences required to speak and write a language.

When someone suddenly is able to speak a language unfamiliar to him or her, the phenomenon is called "xenoglossy."

In 1977, doctors at a state penitentiary in Ohio discovered that a convicted rapist named Billy Mulligan had become possessed by two new personalities, both of whom communicated in different languages. Mulligan was born and raised in the USA and spoke no foreign languages. But when taken over by Abdul, Mulligan could read and write perfect Arabic; as Rugen he spoke perfect Serbo-Croat with a thick Slavic accent.[158]

In another case Ian Stevenson described, in the July 1980 edition of the *Journal of the American Society for Psychical Research*, an Indian woman named Uttar Huddar who at aged 32 spontaneously took on the personality of a housewife of West Bengal who lived in the early 1800s. She began speaking Bengali instead of her own language, Marathi. For weeks, speakers of Bengali had to be brought in to enable her to communicate with her own family.[159, 160]

In 1931, a young English girl from Blackpool, known as Rosemary in the files of the Society for Psychical Research, began to speak in an ancient Egyptian dialect under the influence of the personality of Telika-Ventiu who had lived in approximately 1400 BCE. In front of Egyptologist Howard Hume, she wrote 66 accurate phrases in the lost language of hieroglyphs and spoke in a tongue unheard outside academic circles for thousands of years.[161]

In two other cases, the individuals did have rudimentary knowledge of the language they accessed, but after a trauma accessed the experiences to be fluent in the language.

Rueben Nsemoh, an English-speaking high school soccer player, suffered a head injury, and when he awoke could speak only Spanish "like a native." He could not speak English. Previous to the injury, he knew some basic Spanish but was not fluent.[162]

Matej Kus, a Czech motorcycle racer was in an accident and knocked unconscious. When he awoke he was able to speak English fluently with a British accent. Prior to the accident he had some knowledge of basic English phrases but spoke broken English. After a few days, he returned to speaking Croation.[163]

In these cases, the experiences of vocabulary, pronunciation, and syntax were accessible to these individuals even though they did not have the language abilities in their repertoires of experiences.

People in a state of hypnosis or trance take on other personalities and speak languages they do not know

In a state of hypnosis or trance, a person can access words from a language the person has no knowledge of or speak fluently a language other than the person's native language. Some people have accessed words from ancient languages, while others have accessed the entire lexicon and syntax of a language they don't know, speaking as adeptly as a native-born speaker.

In the first example, Dr Joel Whitton describes the case of Harold Jaworski, who under hypnosis said he was a Viking named Thor in a past life. He wrote down 22 words and phrases he "heard" himself speaking in a past Viking life. Working independently, linguists identified the words as the extinct language Old Norse and translated ten of them. Several of the others were Russian, Serbian, or Slavic. All were words associated with the sea.[164]

The same client, while in hypnotic trance, said he had lived as a Mesopotamian named Xando. Dr. Whitten asked him to write down words for common things like clothing, weather, houses, and so on. Harold held a pencil very lightly and created mysterious Arabic-style figures. When Harold emerged from hypnosis, Dr. Whitten asked him what the figures were. Harold had no idea. They looked like meaningless scribbles to him. Curious, Dr. Whitten gave the figures to an expert in the Iranian/Persian languages. The expert researched the figures and determined they were letters from a language called

Sassanid Pahlavi, used between 220 and 651 CE. The language has long been extinct.[165]

Jaworski accessed the experiences with no knowledge of the language or the period in history. They were experiences accessible from the lives of other people in the distant past, demonstrating that language experiences are accessible from any time.

In other cases, people under hypnosis have been able to access the entire lexicon and syntax of a language not in their repertoire of experiences. Dr. Morris Netherton reports a case of an eleven-year-old Caucasian boy who under hypnosis was taped for eleven minutes speaking in an ancient Chinese dialect. When the recording of the session was taken to a professor at the Department of Oriental Studies at the University of California, it turned out to be a recitation from a forbidden religion of Ancient China.[166]

The famous reincarnation researcher, Dr. Ian Stevenson, documented a study he made of a 37-year-old American woman who, under hypnosis, experienced a complete change of voice and personality into a male. She spoke fluently in Swedish—a language she did not speak or understand. Dr. Stevenson's involvement with this case lasted more than eight years. The woman was studied by linguists and scientists, who meticulously investigated every explanation for her remarkable abilities, finding no reasonable explanation.[167]

Author Lyall Watson describes a case of a ten-year-old Igarot Indian living in the remote Cagayon Valley in the Philippines. The child had never had any contact with any language or culture other than his own. Yet under trance, the child communicated freely in African Zulu, a language the child could never have heard. Watson recognized it because he had spent his early life in Africa.[168]

Peter Ramster, in his book *The Search for Lives Past*, describes the case of Cynthia Henderson, whose only contact with the French language had been a few months of very basic instruction in high school. Yet under hypnosis she was able to carry on a long, detailed conversation in French with a native speaker who commented that she spoke with no English accent and in the manner of the eighteenth century.[169]

The experiences of using the vocabulary, pronunciation, and syntax of a language are accessible in the Universal Intelligence. They can be accessed even though the person has not developed the experiences in his or her repertoire of experiences.

Mediums have been able to speak languages they do not know

Mediums also are able to access the experiences of languages they do not know.

American medium George Valentine under trance conducted séances in Russian, German, Spanish, and Welsh, languages he did not know.[170] The Brazilian medium Carlos Mirabelli spoke and wrote long technical documents in more than thirty languages, including Syriac and Japanese, in the presence of scientists and crowds of up to 5,000.[171]

Foreign accent syndrome

The act of speaking a language comes from recalled experiences with the words, syntax, intonations, and pronunciations. Someone learning a new language will mistakenly use the syntax, intonations, and pronunciations of his or her native language when speaking the new language. The result is what we refer to as an "accent."

There are cases of people suddenly speaking with a pronounced foreign accent, illustrating that all experiences are accessible, including the language-speaking repertoire of someone who speaks with a recognizable accent. The phenomenon is called "foreign accent syndrome," or "dysprosody."

One study identified and studied 62 subjects experiencing spontaneous foreign accent syndrome.[172] The same authors in another study found 112 cases of dysprosody in their meta-analysis of studies.[173] These subjects were suddenly accessing a different repertoire of language experiences because all experiences are accessible, including the experiences of vocalizing a language with the accent of a nonnative speaker.

You can see a video of three people with foreign-accent syndrome at www.earthschoolanswers.com/accent/.

Acquired savant syndrome in mathematics

Performing mathematical calculations with dexterity requires acquiring the experiences in the mathematician's experience repertoire that result in proficient mathematics performance. However, as with the other spontaneous savant examples, mathematics ability can be suddenly acquired; all experiences are accessible.

Jason Padgett received a concussion from a brutal beating. When he recovered, he found that he was able to visualize complicated mathematical and physics concepts. "I see shapes and angles everywhere in real life. It's just really beautiful." He was encouraged by a physicist to take up math studies and is now becoming a number theorist. Various neuroscientists have expressed an interest in studying his brain to understand how he acquired his new expertise.[174]

You can see a video of Jason Padgett describing his abilities at www.earthschoolanswers.com/jason/.

In another case, a man named Jim Carollo was involved in a severe auto accident at age 14 and spent several days in a coma. His injuries were so serious the doctors thought he wouldn't live. However, within a few months after he awoke, he had developed remarkable math abilities. He scored a perfect 100 on his next geometry test without studying, which was surprising because he had never been particularly good at math before the accident. He became especially proficient at remembering numbers and could recite any numbers from memory, including phone numbers, credit card numbers, old locker combinations, and the first 200 digits of pi.[175]

All of these acquired skills resulted from being able to access a far wider range of experiences from the Universal Intelligence.

Acquired savant syndrome in art

Creating art is also a series of experiences the artist brings to Mind as needed. Normally, the experiences have been acquired over a long period of artistic practice, but in some cases an individual with no artistic ability can suddenly access proficient art experiences. This acquired savant condition is known as "sudden artistic output."

One example is Ken Walters. Ken suffered a stroke in 2005. His speech was affected, so he used pen and paper to communicate. His hand spontaneously began to sketch patterns.

> I've never been a doodler. The closest I'd come was copying a cartoon as a child, and I hadn't drawn since. That's why it was so strange. The act was unconscious; only when a nurse asked me what I was doing did I look down to see patterns all over the paper.[176]

Ken used his newfound talent to become a professional artist. His work has been featured in numerous art magazines and displayed in various galleries.[177]

In another example of sudden artistic output, Jon Sarkin, a chiropractor, was able to access proficient art experiences after suffering a stroke in his mid-thirties. After the stroke, he became fixated on drawing. Soon his artwork was being shown in many galleries and typically sells for $10,000 or more.[178]

Another example of sudden artistic output is Ric Owens' case. In 2011, Ric was a professional chef with a successful career. One evening his car was hit by a semi-truck, and although shaken, he didn't seem to have any injuries. Within a week, though, he started experiencing migraines and his speech began to slur. He was diagnosed with post-concussive syndrome. But he also found that he was no longer interested in making food. Instead, he was obsessed with abstract geometric art. Although neither he nor the doctors could explain how it happened, he could suddenly make art with anything he found around the house.[179]

A middle-aged woman from Liverpool, England, named Pip Taylor had her own experience with sudden artistic output. Pip grew up with a passion for drawing but was so bad at it that even her teacher advised her against taking it up as a career. Then, in 2012, she fell down a flight of stairs and hit her head hard. She recovered, but was amazed to discover that she had acquired the ability to draw realistic copies of almost anything. The doctors couldn't explain the change.[180]

In a fifth example of sudden artistic output, a 43-year-old woman with no interest in art or drawing woke up one night in

December 2016 with what she called "the urgent need to draw a multitude of triangles, which quickly evolved to a web of complex abstract designs. I stayed up into the morning with a compulsive need to draw, which continued over the next three days at an intense level." Three days later she was working on a drawing she named "The Mayan," which took her two weeks to complete. Three months later she had created 15 pieces whose styles were similar to artists such as Frida Kahlo and Picasso. She uses a mandala style, even though she had no idea what that was before her remarkable sudden artistic output development. Today she spends about eight hours a day drawing.[181]

In another example of sudden artistic output, a woman in her mid-40s called S. S. began noticing changes in her perception of the world around her. When she looked at things like trees and flowers, she was seeing colors, textures, and shadows in ways she had never seen before. She felt compelled to portray her new visions on paper. She had never painted before in her life and was not comfortable with a paintbrush, so she bought a cheap set of pastel pencils, found a photograph of a gorilla on the cover of an old *National Geographic* magazine, and drew it. The resulting drawing was a rich, complex pastel portrait of the gorilla with uncanny realism. Her creation stunned her friends and family because she had never shown an interest in art or any artistic ability, and she had never taken an art class growing up.[182] She became able to access the experiences required to create great art.

Franco Magnani also experienced a sudden artistic talent. Magnani was a cook in Italy who travelled to San Francisco in 1965 for a vacation. While there, he became seriously ill. After his illness, he suffered from "high fever nightmares" that had the qualities of seizures. During these episodes, he would see visions of his childhood city in Tuscany, Pontito, as it had been before the Nazis came. He described the visions as "rising up" in front of him.

> During this time, Franco began having astonishingly vivid and detailed dreams of Pontito, visions he could actually see before him. He felt called to paint the scenes of his childhood home, and was amazed to find that he

could do so, without ever having had any formal artistic training. He began to create hundreds of "memory paintings" of the buildings, streets and fertile surroundings of his pre-war Pontito, with a perspective unique to him. The scenes he imagined were so real and three-dimensional that Franco would turn his head to "see" them from different angles as he painted, and he experienced the sounds and smells around him. This desire to capture the Pontito of his youth became the driving force of his life from this time forward.[183]

His need to turn his head to have the sight experiences illustrates that he was accessing experiences as a person actually in the city. You can see examples of his paintings at www.earthschoolanswers.com/franco/.

You can view a video of sudden artistic talent at www.earthschoolanswers.com/artistic/.

All experiences that ever were or ever will be are accessible

The Universal Intelligence makes every experience that ever was or ever will be accessible to the individuals who have the sphere of contact to access them. Some people, such as savants, are able to access a much broader range of experiences. In some cases, people are able to access the experiences not in their sphere of contacts, illustrating that all experiences are accessible to the Mind. We just have to be able to access them.

What is "Thinking"?

When we are thinking, we're going through a complex review of experiences in conscious Awareness and subconscious Awareness. We intend to bring an experience into conscious Awareness and it comes. The experience in Awareness cues subconscious and conscious experiences by their association links. We review and organize these experiences in the process of "thinking."

Thinking with verbalization is slowed down by the action of articulating words as though the person were speaking them. However, underlying the words is what is actually influencing the thinking and outcomes: the subconscious memory experiences and interpretations. The conscious mind's verbalizing is only a codification of what has already come to mind from the subconscious.

And so, in the case of someone who must decide whether to spend an extra $200 on a computer to get a touch screen, when she thinks of spending the $200, her subconscious Awareness is flooded with cued concerns over money, money amounts, feelings that she doesn't need such a luxury, recalling that the rent is due in a week, and on and on. The conscious Mind is hardly engaged. The subconscious experiences carry interpretations that give rise to the feelings or emotions that may "tie her in knots." The reason is that the subconscious Awareness is accessing experiences at a faster rate than conscious Awareness can process them. They create confusion.

Conscious Awareness is initially dominated by these subconscious thoughts that flood in unbidden, but the conscious Awareness is where our free will resides. After receiving the flood of experiences from the subconscious, the person can begin the part of the thinking process that is more deliberative. She can ask herself, "Will the touch screen be worth the $200?" Immediately, a flood of new subconscious experiences flows into the mind having to do with the pleasure of having the touch screen, the extra money coming in from a tax return, the image of her father telling her to be frugal, and on and on. The subconscious experiences fill the subconscious Awareness while the conscious Awareness is ponderously articulating a single strand of thought stimulated by the subconscious experiences.

Using her conscious Awareness, she evaluates the subconscious experiences about the touch screen until she arrives at a combination of experiences that feels comfortable. The comfortable-feeling thought in the conscious Mind provides a compromise that stems the flood of experiences coming into the subconscious. If her decision feels good, she has built a structure out of the subconscious experiences that enables her to have the emotional response, "That feels OK." The feelings are the temperature gauge for our life in Earth School.

"Thinking," then, is a complex process involving conscious Awareness's evaluating and rearranging the experiences and interpretations of experiences welling up from the subconscious to arrive at a conclusion that feels good. It's as though someone had assembled 20 workers to build a house. One is good at nailing together wood to make the wall frame. One is good at using cinder blocks to make a foundation. One is good at installing windows. And all the other workers are each good at something else. Everyone immediately gets busy in his or her area of expertise without a plan; there is chaos. Windows are being built when the walls aren't even up. The foundation is being laid before the plans are complete. Every worker is doing what he or she is best at, regardless of what the consequences are for the house.

Those workers are the experiences and interpretations flooding Awareness from the subconscious. A general contractor must come onto the scene and sort out who does what when and give orders. That's conscious Awareness. As conscious Awareness is assembling the workers in a plan that will be satisfying to build the house, the workers are all still clamoring for attention. Finally, over the din of noise from the workers, the general contractor announces the plan that feels right. That quiets all the workers.

In the same way, the subconscious Awareness's experiences, interpretations, and emotions are the workers, each intent on having its experience and interpretation influence the outcome. The first response the person has to an experience will be from the subconscious interpretation that is strongest. What comes to us through subconscious Awareness is very fast, at 11 or 20 million bits per second, so conscious Awareness, processing information at 60 or 120 bits per second, is not involved until the subconscious experiences have made their entrance.

Someone who is impetuous or closed-minded will respond based on that first subconscious experience and interpretation, without considering the other experiences in the repertoire of experiences. Another person who realizes the need to examine the other experiences in the repertoire might say, "I have to think about this." The thinking will be allowing the other experiences in the person's repertoire to come into Awareness where the person can feel how they fit. The person then tries out different experiences, much like putting pieces into a jigsaw puzzle.

The subconscious experiences and interpretations that are strongest will be most influential. Conscious Awareness must review each experience and interpretation, weigh it based on reason and feeling, and as rationally as possible make the final decision. The final decision will be based on what feels comfortable or right or logical. That comfortable feeling is the goal of the thinking.

The experiences in subconscious Awareness are felt more than rationally considered because of the speed with which they come into Awareness. The roles of conscious Awareness are to realize the decisions already framed by the combination of experiences and interpretations in subconscious Awareness that result in the most comfortable feeling, then articulate the decisions as rational, carefully considered conclusions. However, the rational explanations come after the feelings about the alternatives have already made the decision.

Even a quantum physicist, puzzling through the notion of quantum gravity or string theory, is having experiences flood awareness from the subconscious with theories, data, knowledge, feelings about what colleagues might think, and a host of other subconscious experiences. The technical, evidence-based nature of the thinking affects the content, but the process is the same as less technical deliberations. The quantum physicist is comparing, combining, weighing, reconstituting, and eliminating the very technical subconscious experiences at great speed. Conscious awareness is slowing the process to corral the subconscious experiences and bring them into some order. A conclusion, then, is made up of the 95 percent subconscious experiences articulated by the 5 percent of the rationalizing that is conscious awareness, whether the thinker is a mother making a decision about what to make for her child's lunch or a quantum physicist writing a paragraph about quantum gravity. The resulting decision or solution fits with the feelings about the subconscious and conscious experiences. This decision about my child's lunch feels OK. This conclusion about my writing on quantum gravity feels OK. The process is the same. Only the content is different.

Scientists like to think of themselves as objective and thoroughly rational, but the truth is that they rely on the same "It feels OK" decision as anyone does. And in areas not in their technical area of expertise, they are as emotional and biased as every other human being is. Witness their attitude towards all things having to do with psychic abilities in the face of overwhelming evidence of the validity of psychic phenomena. Their subconscious experiences dominate, so they lose their rationality about data outside the boundaries of the experiences that make them feel OK.

However, among the subconscious experiences coming to the scientist are insights and guidance from scientists living in the next realm of life who are dedicated to helping humankind advance in its knowledge of the world. They are inspiring the "aha" moments. The scientist just has to be open to having them come into conscious Awareness as possibilities for consideration.

How do we use experiences in speaking?

These experiences that come into subconscious Awareness result in automatic activities such as speaking. Speaking is a complex set of experiences that come into subconscious Awareness and result in vocalizations. When we see a dog, the sight triggers subconscious experiences and interpretations that come into Awareness in a flurry: "cute," "pet it," "come to me," "friendly?" "hurt me?," and a variety of other interpretations. These experiences are not related to language. They are experiences and interpretations that enter the now point of Awareness and cue other experiences that come into subconscious Awareness. Words are coming to mind continually as we go through our day, but virtually all of what we experience is not accompanied by words. The words are just codifications of a small part of what is coming into our Awareness.

At some point, the person may intend to have the experience of speaking. We have a concept we want to state that is in Awareness, but the totality of the vocalized explanation happens in subconscious Awareness. If we dragged the explanation into conscious Awareness to assemble it, we would dither for hours to voice a simple concept.

Instead, we have a concept we access from our memory experiences and rely on the subconscious to give us words and syntax in an instant to match the message we want to communicate. We begin sentences, assemble the words using language syntax, and vocalize adeptly without being consciously aware of the process. It just happens. When we begin a sentence we don't know in conscious Awareness how it will end, but subconscious Awareness has it all mapped out.

An important component in the freewheeling activity of speaking is the inspiration of the Universal Intelligence. The Universal Intelligence is the creative energy that brings experiences into being. It is always available to give us the capabilities that go beyond our own experiences to create what we ask to be created. The complexities of speaking and writing are augmented by the Universal Intelligence. That is why we can make such complex combinations of words using correct syntax quickly.

Skills such as speaking, playing an instrument, and playing tennis are made up of these complex, rapidly assembled sequences of experiences brought into action without conscious Awareness being much involved. Conscious Awareness then uses its slow, ponderous rationalizing to realize what subconscious Awareness has already determined and has already performed.

8

What Determines the Experiences We Bring into Awareness?

The infinite points of now Awareness are continually being filled with experiences. The experiences that can come to us are those in which we have a personal investment; they are in our sphere of contacts. They can be experiences we are having in Earth School, experiences we have had in Earth School that are now accessible as memories, experiences we create through imagination, experiences coming through psychic knowing, and experiences brought into our individual Minds by sources such as guides, helpers, people interested in us living in other realms, and our loved ones living in the life after this life.

To have them enter our Awareness, we must be able to access them. We are not able to bring into mind the feel of a rock on Mars or a song sung by an ancient Egyptian. However, those experiences are accessible. No experiences are lost, including thoughts and events, and including experiences no human has ever experienced. But to access any experience we must have some connection to it and the ability to access it.

The presence of cues and affiliations

The experiences come from our activities during our days in Earth School and from cues that bring experiences into Awareness from what we call "memory." During our journey in Earth School, we might see a bird, hear the bird's song and the rustling of leaves, smell the pleasant natural smell of a forest, taste the mint we have in our mouth, and feel a cool breeze across our arms. Every now instant, the experiences in Awareness change to a new set of Earth School sensory experiences.

Our Awareness is also filled with memory experiences and insights. The bird singing may bring to mind Mom's love of cardinals, which might cue into Awareness Mom's face, which might cue into Awareness the image of Mom's ceramic cardinal, and on and on. The experiences in Awareness are a form of intention we do not manipulate. Having an experience in Awareness is the cause of other experiences that are brought into Awareness by the Universal Intelligence. The experiences come to us because we are engaged in the experience of Mom.

The association of memories with other memories is called "associative networks":

> Associative networks are cognitive models that incorporate long-known principles of association to represent key features of human memory. When two things (e.g., "bacon" and "eggs") are thought about simultaneously, they may become linked in memory. Subsequently, when one thinks about bacon, eggs are likely to come to mind as well. Over 2,000 years ago, Aristotle described some of the principles governing the role of such associations in memory. Similar principles were elaborated by British philosophers in the 1700s, and contributed to a variety of psychological theories,

including those developed by contemporary cognitive psychologists to model memory.[184]

Cues increase the chances that we will be able to bring experiences into Awareness. The cues are much like intentions. When we have an experience in Awareness, the experience cues other experiences related to the experience. As we are trying to remember something, we are scanning our experiences to see whether one of them fits. Each time we bring a memory experience into Awareness, it is a cue for other memory experiences. We perform this activity when speaking. We scan our repertoire of experiences looking for the word that is associated with the concept we have in mind, or we scan our repertoire by thinking of the concept hoping that will be a cue to accessing the word. The associated experience memories come into Awareness automatically as we go through the process of "re-membering" and speaking.

Experiences come based on probabilities

The experiences come into our Awareness based on probabilities. The highest probabilities are experiences from our presence in Earth School in the form of sights, sounds, smells, tastes, touches, senses of motion, senses of position, and bodily sensations. While we are in Earth School, they dominate our Minds because we must attend to them to navigate through the Earth School experiences and learn lessons. They are more often 100 percent probable to come into Awareness than any other experiences.

However, other experiences come to us as thoughts, impressions, sentiments, memories, and any of the other experiences we call "inner experiences" or "mental experiences." When we intend to have an inner experience, it immediately comes to 100 percent probability because of our intention to have the experience. Conscious Awareness is always occupied by some experience unless we are sleeping, anesthetized, or in a coma. If we intend to remember someone's face, the face occupies that point of now in conscious Awareness. Our conscious Awareness, with its limited capacity, is not attending to anything else around us as long as we are focused on the face, although our attention can be interrupted by someone's voice, a loud sound, or other stimulus.

The experiences we are able to access and the probabilities that we will experience them make up our Earth School Mind. The experience memories with highest probabilities for being accessed will come to mind when we're thinking, solving a problem, interpreting what someone has said, making a decision, and every other normal daily activity. When we see our spouse or child, there is a 100 percent probability we'll have the experience of the person's name come to mind. When we see a person who looks familiar, but we can't remember who that person is, the probability of experiencing the person's name drops to 10 percent or some other lower percentage. Other higher-probability experiences will come into Awareness: "I think her name is Joan, or maybe Jane." We then must go to some 100 percent probable experiences to recall the name, such as scanning our repertoire of experiences about places we might have seen the person. A cue from one of the experience will result in the person's name coming into 100 percent probability—we will "re-member" it.

People with hyperthymesia, who remember virtually every event on every day of their lives, have high probabilities for a huge number of memory experiences. People with Down syndrome have very low probabilities for recall of most memory experiences in their lives. We chose the level of ability to access memories we have in Earth School during our pre-birth planning.

We acquire the probabilities from events in Earth School and from our past experiences. We can change the probabilities; we are masters of our Minds. But we must change the probabilities through effort. To change the probabilities, we must make the probabilities of accessing certain experiences higher so they are more prominent than other experiences. Experiences that have lower probabilities don't disappear. The new experiences have higher probabilities, so they come up first in conscious Awareness. When we feel we have forgotten something, it isn't that the memory isn't accessible. It's just that when we try to access it, other experiences interfere with the access.

So we practice the piano to develop adept experiences that have 100 percent probability of coming into subconscious Awareness while we're playing a concerto. Developing these experiences takes time and repeated trial and error. Once experienced however, all the 100 percent probable experiences of the correct notes, sequencing, posture, timing, pressure on keys, pressure on foot pedals, and all the other experiences involved in playing result in a virtuoso performance. The performance is just a complex recall of the 100 percent probable experiences aided by the creativity of the Universal Intelligence.

Interference and "forgetting"

The probability an experience can be accessed reduces when the experience has not been accessed for a period of time because other experiences become more prominent. Experiences do not cease to exist. They are just less likely to be experienced than are other experiences.

This is called the displacement explanation of why people forget or why memories lose their potency. Another related explanation is termed the "interference" explanation, suggesting that new memories interfere with remembering old memories.

> Interference is an explanation for forgetting in long term memory, which states that forgetting occurs because memories interfere with and disrupt one another. In other words, forgetting occurs because of interference from other memories.[185]

There are two types of interference with accessing memory experiences: proactive interference and retroactive interference. Proactive interference occurs when we have difficulty bringing new experiences into Awareness because old memory experiences interfere; they have a higher probability of being experienced. When we intend to remember something, or when our Minds are searching subconsciously for the next experience to bring into play during automatic activities such as playing sports or speaking, we may keep bringing old experiences into Awareness because as we attempt to access the newly learned experiences, the old experiences have a higher probability of being accessed—they are "stronger." So the old memory experiences come into Awareness before the new memory experiences and block the new memories. "I can't recall the restaurant's name. I keep remembering the restaurant on the other side of town." "I know I have an appointment Thursday, but I keep remembering the appointment Wednesday when I try to recall what's going on Thursday."

Retroactive interference occurs when we intend to bring into Awareness an old experience and a new experience with a higher probability of being accessed keeps filling conscious Awareness, blocking the older memory experience. "Where was that festival in 2018? All I can think of is where it was this year."

You must have some experience in mind to serve as a cue to bring another experience to mind. You may not be able to recall an experience because you have forgotten the cue experience. You may be driving in an unfamiliar town and know there's a big building where you must turn, but can't bring into Awareness what the building is or what it looks like. The experience is in your repertoire; you just don't have the cue. As you scan your memory experiences of the town, you may chance upon a cue. You recall that you thought you might go back to the building the next day. That's the cue. "Oh, right. It's the post office. I'll take the package in and mail it tomorrow." The cues cascade into other memory experiences that cue each other.

The highest probability experiences are Earth School experiences we encounter continually as we live in the Earth School environment. Next are experiences in memory. When we recall an experience into Awareness, we are creating a new experience that will acquire a higher probability. When we scan our experiences, the new experience will more likely come into Awareness. However, both the new experience we just had in Awareness and the old experience are accessible. It's just that we will usually have retroactive interference when we attempt to bring into Awareness the old experience; the new experience will keep interfering.

You may recall that earlier in this book I wrote about accessing experiences with a room you lived in during your childhood. If someone were with you experiencing your room at the same time, the two of you would each have unique experiences of the room, but neither set of experiences would be a facsimile of a room external to your Mind. There is nothing external to your Mind. There are only experiences your Mind has, and the experiences are unique to you.

Decades later, when you and your friend are reminiscing, you may share memories of the room. However, you are not accessing the same experience—it isn't the same room. You are accessing the memory experience you each have that was the cluster of sensory experiences relevant to you. While many of your recollections will be the same, the experience you are accessing is your unique experience, not an experience related to the other person's experience. Experiences, with all their unique properties, have lives of their own. They are accessible.

We have access to innumerable sensory experiences in each environment, available from the Universal Intelligence, but we perceive only those important to us. In the same way, when you access the experience of the room now, you will access the experiences that fit for you now. You will not bring into conscious Awareness experience memories that don't fit. That is why we know memories of events change over time. There is not a single memory experience; there is a new memory experience every time an old memory experience is accessed. We may have earlier memory experiences that are superseded by later memory experiences of the same thing, but when we're intending to recall the earlier experience, retroactive interference may keep us from cueing it into Awareness.

Also, living in your room for years, you would have had many daily experiences with the room. Today you could sit quietly and reminisce about your room's walls, windows, floor, furniture, and other features of the room. During your reminiscing tour, you would cue other experiences so you might bring into conscious Awareness features of the room you had forgotten about, created from an uncountable number of experiences over the years.

Reexperiencing experiences

When someone brings to Mind an experience, the person is experiencing the experience anew. The interpretations and emotions are renewed with the new experience, so the new experience takes on a higher level of probability of coming into Awareness. Each time an experience is reexperienced, it generates the same interpretation and emotional response the experience originally had, so it increases the probability it will be experienced again. Each new experience becomes a different, fresh experience and takes on a higher probability of coming into the subconscious Awareness. Time hasn't healed that wound. It's been revived in a new wound that has the same potency as the old wound.

In deep grief, the person reexperiences the trauma of loss and images connected with a tragic event such as a death, renewing the experience. When an experience is reexperienced, the interpretations and emotions are the same. The interpretations and emotions don't distinguish between an event in Awareness happening now in Earth School and the event in Awareness being recalled as a memory. The interpretations result in emotions that are felt as they were felt during the original experience, and new interpretations can make the anguish even greater. The disturbing image of the car accident that results in the interpretation that a loved one suffered and the resulting grief can take on additional interpretations that the loved one may have been in pain and fear for a long time. That would result in a new experience with additional feelings of grief. The new experience has more dire interpretations resulting in more disturbing emotional responses than the original.

The same is true of more trivial experiences. What was originally an experience of seeing a branch from the neighbor's tree in my yard that resulted in a neutral interpretation, "Things happen and that's OK," could when recalled become the experience of seeing the branch with the sudden interpretation that the neighbor needs to take care of her own tree branches. The new experience with the new interpretation would result in frustration, perturbation, and even anger. The experience that now comes into Awareness is the newly minted experience with the new interpretation.

However, the new experience could become a positive experience. For example, someone may have the experience pop from subconscious Awareness into conscious Awareness that she felt bad because she spoke angrily with her brother in a phone conversation. She would interpret it as feeling a separation and loss of love and sadness. Then she might later remember that conversation experience, but recall that he ended it by saying he loved her and knew she didn't mean anything. She would interpret that as loving and would feel happy. The next day, she might spontaneously remember the anger again but quickly recall the loving ending. Both experiences are accessible. However, the later, positive experience will have a higher probability of coming into conscious Awareness, so she soon will not recall the older, negative experience.

What we call "memories" are not stable facsimiles of a situation. Reexperiencing the memories results in the same selections of details people go through when first experiencing something in Earth School. Among all the details in the total experience, five may be missing when it is reexperienced and two may be added. The interpretations may change because of a perspective on the experience. The reexperienced experience then would be recalled differently and interpreted differently. It could be a "false memory" or a distorted memory, like the change in a story that happens when you whisper a story down the line from one person to the next until the last person vocalizes a version that is vastly different from the story articulated by the first person in the line. Reexperiencing can create new experiences that are increasingly different from the original experience. However, all the experiences still are accessible, both all the old and all the later reexperiences. The later experiences just have a higher probability of being accessed when cued.

A dramatic example of the change in a reexperience and the resulting change in interpretation is in the book *Induced After-Death Communication* I co-authored with psychotherapist Dr. Al Botkin. The IADC procedure brings the client into a state of mind in which an after-death communication occurs with the person for whom the client is grieving. The method dramatically reduces grief and changes lives.

One case in the book describes a Vietnam War veteran who saw a Viet Cong enemy soldier running toward him, so he saw the young man's face clearly. The veteran raised his gun and shot the young man dead. Years later, the veteran came to Dr. Botkin profoundly disturbed by the memory. He thought of the young man's family and his suffering on the battlefield. He said he had nightmares in which he saw the young man's face as he had seen it before he shot him.

This is the account of what happened. The veteran was put into the state of mind to have an afterlife connection and closed his eyes to allow the connection to occur.

> With [the veteran's] eyes still closed on the second induction, he began to describe what he saw. "I can see him, the guy I killed, but it doesn't look like the face I saw in 'Nam and what I see in my nightmares. I see him smiling and happy." Mike sat quietly for a moment, then opened his eyes. "He communicated to me that he is very content where he is, and he understands that I had to do what I did."

> After that session, the look on the enemy VC's face before he died that had haunted Mike for over 25 years was replaced by the smiling and happy face he experienced in his IADC. He told me at the end of the session, "I'm trying to remember the old face I always saw in my nightmares, but I can't."[186]

The new experience of the smiling young man had gained a higher probability of being experienced when the veteran intended to bring an image of the young man into conscious Awareness. The old experience of the face in his nightmares was still accessible, but had faded in its probability of being experienced to the point that only the new experience came to the veteran.

The probabilities change with different states of Mind

We have been given the ability to enter different states of Mind. We are in Earth School because we planned to have the Earth School experience. We decided our life's circumstances, family of origin, general circumstances, and other details. We then entered a state of Mind to have the Earth School experience. We might call it the Earth School state of mind. Some have likened the state of mind to tuning a radio to a frequency. We can listen to the radio shows on that frequency, but cannot listen to the radio shows on another frequency as long as we're tuned into that frequency. The other frequencies are accessible in our radio now. We've just decided to tune to one set of radio experiences.

The same is true of the Earth School state of mind. All the other states of mind that are other realms are here and available, but we're not choosing to be in those states of mind; we're not tuned to their experiences. We are constrained from stepping out of the Earth School state of mind by our own free-will choice before we entered Earth School so we spend this time loving, learning, and enjoying the journey.

While we are in the Earth School state of mind, we have access to the experiences others are having in the Earth School state of mind. We all have the experiences of tables, buildings, scents, sounds, tastes, rivers, mountains, a moon, and stars because we are in the same state of Mind. Other people are in other states of minds, such as the realm of the life after this life, so they have experiences with their fellow travelers in those states of Mind. They have their own tables, buildings, scents, sounds, tastes, rivers, mountains, a moon or two, and stars if they want them. There are millions of other states of mind. But they are all here. There is only here.

Within the Earth School state of mind, we have the ability to will ourselves into many varieties of states of mind that allow us to have different experiences, just as we would have different experiences if we were in the state of mind to attune ourselves to another realm. These states of mind are commonly known, so we have words in English for them: awake, sleep, dream, daydream, nightmare, hypnogogic dream, fantasy, imagination, imagining, trance, reverie, meditation, problem-solving, focus, in the zone, pipe dream, psi or psychic ability, mediumship, ecstasy, orgasm, hypnosis, deep in thought, coma, near-death experience, out-of-body experience, spiritual experience, concentrating, brooding, oceanic boundlessness, nondual awareness, and others.

We are able to will ourselves into these states of mind. Many will themselves into meditation, self-hypnosis, and other states that relax the Mind so they have experiences more fully that are accessible in that state of mind, such as peace, calm, communication with people living in other realms, psychic experiences, nondual awareness, and kundalini awakening.

Entering a creative state of mind can result in creativity, visions, fantasies, art, music, writing, and the other fruits of this state of mind. When someone is in a creative state of mind, among the millions of experiences the conscious Awareness and subconscious Awareness can access in the point of now, creative experiences will have higher probabilities. In this state of mind, creative minds living in the life after this life may inspire the person and even compose music and literature through the person. Entering the creative state of mind gives the person access to experiences outside of his or her repertoire that result in creative masterpieces.

Pearl Curran, the housewife from St. Louis, Missouri, entered a state of mind in which a woman named Patience Worth, who lived in Dorsetshire, England, from 1649 to 1694 dictated literary works through her.[187] I explained Curran's works on pages 123-124 of this book. Entering other states of mind doesn't normally have the dramatic results Pearl Curran had, but nonetheless opens the person to the subconscious experiences in the Universal Intelligence that result in remarkable creations.

A businessperson enters a state of mind to solve a problem or develop plans. In this state of mind, novel experiences of insights and solutions come to mind in "aha" moments. While working on the problem, the person seems to be in a different world and loses track of time. Those are the signs of being in a different state of mind.

Getting into the zone in athletics and the performing arts can result in brilliant performances that seem to be inspired by a creative impulse outside of the person. The performer has learned how to enter an alternate state of mind in which the experiences come so the performance occurs flawlessly.

Out-of-body experiences allow people to enter a state of mind in which they experience other locations, even in other dimensions and in the life after this life realm.

Most of the states of mind have in common that the person intends to enter the state of mind and loses track of time, the surroundings, and normal Earth School functioning. The person may be difficult to reach even for someone who is with the person. The person is experiencing in a microcosm what we are experiencing when we immerse ourselves in the Earth School state of mind and lose ourselves in it.

We are living in a reality created by those who came before us, and we are evolving that reality ourselves by creating new experiences

There is nothing but Mind and experiences. We are the Universal Intelligence living as the individual Minds we have chosen to become to participate in Earth School experiences so we can love, learn, and enjoy life. My Earth School experience repertoire is unique to me. Your Earth School repertoire of experiences is unique to you. These Earth School experiences in our repertoires became accessible when we were participating in Earth School experiences together. When we had the sight experience of the Grand Canyon, we were each having our own experience of the Grand Canyon with details chosen from all those available to all of us in the Universal Intelligence. We chose the details of the shared experiences that became our unique experience of the Grand Canyon. The Universal Intelligence had, say, 4,000 sight details, many accumulated through other people's experiences with the Grand Canyon. I chose to notice 215. You chose to notice 186. We had 93 in common. So from the totality of all sight experiences ever experienced, the highest probabilities for us were experiences that fit our time of having sight experiences of the Grand Canyon. Each of us came away with a unique set of details that was our sight experience of the Grand Canyon. When we reminisce later, we would each describe our different set of experiences, but would agree we had a shared experience of sights of the Grand Canyon.

When we saw a portion of the wall of the Grand Canyon collapse, the sight experience of the rocks in a pile on the canyon floor became a sight experience in the Universal Intelligence. Someone coming to the Grand Canyon the next day would have the experience of the pile of rocks and surmise, "The rocks must have fallen from the wall of the canyon." We are creating new experiences others will access.

When we change the environment, the change becomes an experience others will have when they access experiences of the location. When we look at our house, we experience the house as it is now in our common set of experiences. However, the experiences of our house include all the experiences had by the builders and previous owners of the house. Those experiences are accessible, but we will experience the set of experiences of our house we hold in common as it is now. We must do so to have experiences together in Earth School. However, I could paint the house blue when you weren't there to see it. When I painted it blue, the new color sight would be accessible from the Universal Intelligence with 100 percent probability when you came the next day to see the house. I created a new experience that you shared the next day. There is no house outside of us. We each have the sight experience of the house from the Universal Intelligence.

And so the sense of past is those experiences accessible now that we and others have created. We are maintaining the experiences by perpetuating them through experiencing our repertoire of experiences that has causes, effects, and continuity. The Universal Intelligence accommodates our need for causes, effects, and continuity by co-creating Earth School with us. We are then creating new experiences that become part of the accessible set of experiences of everything in our Earth School life.

We are creating the world of love and other-centeredness or the world of insensitivity and self-centeredness

Among the experiences we have are subtle experiences that are not the normal sensed experiences such as sight. They are subtle positive experiences, including love, healing, and peace, or negative experiences such as fear and foreboding. These subtle experiences are also part of the shared experience we have in the Universal Intelligence. When we have experiences of a location, included in the experiences are the subconscious feelings described as "positive energy," "positive vibrations," or "bad vibes."

Tiller's experiments

One example of these subtle experiences comes from work by William A. Tiller, PhD, Stanford University Professor Emeritus in physics. Tiller performed experiments to discover whether conscious intention influences the Earth realm. In carefully controlled experiments, people were asked to focus on specific things, trying to influence their composition. The focused attention of subjects had these effects on the things:

- The acidity (pH) of water was intentionally raised or lowered by one pH unit.

- The activity of a human liver enzyme was increased by 15 to 30 percent.

- The larval growth rate of a fly was increased by 25 percent.

The results were highly significant; the possibility of occurrence by chance was less than one in 1,000.[188]

Tiller's experiments had one other finding that showed how we are creating subtle positive experiences. The spaces in which the experiments were conducted seemed to become increasingly conducive to enhancing the positive experiences the more they were used. People's focused attention on positive experiences in spaces was resulting in the experiences of the spaces becoming more positive. Even when no people were involved in the experiments, just magnets, the spaces were more conducive to having positive effects. As Tiller put it, in those spaces the laws of physics no longer seem to apply.[189] The experiences of the spaces available for our access in the Universal Intelligence include the subtle positive experiences. That means anyone having experiences in those spaces will experience the feeling of the positive nature of the space.

More indications of subtle experiences by Radin, Taft, and Yount

This development of positive subtle experiences in a space was demonstrated in experiments by Dean Radin, senior scientist at the Institute of Noetic Sciences, and Ryan Taft and Garret Yount, of the

California Pacific Medical Center Research Institute. The results were published in *The Journal of Alternative and Complementary Medicine*.[190]

In this study, the experimenters placed flasks of living astrocyte central nervous system cells into a chamber over a period of three days to see whether the brain cells were influenced when spiritual practitioners directed healing to make the cells grow strongly in the space. He also placed an inanimate object in the space, a random-number generator, to see whether the spiritual practitioners' healing intentions would influence the numbers it produced. A random-number generator creates a stream of numbers at random. If the numbers start to show some order, that means something has influenced the machine.

In shifts, spiritual practitioners focused on the brain cells and the random-number generator in the healing space chamber, intending to have the brain cells grow more strongly and give the numbers produced by the random-number generator some order. Between healing-intention sessions, the spiritual practitioners entered the chamber and performed spiritual chanting.

On the first day of the experiment, there was negligible growth of the cells and negligible change in the random-number generator outputs. On the second day, there was more notable growth of the cells and more notable changes in random-number generator outputs. On the third day, the improvement in the cells was most pronounced and the output of the random-number generators was most notable.

As the experiment progressed and the spiritual practitioners repeatedly focused healing energy on the chamber, the cells grew more strongly with each day that passed, and more ordered numbers came from the random-number generators over time. That most likely showed that the experience of having the spiritual practitioners focus healing intentions in the healing space changed it, so over repeated healing sessions it became more conducive to healing.

What we're calling the "chamber" was an experience of a chamber, provided by the Universal Intelligence. We are experience makers. As we live our lives in Earth School, we are creating experiences that modify and add to the experiences the Universal Intelligence has that are then accessible by all other Minds. As the

Minds of the spiritual practitioners sent loving, caring, healing thoughts and intentions, the experience of the chamber gained the subtle experiences of loving, caring, and healing. The sentiments of loving, caring, and healing modified the experience of the chamber being accessed from the Universal Intelligence. The reexperiencing over three days resulted in the chamber experience's becoming more strongly loving, caring, and healing. The experience of the chamber was not wood, plaster, and fixtures in a material world outside of our Minds. It was an experience that affected each person's sentiments when the chamber was experienced. The subtle loving, caring, healing experiences in the chamber also affected every other part of the experience, including the cells and random-number generators. Loving, caring, and healing feelings and intentions create a world of experiences that are more loving, caring, and healing. Loving, caring, and healing feelings and intentions influence the reality we are creating together.

Masaru Emoto's experiments demonstrating subtle experiences

Another well-known set of experiments demonstrates that subtle positive experiences, including love, caring, and healing, become part of the shared experience associated with something that is then accessible to our Minds from the Universal Intelligence. Dr. Masaru Emoto conducted thousands of experiments with water crystals, showing that spiritual intention experiences affect how people experience frozen water crystals.[191]

When tap water is frozen, it doesn't form clear crystals; the forms are disorganized. But when the same water is prayed for, the water crystallizes into beautiful, delicate crystals. The subtle experience of prayer influences the experience of the water crystals in the Universal Intelligence.

When Emoto took a sample of water from a Japanese city reservoir (Fujiwara Dam) and froze the sample, it showed misshaped crystals. Kato Hoki, a Shinto priest, offered an hour-long prayer on the edge of the reservoir. A film crew had the sight experience of the water becoming clearer as they watched it. They were even able to make out the foliage at the bottom of the lake that had been hidden by the cloudy water.

This experience of a prayer over the reservoir resulted in a subtle experience accessed by those assembled who were experiencing the reservoir.

When the water from the reservoir sampled after the prayer was frozen, the crystals were in beautiful, snowflake-like shapes. The experience of the water had changed.

You can see an explanation of Dr. Emoto's water crystals at www.earthschoolanswers.com/emoto/.

Dr. Emoto's results were replicated by Dean Radin, senior scientist at the Institute of Noetic Sciences, in double-blind experiments performed by a team that included Dr. Emoto.[192]

The Maharishi Effect

Another example of the subtle positive experiences of love, caring, and healing is the Maharishi Effect. Large groups engaged in the advanced Transcendental Meditation program were associated with significant reductions in U.S. homicide and urban violent crime rates during an intervention period of 2007-2010.

During the time when large groups were engaged in the advanced Transcendental Meditation program in the U.S., there was a drop in the homicide rate of 21.2 percent. A rising trend of U.S. homicides during the 2002-2006 baseline period was reversed during the 2007-2010 period of the study. The decrease in the violent crime rate was 18.5 percent for a sample of 206 urban areas nationwide with a population over 100,000.[193]

In another study, as a group of 4,000 people meditated in calm and peace, the minds of the people in the geographical area seemed to be influenced by the subtle positive influence, even though they had no knowledge of the meditation or positive influence:

> A 1993 study found that, when 4,000 people meditated together, violent crime in Washington, D.C., declined 23% over the course of the experiment, in contrast to its rising in the months before and after. The results were

shown not to be due to other variables, such as weather, the police, or anti-crime campaigns. The predicted effect had been posited with an independent review board, which had participated in the study design and monitored its conduct.[194]

The findings were replicated in a study of 24 U.S. cities:

A similar effect was shown in a study of 24 U.S. cities, in which 1% of the urban population regularly practiced TM [transcendental meditation]. A follow-up study demonstrated that the 24 cities saw drops of 22% in crime and 89% in the crime trend, compared to increases of 2% and 53%, respectively, in the control cities.[195]

Another study was performed in Israel using a transcendental meditation group:

During a two-month period in 1983 in Israel, on days when a TM-Sidhi [meditation] group equaling the square root of 1% of the surrounding population meditated, independently published data showed that war-related deaths in Lebanon dropped 76%, and conflict, traffic fatalities, fires and crime decreased. In Israel, the national mood increased, as measured by a blinded content analysis of the emotional tone of the lead, front-page picture story in the *Jerusalem Post,* and the stock market increased. Other potential causal variables were controlled for.[196]

The subtle experiences of the meditators' intentions and sentiments became part of the experiences accessible from the Universal Intellect. People in the geographical area were accessing experiences at the subconscious Awareness level that affected their interpretations and behavior. It illustrates the fact that we are influenced by experiences at several levels, like the instruments in an orchestra, and these subconscious experiences come without our intent or detection. Our loving, peaceful acts and gestures affect the subconscious experiences being accessed by people around us without their knowledge of the effects.

Experiences are affected, not "people"

It may seem that the effects of healing messages and spiritual practices are affecting people. However, when we think of "people," we must realize that we are the soul in Awareness. We are assuming the role of the individual in Earth school to love, learn, and enjoy the experiences. However, the experiences come into Awareness and are immediately replaced, in a continuous stream of changing experiences. We develop a repertoire of experiences and interpretations that we can change to be more loving, caring, and healing as we live our lives and overcome challenges in Earth School.

Our soul is not making the decisions or being influenced by healing messages and spiritual practices. Instead, the experiences we have in Earth School and in our repertoire of memory experiences change, and the interpretations we have of experiences change. The experiences and our interpretations become more loving, caring, and healing. As a result, we feel loving, caring, and healing in more of our now moments, and the world we live in has more loving, caring, and healing inherent in experiences.

So instead of saying the effects of prayer, meditation, and spiritual practices change people, we must say they change the experiences and interpretations people have.

The apparent evidence of the past doesn't mean things "happened"

If a tree falls in a forest, does it make a sound, or does a sound exist? Existence is a slippery concept. If we walk into a forest no human being has ever walked into, the experience of a tree lying flat on the ground becomes 100 percent accessible to us. The experience is given by the Universal Intelligence that provides experiences in Earth School to give us an environment resulting from apparent cause, effect, and continuity.

However, there are no experiences of a tree seed on the ground, a sapling growing, a tall tree rising through the canopy, the tree falling into decay, the tree falling to the ground, and the sound it would make when it fell to the ground if someone were there to hear it. Those experiences didn't "happen" as we think of "happening" that occurs when someone is having an experience. The first experience of the tree is the sight of the tree lying on the ground, experienced by the person venturing into the forest. The tree sight experience has the characteristics of the tree's having grown and fallen, but the characteristics were not collapsed into reality until someone had the sight experience of them. After seeing the tree, the memory sight experience was easily accessed by the person having the experience because the sight was in her repertoire of experiences. In other words, it became a memory that could be accessed with 100 percent probability when the person intended to remember the tree lying flat on the ground.

If that person then carved her initials into the fallen tree, she would have added an experience to the tree. When someone else entered the forest the next day, the sight experience of the tree lying in the forest with the initials carved into it would be accessible from the Universal Intelligence, so the person would experience the tree lying there and notice the initials. However, there is no tree outside of our Minds.

If someone could enter a state of mind in which he or she had a "past" experience of the forest, as happens in what we call a past-life regression, we can assume that the experience of seeing the tree falling would be accessible. But the experience of a tree falling would be accessible only because the person was observing it. The Universal Intelligence gives us the experiences we expect to have, even if the experience likely didn't "happen" in a sunrise, sunset, sunrise, sunset of days that exist apart from us. We can't demonstrate that they did "happen."

John Wheeler, American theoretical physicist and professor of physics at Princeton University, noted that the observation of a quantum system not only defines the state of the system at that moment, but also defines its history:

Could our asking about the origin of existence, about the Big Bang and 13.8 billion years of cosmic history, could that create the universe? "Quantum principle as tiny tip of giant iceberg, as umbilicus of the world," Wheeler scrawled in his journal on June 27, 1974. "Past present and future tied more intimately than one realizes. . . . .

And just as observers can make measurements that determine a photon's history stretching back billions of years, the history of the universe only becomes reality when an observer makes a measurement.[197]

The work by Dean Radin, shows that an experience can come into being when someone just thinks about it, demonstrating that going into a state of attention can cause an experience to come into reality even if the person is not there at the time of the experience.

Dr. Radin set up an experiment based on an experiment performed by Thomas Young in 1801 called the "double-slit experiment." In the double-slit experiment, when someone is observing or measuring light going through two very narrow vertical slits, the light casts two vertical lines of light on a back wall, showing the light is going through the two slits as particles. We must have particles to create the reality of sight experiences. However, when no one is observing or measuring the light going through two slits, the light casts several light and dark vertical bands on the wall, showing that the light went through the slits as waves, like ripples going out from a pebble dropped into a pond. Since there are two slits, the light going through each slit acts as though a pebble had been dropped in water at each slit. The waves travel out from each slit. Since there are two sets of waves, they meet and interfere with each other. The result is the alternating dark and light bands on the wall. There are light bands where the crests of two of the interfering waves come together; there are dark bands where the troughs of two waves come together. The alternating light and dark bands show the light must have gone through the slits as a wave. If there are two vertical columns of light, it shows the light must have gone through the slits as particles.

How can the light be going through the slits as particles making two vertical light columns at one moment and then go through the same slits as waves, making dark and light wave bands at the next moment? Quantum physicists suggested that observing or measuring the light causes it to change. When the light is observed or measured it turns into particles that give us the sight experiences we have. When we're not looking, the light is in waves that are not the solid world we see—the wave world is just possibilities that the particles could be at some place if someone observed or measured the location. The world in waves doesn't "exist." It's just possibilities that one experience could exist if the wave collapsed into particles because someone experienced it. It sounds crazy, but that's the weird world of quantum mechanics.

Dean Radin set up an experiment in which light particles were sent through two slits and shined on the back wall as Young had done. If someone observed or measured the lights going through the slits, there would be two vertical lighted columns on the back wall—the light would be particles. If no one was observing or measuring the lights, there would be several vertical bands of light and dark on the back wall, showing the light was going through the slits as waves. In a clever experiment, Dr. Radin had meditators in other locations focus on the two slits. The results were that just meditating on the slits resulted in the light's becoming particles and showing on the back wall as two vertical light columns. When the meditators stopped focusing on the two slits, the light on the back wall turned back into bands created by interfering waves. The meditators had caused the light that was just possible experiences in a wave to become particles necessary to have one experience. The meditators had created reality even though they weren't at the location.[198]

The finding suggests that any potential experience from any time could become a real experience if a person intended to have the experience and had it, even though the experience may not have "happened" as we think of things happening. When we experience something, it becomes a reality at that moment.

Shrödinger's cat is an example of the fact that the history is written when a person has the experience. Erwin Shrödinger, the Nobel Prize-winning Austrian-Irish physicist who developed a number of fundamental principles of quantum mechanics, couldn't accept the assertion by the pioneers in quantum mechanics that things don't come into existence until they are observed or measured, as the double-slit experiment showed. Until they are observed or measured, quantum mechanics states that they are in "superposition" waves, which means all states of the object are possibilities but none "exists." One of the states becomes the experienced state in particles when an observer has the experience—then it exists.

Shrödinger created a thought experiment to show how absurd, in his estimation, that is. Imagine a cat is in a sealed box. In the box is a flask of poison, a radioactive source, and a Geiger counter. The radioactive source could have an atom decay and fly off it at any time, or have no decay and no atom fly off during the time the cat was in the box. If the Geiger counter detected a single atom decaying from the radioactive source, the flask would be shattered and the poison would kill the cat.

Fast forward into the future. The cat has been in the box for some time. Quantum mechanics asserts that whether the cat is alive or dead will only be determined when someone opens the box and observes the cat. Until that time, the cat is in the superposition of both aliveness and deadness, but is neither alive nor dead. When the box is opened, the experience of seeing the cat collapses the alternatives into one: the cat is dead or alive. Reality doesn't exist for the cat's status until sight of the cat is experienced.

However, at that moment when the cat is experienced so reality is created, a whole history of the cat's being dead or alive is created. If the cat is alive, the sight experiences of being alive will appear: the food bowl is empty, there are excrements, there are scratches on the sides of the box in its attempt to get out. If the cat died quickly, the sight experiences of a quick death will appear: the food bowl has food in it, there are no scratches on the sides of the box, the body is cold, and there are no excrements. Did either set of events "happen" before the box was opened?

"Happen" is another slippery concept. Nothing "happened" as we think of it. All we know is that the experience of seeing the cat alive or dead in the box and the experiences that accompany a cat's dying quickly or the experiences that accompany a cat's being in the box for a while become accessible at that moment. Thus, the historical events that have not been observed are simply part of the story the observer surmises "happened" based on the conditions in the experience of the world when observed. The evidence that something "happened," such as an empty food bowl, could as easily be part of the creation by the Universal Intelligence to give us the cause and effect relationship we expect in Earth School. If the cat is alive, we expect to see signs of a period of aliveness. If the cat is dead, we expect to see no signs of a period of aliveness. The Universal Intelligence gives us causes, effects, and continuity.

View a video about Shrödinger's cat at www.earthschoolanswers.com/cat/.

Another demonstration that the appearance of a history is made part of the experience when reality is accessed through observation is the delayed choice experiment. The experiment is based on the experiment by Thomas Young described earlier, called the "double-slit experiment." The experiment showed that light is a wave or probabilities if we're not observing it, and a particle if we're observing it. For us to have the world we experience, the light must be particles. When the world is a wave, it isn't being experienced; it just has the potential to be experienced when it collapses into reality. We must observe the light for it to collapse into the real world. The observation results in the experience.

Scientists thought they would fool the light and trick it into staying a wave even when it was observed before it hit the back wall. They would allow the light go through the slits when no one was observing, then quickly look at the slits before the light hit the back wall. That way, the light would already have gone through the slits as waves since it wasn't being observed at that time and would show up on the back wall as the light and dark bands of interference patterns, even though there was an observer looking at the light before it hit the back wall. The experiment is called the quantum eraser experiment.

It didn't work. If the scientists let the light go through the slits and quickly observed the light before it hit the back wall, the light produced two vertical columns, showing the light was in particles. If they didn't observe the slits at any time, the wall showed the light and dark vertical bands made by waves. How could that be. It's as though the light foretold the future and knew whether an observer would look at it before it hit the back wall. What happened was that the history of whether the light was going through the slits as a wave or as a particle was written into the experience of what appeared on the back wall. Bands of light, dark, light, dark created a history of the light coming through the slits as a wave; two vertical columns of light created a history of the light coming through the slits as particles. The history was created at the moment of the sight experience of the back wall.

Another indication that the evidence of a history of experiences unobserved is created when a person has the experience is in studies by Helmut Schmidt, a German physicist. Schmidt knew the often-replicated research showing that a person can influence the types of light flashes produced by signals from random-number generators. For example, if the random-number generator is producing random light flashes of red and green, you would expect an equal number of red flashes and green flashes because they are occurring at random. When a person intends for there to be more red flashes or more green flashes, the intention consistently results in more of the intended color flashes.[199] It is an example of what is commonly called "mental influencing" or "psychokinesis."

Schmidt wondered whether the same mental influencing would occur if someone observed flashes from a previously recorded session that created a recording of the signals to produce the flashes. We would expect that since no one watched the original event, the recording would have 50 percent red and 50 percent green signals for flashes. Schmidt created two sets of recordings: a control set and an experimental set.

Two days after making the recordings of signals from the random-number generators, Schmidt had a volunteer watch the experimental recording and consciously focus on having more red or more green signals as the recording played. Consistently, the experimental recordings influenced by the volunteer had more flashes of the color the volunteer intended to have occur, in spite of the fact that the recordings had been made two days earlier. The control recordings were also played, with no effort to have more red or green flashes. The number of flashes of each color in the control recording was consistently equal: 50 percent of one and 50 percent of the other.[200]

This phenomenon is called "retrocausality." The description of retrocausality in the literature implies that the future observation causes a change in the past event. However, what is actually happening is that the experience is not created until an observer performs the observation. Until then, the recordings were in superposition, meaning all the possible outcomes were possibilities that didn't exist as we think of existence. Existence was created when the volunteer attempted to influence the number of red or green flashes. That means that someone seeing the resulting data would assume there had been a history in which someone attempted to influence the number of flashes of one or the other color. There was no such history. The evidence of such a history was created when the flashes were experienced, but such an event did not "happen."

Shrödinger's thought experiment, the delayed choice erasure experiment, and Schmidt's mental influencing effects show that all the signs of a history in characteristics present in the experience may suggest a history, but since no one was observing the history to collapse it into reality, we can't say the history "happened." What the observer experienced was the cause, effect, and continuity characteristics we expect in our reality, so the Universal Intelligence gives them to us.

For example, we experience coal, with all the signs that plants fell to the ground 360 million years ago and over millions of years compressed into coal, but the characteristics suggesting this evolution of plants into coal were only accessed when someone first observed coal. So whether there was a history of plants falling 360 million years ago and developing into coal isn't necessarily a sunrise, sunset, sunrise, sunset of days for millions of years. Whether the Carbiniferous Period really "happened" over millions of years is impossible to determine. It appears unlikely, just as it's unlikely Shrödinger's cat had either the actual events of the cat's being alive or the actual events of the cat's being dead in the box before the observation; whether the cat was alive or dead wasn't established until someone looked inside to see the cat.

Earth School is the realm of causes and effects. For every effect, we will have the experiences of causes, even if the causes themselves were never experienced by a person. Our minds are so formed by the notion that causes must have "happened" that we assume there have been 13.7 billion years of actual experiences, with 4.5 billion years of solar system experiences, 175 million years of sunrise, sunset experiences since Pangea started evolving into the continents we see today, and eons of experiences of all the other events that seem apparent in rock stratification and the fossil record. However, we can say only that we have the experience of the present signs in the Earth that would give us the impression everything "happened" in vast geologic time.

And so the musing about whether the universe had a beginning or whether it will have an end is only a mind game played by the Earth School intellect. Beginnings and endings are just part of the Earth School scenery. The Universal Intellect and we are eternal.

We now have our personal repertoires of experiences

We are living in the Earth School now that has experiences we are choosing to access. They are the experiences at the highest probabilities of being experienced by each of us based on our experiences in this Earth School life. We have similar experiences in Earth School because we are accessing the same sets of experiences accessible in the Universal Intelligence, but the details we experience from the accessible experiences depends on our unique life perspectives, needs, and expectations.

The experiences have been accumulated by other people who have lived in Earth School and have built on the experiences that were available to them by changing the experiences as they went through their lives. We are creating experiences that build on the experiences already available in the Earth School dream. We are creating reality.

9

What Effects Do the Experiences Have on Our Lives?

These experiences in Awareness are accompanied by interpretations we have learned to associate with the experiences. The interpretations result in emotions. The combination of experiences, interpretations, and emotions is unique to each of us. The interpretations and resulting emotions are not in the experiences. The person has learned the interpretations in childhood based on early experiences in similar situations, the reactions of others to the experiences, and overt teaching that molded the interpretations. These interpretations and the accompanying emotions arise spontaneously and immediately when similar experiences come into Awareness. They may result in conditioning so the emotion is triggered without a clear perception of the experience and interpretation.

We can change the experiences and interpretations. We cannot change the emotions in themselves. Mood-altering drugs change the script in the Earth School experience so we have the reaction experiences in Earth School that the drugs have caused, and we have an expectation the drugs will make us feel better, so we have a placebo effect.

However, to have a lasting effect on the emotions without the support of drug experiences and our expectation that drugs will make us feel different, we must change our interpretations of experiences. The emotions arise from the interpretations of experiences spontaneously. If we change the interpretations, the emotional responses will change. If we want to change the magnitude of love, compassion, peace, and joy in our lives, we must change the interpretations we have of experiences so they are loving, compassionate, peaceful, and joyful.

This chapter explains interpretations, beliefs, body experiences resulting from beliefs, emotions, response strategies, conditioning, and rationalizing.

Interpretations

Interpretations arise with the experiences. I use the term "interpretation" because the interpretation is a personal assessment of the experience. Each person has a unique repertoire of interpretations of experiences.

The famous Vedantic rope and snake story called Rajjusarpa Nyaya (The Rope and the Snake) is an example. I have adapted it for this explanation. A man living in a region with many poisonous snakes walks into a dimly lit shed. He can barely make out something coiled in a corner. If his interpretation is that it is a snake, he will feel fear. If his interpretation is that it is a rope coiled up, he will feel no emotion. However, the emotion is a result of the interpretation, not anything in the experience of the coiled-up thing. Once he discovers what the coiled-up thing is, the next time the man enters the dimly lit shed, he will immediately experience the emotion: fear or calm. That is the conditioned component of the experience. If he first thought the coiled-up thing was a snake, but then learned it is a rope, he will feel calmer, but may have some trepidation about going into the shed. The conditioning must be overcome by repeated experiences with the harmless coiled-up rope.

These interpretations can be social and interpersonal. A woman sees a friend turn away when she approaches. Her interpretation is "She doesn't like me." The result is feeling rejected and sad. She could have had the interpretation "She didn't see me," with neutral or loving emotions and the response of going to the woman to have a friendly interchange. The interpretation came from similar experiences with people in the woman's past or similar experiences with this friend in the past. Interpretations are learned.

The experiences coming into conscious Awareness and subconscious Awareness trigger the person's unique interpretation resulting in the emotions the person feels in situations. The experiences and interpretations coming into subconscious Awareness may cause generalized anxiety, worry, and a sense of dread even if the person is not consciously aware of the reason for the negative emotions.

The interpretations indicate how much our lives are characterized by love, compassion, empathy, sympathy, other-centeredness, kindness, and altruism on one hand and fear, self-absorption, disdain, envy, greed, insensitivity, lack of sympathy, lack of remorse, and lack of guilt on the other hand. The types of interpretations we most commonly have are what characterize our nature. We use a form of "to be" to describe this nature: "He is loving," "She is self-absorbed." However, no one "is" something. Instead each of us has interpretations of experiences that result in loving actions or self-absorbed actions. Some have more interpretations of one or the other.

One person may see an injured squirrel on the side of the road and interpret it as distasteful, with no sadness or empathy. Another person with the same experience may interpret the image as a suffering animal that needs help, and so feel sad and empathetic. The difference is in the interpretation, not the experience.

Some tendencies to have interpretations are inborn

While the interpretations are learned, the propensity toward having negative interpretations can be built into the person based on the pre-birth plan for the person's life. For example, people with antisocial personality disorders, called sociopaths and psychopaths, have conditions that are inborn and cannot be changed easily. Their learning in childhood may exacerbate the condition, but it is part of their life plan.

The interpretations that come into Awareness for the person with an antisocial personality disorder will be molded by the inborn condition. A sociopath has automatic interpretations that are followed by antisocial behavior, such as failure to conform to social norms, unlawful behavior, deceit, repeated lying, impulsiveness, aggression, and irresponsibility.

A psychopath can be very well organized and have normal relationships and career success. However, the interpretations that automatically come to the psychopath's Mind are characterized by self-gratification, self-absorption, impulsivity, aggression, anger, lack of remorse, perversion, criminal thoughts, and amoral behavior. They are said to have no conscience.

Both sociopaths and psychopaths chose to live with their conditions when they were planning their time in Earth School. No one plans violence during the pre-birth planning, but the propensity to be violent is acknowledged among all who will be part of this person's life. During the life planning, this person and all who will be involved in life with this person have agreed in love to accept the possible negative behaviors. The likely hope of all involved in the life plan is that the person will endeavor to change his or her interpretations so the person develops some measure of other-centeredness and sensitivity.

Interpretations we call beliefs

Many of these interpretations are codified into what we call "beliefs." The beliefs are articulations of the spontaneous interpretations that come into Awareness from the subconscious when we are confronted with an experience. Perhaps someone believes people may eat a fish but not a cow, or eat a cow but not a dog. Or someone else may believe people should not eat animals at all. We feel these are rational beliefs, but they are simply the interpretations that come into Awareness spontaneously on thinking of eating a fish, a cow, or a dog because of our learning from our family, institutions, and society or our unique development of the interpretations resulting from experiences.

In childhood, we rely on others to tell us or demonstrate to us the interpretations we should have about experiences that result in beliefs we and those around us articulate. Our families, institutions, and society mold our interpretations, and thus our beliefs. That socialized set of interpretations results in articulated beliefs that make possible the progress we have made as human beings. We learn from others and accept their beliefs so we can move forward socially to build on what we all have learned. We believe tiny, invisible organisms cause disease, so we wash our hands and cook food thoroughly. We haven't seen the little organisms, but we trust those who have taught us about them and follow their direction in taking care to avoid contracting illnesses. So it is with virtually all of our beliefs.

Beliefs affect the body experience

We are creating this reality. We expect our houses to be where we left them when we return home from work. That doesn't mean there is a house in a world outside of us that we leave and return to. It means our experience of the house is among the experiences we all have in our repertoire from the Universal Intelligence based on the experiences those before us in Earth School made accessible by their activities. We then expect that when we leave our house, it will be there when we return. Our experiences, beliefs, and expectations are creating the reality we all share as individuals.

However, our beliefs and expectations can also affect the personal area of the world that is our body experience. Creation of our body experience that reflects our beliefs and expectations will not affect someone else, so our body experience can change to fit our unique, personal beliefs and expectations about ourselves.

The most dramatic demonstrations of that fact are changes in the body resulting from beliefs and expectations generated by psychological suggestion, the placebo effect, and changes in body chemistry of people with dissociative identity disorder (multiple personality disorder). The changes are evidence that there is only mind and experiences, and the experiences can result from our beliefs and expectations.

Body experience changes from psychological suggestion

Accounts in the literature describe people's physiology changing when they are given the suggestion that something is true about their bodies. When a person's interpretations of experiences or beliefs change, the body experiences may change to match.

In one study reported in the *American Journal of Psychiatry*, a combat veteran was placed into a hypnotic trance. He was then told he was back in combat and a shell just exploded, dropping a small particle of molten shell fragment on his hand. When he came out of the trance, the veteran complained of a pain in his hand as though he had a cigarette burn. Four hours later, a full blister about one centimeter in diameter had appeared on his hand, just as though a small particle of molten shell fragment had landed on his hand. Of course, none had. His beliefs and expectations changed the experience of his body.

On the day after the burn had healed, he was again taken into a hypnotic trance and told his right hand was perfectly normal, but his left hand was anesthetized and drained of blood. When he was brought out of the hypnotic trance, a finger on his right hand was pricked with a needle. He winced and bled. A finger on his left hand was pricked. He felt nothing and no blood emerged from the wound.[201]

The beliefs resulting from interpretations changed the combat veteran's body experience. The body experience is in the Mind, as are all experiences, not in a world outside of the person. There are no bodies in worlds outside of the Mind. Since the body experience is in the Mind, changes in beliefs and expectations can result in changes in the body experience. In this instance, the person believed he had a burn and believed he had no blood in his left hand so his body experiences fit his beliefs and expectations.

Body experience changes from the placebo effect

In the placebo effect, a person can be convinced something is true and the body experiences will reflect whatever the suggestion is.

People's body experiences can change to fit their beliefs about experiences.

In a Baylor School of Medicine study reported in the *New England Journal of Medicine,* patients with severe and debilitating knee pain were divided into three groups. Surgeons shaved the damaged cartilage in the knee of Group 1. Surgeons flushed out the knee joint for Group 2. Group 3 received a fake surgery; surgeons made incisions and bandaged the knees, but performed no surgery. The three groups had no knowledge of the procedure that happened to them.

All three groups went through the same rehab process. The result was that the placebo group improved as much as the other two groups that had surgery. The authors concluded the following:

> The new findings could transform the treatment of osteoarthritis. "This study has important policy implications," remarks lead investigator Nelda Wray of the Houston VA Medical Center and Baylor College of Medicine. "We have shown that the entire driving force behind this billion dollar industry is the placebo effect. The health care industry should rethink how to test whether surgical procedures, done purely for the relief of subjective symptoms, are more efficacious than a placebo."[202]

In another example of beliefs affecting the body experience, psychologist Dr. Bruno Klopfer describes a patient named Mr. Wright with an advanced lymph-node cancer called lymphosarcoma. Wright's neck, armpits, chest, abdomen, and groin were filled with tumors the size of oranges, and his spleen and liver were so enlarged that two quarts of milky fluid had to be drained out of his chest every day.

Mr. Wright learned about a drug called Krebiozen that was being used to treat this specific type of cancer. He begged his physician, Dr. West, to give him the drug. Dr. West reluctantly injected him with Krebiozen. Ten days after the first dose of Krebiozen, Mr. Wright left the hospital, apparently cancer free.

Two months later, Mr. Wright chanced upon a copy of a study reporting that Krebiozen is worthless for the treatment of cancer. Upon reading it, his cancer quickly returned in full force.

Dr. West knew his patient was failing, so he tried an experiment. He announced to Mr. Wright that he was giving him a new variant of Krebiozen called "ultra-pure Krebiozen." Actually, he injected Mr. Wright with harmless saline solution. Sure enough, the tumors melted away and the fluid in his chest disappeared. He was once again cancer free.

A short time later, the American Medical Association announced without a doubt that Krebiozen was utterly worthless. Mr. Wright saw the study and his cancer returned. He died two days later.[203]

Mr. Wright's interpretations of the experience of being injected with Krebiozen changed him physiologically. Such is the power of our beliefs and expectations resulting from our interpretations of experiences.

The bodies of people with dissociative identity disorder (multiple personality disorder) change when they change personalities

People's beliefs and expectations create their reality. Physiological changes occur when people with multiple personality disorder (now called dissociative identity disorder) believe they are another personality with a different physiology.

Dr. Pamela J. Maraldo describes the result of her research into the changes that result when a dissociative identity disorder patient changes personalities:

> By changing personalities, a drunk person can instantly become sober, and different personalities within someone with multiple personality disorder also respond differently to various drugs. Braun records a case in which five milligrams of Valium sedated one personality, while 100 milligrams had little or no effect on another. Often one or more personalities of a multiple are children. While an adult personality is in the fore and takes an

adult dose of medicine, he or she is fine, but if one of the child personalities abruptly takes over, he or she may overdose.

With a change of personalities in multiples, scars appear and disappear; burn marks and cysts do the same. The "multiple" can change from being right-handed to being left-handed with ease and agility. Visual acuity can differ so that some multiples have to carry two or three different pairs of glasses. One personality can be color-blind and the other not. Even eye color can change. Speech pathologist Christy Ludlow has found that "the voice pattern for each of a multiple's personalities is different, a feat that requires such a deep physiological change that even the most accomplished actor cannot alter his voice enough to distinguish his voice pattern."

. . . . Robert A. Phillips, Jr., a psychologist, reports that he has even seen tumors appear and disappear.

Multiples tend to heal faster. For example, there are several cases on record of third-degree burns healing with amazing rapidity. Most incredible of all, at least one researcher, Dr. Cornelia Wilbur, the therapist whose pioneering treatment of Sybil Dorsett (of the book and movie *Sybil*) is convinced that multiples do not age as fast as other people.[204]

Sybil was a psychiatric patient of Dr. Wilbur who had dissociative identity disorder with 16 distinct personalities that emerged over 40 years. One of her personalities was diabetic, while another was not. Sybil's blood sugar levels would be normal when she was in her non-diabetic personality, but when she shifted into her diabetic alter ego, her blood sugars immediately rose and all medical evidence demonstrated she was diabetic. When her personality reverted to the non-diabetic counterpart, her blood sugars immediately normalized.[205]

Dr. Francine Howland, a Yale psychiatrist specializing in treating dissociative identity disorder, describes a patient who showed up at an appointment with one eye swollen shut from a wasp sting. Dr. Howland called an ophthalmologist to treat the patient, but as they were waiting for the ophthalmologist to arrive, the patient changed to another personality and the pain and swelling ended in a short time. When the ophthalmologist arrived, he confirmed that there were no signs of the wasp string or other trauma to the eye. When the patient returned home, the personality that suffered the wasp sting came back and the pain and swelling returned with a vengeance. The patient went to the ophthalmologist and was treated. The ophthalmologist attested to the fact that the patient indeed had an eye swollen shut from a wasp sting. He was perplexed and had no explanation for the strange phenomenon.[206]

Psychiatrist Bennett Braun, author of *The Treatment of Multiple Personality Disorders*, describes a patient named Timmy who had multiple personalities. One personality who was allergic to orange juice would break out in blistering hives shortly after drinking it. However, when he changed to another personality who was not allergic to orange juice, he was able to drink it uneventfully. If the allergic personality was in the midst of an allergy attack and shifted back to the non-allergic personality, the hives would disappear instantly.[207]

The people with dissociative personality disorder change the sets of beliefs and expectations that come to them when they change personalities. The experiences, such as drinking orange juice, remain the same. However, the beliefs and expectations result in changes in the body experience. Mind cannot change matter, so the material body must be made of Mind stuff. That means Earth School is made of Mind and experiences only. Matter and energy are just Mind stuff.

We are affecting our body experiences every day. What we believe deeply, without reservation, about our body experience is what the body experience becomes. The literature on healing attests to the fact that the body experience can become what we want it to become. Our belief makes us whole.

Emotions

Emotions result from the interpretations of experiences. Fear, joy, anxiety, frustration, grief, delight, and the other emotions are not in the experiences; they result from the interpretations of the experiences.

Emotions are fundamental to the Mind. We cannot dissect emotions to identify what they are made of. There are body experiences that correlate with emotions, but the physical correlates result from the emotion; the emotion doesn't result from the physical correlates. A feeling is entirely subjective and can be described only as itself: "I feel sad." "I feel happy." Some emotions feel pleasant and comfortable. Others feel disturbing and uncomfortable.

The emotions are indications of how we interpret each experience. They are the thermometer showing us our Mind's state in Earth School. Our interpretations of experiences might precipitate negative emotions such as fear, sadness, annoyance, guilt, anxiety, discouragement, and frustration. We can seek experiences that have more love, peace, and joy inherent in them, but we will still encounter the other experiences that we attach negative interpretations to. To feel more love, peace, and joy in our lives and eliminate the negative emotions, we must change the interpretations of experiences.

One spiritual goal in Earth School is to grow to have interpretations of life, who we are, and who other people are that cause every experience that comes into Awareness to bring us love, joy, and peace. When we interpret experiences as being loving, joyful, and peaceful, we will most often feel happy. We will choose strategies for our behavior that result in others feeling loving, joyful, and peaceful, and they will respond with love.

Some people have interpretations and emotions that are socially unacceptable. Sociopaths and psychopaths, for example, feel little sadness, regret, or remorse from their behaviors. The lack of emotional sensitivity allows them to continue antisocial behavior without emotional consequences. The tendencies are inborn components of their life plans.

Some experiences we interpret negatively come into subconscious Awareness without rising to the level of conscious Awareness where we can identify them. We may feel anxious or fearful and don't know why. The words for the resulting feelings from these subconscious experiences are worry, anxiety, stress, hopelessness, depression, brooding, gloom, anguish, despair, discouragement, foreboding, misery, sorrow, woe, despondency, downheartedness, low spirits, malaise, blues, unsettled feeling, uneasiness, and loneliness.

The negative responses can take a toll on the Mind and body. We know experiences in subconscious Awareness affect the body because of the studies performed by Dr. Dean Radin and others (see pages 50-51). The studies showed that many people reacted to pictures shown on a computer monitor six or seven seconds before the pictures were selected by the computer and shown, even though the people insisted they didn't know what the pictures would be. If the pictures were of disturbing images, the subjects' body experiences showed tension. However, they had no idea a disturbing image was about be shown. Their body experiences showed the effects from experiences coming to subconscious Awareness that never rise to conscious Awareness.[208]

There are other indications that subconscious experiences and interpretations affect us. In many studies, twins have felt sensations in the body because of their twin's experience even though the reason for the feeling did not rise into conscious Awareness.[209]

Feelings of tension or negative emotions can be sent from one person to another causing the receiver's body to react, even though the receiver realizes nothing in conscious Awareness.[210]

The experience and interpretation coming into subconscious Awareness result in a body experience and underlying emotions.

Response strategies

The responses the person has to the interpretations are learned from models in childhood and repeated success or failure in using the responses. The response strategies arise in subconscious Awareness and affect the person's behavior without consideration for whether they are appropriate or not. They're just the way things have to be.

A woman may have learned through experiences that she is able to obtain love or help from a man by taking on a helpless role. She may have experienced Mom doing that, or she may have learned in childhood that when she took on the helpless role, Dad would always step in. She had learned through experiences to cope with a child's needs in a child's world using a child's strategy. The strategy resulted in interpretations of the resulting experiences that made her feel satisfied, comfortable, and happy.

She grew into adulthood without changing the strategy. As a result, now when she wants her husband to do something, the experiences from childhood spontaneously come into her subconscious Awareness and she uses the child's strategy of acting helpless. However, the child's strategy is not appropriate for the adult she has become. She has not learned to be confident and self-reliant, so she may have conflict with her husband because of her feigned helplessness.

When the strategy is successful, experiences result that make her feel satisfied, comfortable, and happy. However, the strategy also results in experiences she interprets as threatening her security and feeling of belonging, so when those experiences with her husband result, she feels fearful, rejected, and sad. The system isn't working with the childhood strategy. If she doesn't change the strategy, she will continue to engender experiences that result in unhappiness. She may blame her husband and God and any manner of other perpetrators, but the fact is that she is a prisoner of her childhood. She will not be happy until she breaks out of prison by changing the strategy she uses to cope with the experiences, interpretations, and emotions.

The subconscious memory experiences of strategies that worked in childhood may be dysfunctional for an adult. Unfortunately, people go through their entire lives with the interpretations of experiences, emotions, and strategies that they learned in childhood to mitigate the emotions. They never learn to be self-confident, loving, compassionate adults. They may anesthetize the resulting emotions with alcohol, anger, sex, work, recreation, and other temporary measures that leave the underlying interpretations and strategies that will continue to arise when similar experiences come into their lives.

Conditioning

The experiences can become conditioned. As soon as the experience comes into Awareness, the conditioning gives rise to the emotional response. These emotional responses can come to the body experience even when the experience itself doesn't come fully into the Mind. As a result, someone may have a nagging fear or a free-floating anxiety.

The results of these chronic emotions can be debilitating to the body experience.

Rationalizing and balancing interpretations to change emotions from negative to positive

We often seek ways through conscious Awareness of making the experiences coming through subconscious Awareness give us satisfying, positive emotions. We do so by manipulating the interpretations. We barter with ourselves.

For example, I feel I need to call my sister because I haven't talked to her in several months. My conscious Awareness is "I need to call Fran." The flood of experiences comes into the subconscious Awareness: Fran will comment that I haven't called, image of Fran being angry, image of Fran as a child throwing something at me, sound of my wife in the kitchen, frustration Fran isn't more gentle, itch on my left ear, image of the telephone, feeling guilt for not calling Fran.

My feeling of guilt and the interpretation that Fran will be angry are giving me discomfort. I don't like discomfort. I want to feel happy. So I review the experiences coming into my subconscious Awareness and juggle the interpretations using my conscious Awareness: "I sent Fran a birthday card two weeks ago." With that thought in conscious Awareness, experiences flood into subconscious Awareness: content of the card, sentiment of love in the card, feeling of love for Fran, image of her smiling when she got the card, seeing leaves blow across my window, feeling I have to rake the leaves, good feeling about sending Fran the card. My interpretation of the experience that I didn't call Fran has changed. Fran won't be angry.

In an instant, I have a good feeling from the image of her smiling at the card and think, "The card will do for my contact now. I won't call her. I'm happy." My subconscious Awareness floods with a feeling of satisfaction, image of her smiling when reading the card, thought of where my rake is.

The interpretation that the card will take care of my connection changes the interpretation of Fran's reaction, thereby changing my emotion. That is a rationalization. I used rational thought to juggle my interpretations of experiences to make me feel happy.

Our day-to-day thinking often contains these episodes of juggling the subconscious experiences in conscious Awareness so the resulting feelings are comfort and happiness. The situation has not changed. The Mind is just rearranging the interpretations of experiences to give a satisfying result.

10

Who Are We?

But if the needle point of now Awareness is continually changing experiences resulting in different interpretations and emotions from instant to instant, then who are we?

Each of us has a repertoire of experiences that come into the now point of Awareness so we can accomplish tasks, overcome challenges, learn, and grow while in Earth School. We acquired the repertoire from the day of our birth until now. The experiences allow us to perform as accountants, physicians, mechanics, teachers, pianists, fathers, mothers, writers, and all the other roles we play. They are unique sets of experiences that come into our now point of Awareness when needed and are replaced by new experiences instantly.

Knowledge experiences allow us to solve problems and perform tasks. Interpersonal experiences influence our relationships and encounters with other people. Experience memories result in interpretations that give us feelings of happiness and wellbeing or fear and sadness. All the experiences and their interpretations we have accumulated in our repertoires give us the capabilities and emotions we experience in our daily lives.

The interpretations result in emotions that let us know how well we understand that we are eternal beings who have enrolled for a short time in Earth School, and how much love, compassion, and other-centeredness we have in our nature. However, the unique experiences and interpretations are transients; they come into Awareness and are instantly replaced. When they are not in the now point of Awareness, they are potential experiences and interpretations, accessible but not stored in some depository with our name on it. They don't "exist" as such. They are just potentials. They are not who we are.

Then who are we? We are the aware soul having the experiences, an individualized manifestation of our higher self or oversoul that is part of the Universal Intelligence. As the soul, we have accepted the role of an individual self so we can love, learn, and be happy in Earth School. During Earth School, our individual selves grow spiritually by coming to understand who we are in eternity and adjusting our interpretations of experiences based on the understanding. We know we are being successful when we feel love, compassion, peace, and happiness naturally and spontaneously as experiences come into Awareness. If our interpretations of experiences are filled with love and compassion, we will automatically feel love and compassion during experiences and act in loving, compassionate ways. That will be our nature.

If our interpretations of experiences show disdain, greed, self-absorption, and hostility, we will live in the disdainful, greedy, self-absorbed, hostile world we have created. Every experience will set off negative interpretations resulting in negative emotions. But we are creating that awful world. Our actions show the nature of our interpretations.

This paraphrased story by a great teacher illustrates. He was asked which people in the story are loving and compassionate toward others. He told this story to teach those listening about how their interpretations of experiences display their spiritual natures.

> A man was attacked by robbers who stripped him of his clothes, beat him, and left him for dead on the side of a road. A clergyman happened to be going down the same road, and when he saw the man, he passed by on the other side. Then a deacon in the local church walking the road saw him and passed by on the other side of the

road. But a member of a sect deemed heretical came to where the man was; and when he saw him, he felt pity and sadness for the man. He abandoned his plans for where he was going and put his coat around the suffering man. He supported him as they walked to a motel where he found some medical supplies, bandaged the man's wounds, and had a meal brought to him. He paid for a room for the night. The next day, he came to the motel to see how the man was doing out of great concern for him. As he was leaving, he gave the clerk his credit card information and said, "Look in on him and let him stay tonight if he wants to. Let him order food and take it all out of my credit card."

The first two men were religious officials. The third was a heretic to them. Which of these three do you think was a spiritual man? (My recast of the story in Luke 10:30-36)

The interpretations of the experience of seeing the beaten man by the clergyman and deacon were "How disgusting. He's dirty and may have germs." Those automatic interpretations of the experience were their nature. The member of a sect deemed heretical felt pity and sadness: "That poor man. I have to do something for him." That automatic interpretation of the experience was his nature. Our interpretations of experiences are our spiritual nature. They arise spontaneously and unbidden when we have experiences.

Since these interpretations arise spontaneously at every moment, without our control or intention, it may seem we are determined, with no free will. However, we do have free will. When we act and react based on interpretations of experiences that come to us without our deliberation or control, we are then able to use our conscious Awareness to examine these experiences and decide whether we want to continue to have them as our nature. We decide of our own free will who we want to be.

The purpose of our lives in Earth School is to live with the realization that we are eternal beings, one with the Universal Intelligence, and one with each other. We fulfill our purpose by desiring to become a naturally loving, compassionate person, then remaking ourselves to be that person. We must grow to have interpretations of experiences that result in our being spontaneously loving and compassionate, peaceful, other-centered, and happy, even with obstacles and setbacks.

We are the masters of our destinies and ultimately the destiny of humankind. We can and must become what we want the world to be: loving, peaceful, and joyful.

Endnotes

1 David Schilling, "Knowledge Doubling Every 12 Months, Soon to Be Every 12 Hours," Industry Tap Into News, April 19, 2013, http://www.industrytap.com/knowledge-doubling-every-12-months-soon-to-be-every-12-hours/3950.

2 Adam Taylor, "47 Percent of the World's Population Now Use the Internet, Study Says," *Washington Post*, November 22, 2016, https://www.washingtonpost.com/news/worldviews/wp/2016/11/22/47-percent-of-the-worlds-population-now-use-the-internet-users-study-says/?utm_term=.ff4a94128b32.

3 Business Insider, "Here's What the Internet Will Look Like in 5, 10, and 15 Years," https://www.businessinsider.com/sc/future-of-the-internet-in-5-years-2015-2.

4 Carolyn Duffy Marsan, "10 Fool-Proof Predictions for the Internet in 2020," *Network World*, January 4, 2019, https://www.networkworld.com/article/2238913/10-fool-proof-predictions-for-the-internet-in-2020.html.

5 William Ely Hill, "My Wife and My Mother-in-Law, *Puck,* November 6, 1915. Image adapted from a German postcard.

6 Nika Shakhnazarova, "Old or Young? Whether You See a Young or Old Woman in This Classic Optical Illusion May Depend on Your Age, Researchers Say," *The Sun*, https://www.thesun.co.uk/news/7307450/optical-illusion-young-or-old-woman-depends-on-age/.

7 Donald Hoffman, cited in Amanda Gefter, "The Evolutionary Argument Against Reality," QuantaMagazine.org, https://www.quantamagazine.org/the-evolutionary-argument-against-reality-20160421.

8   Robert Lawrence Kuhn, "Is Consciousness Ultimate Reality?" An interview with Deepak Chopra. Closer To Truth, May 2, 2020. Video at https://www.youtube.com/watch?v=ske-PYBCq54.

9   R. Craig Hogan, *Your Eternal Self* (Normal, IL: Greater Reality Publications, 2008).

10   Daniel Dennett, quoted in Reuben Westmaas, "There's No Such Thing as Consciousness, According to Philosopher Daniel Dennett," *Curiosity makes you smarter*, https://curiosity.com/topics/theres-no-such-thing-as-consciousness-according-to-philosopher-daniel-dennett-curiosity/.

11   Francis Crick, "Taking an Inward Look: A Scientific Search for the Soul," *Telicom*, October 1994.

12   Hogan, *Your Eternal Self*.

13   Amit Goswami, *The Self-Aware Universe: How Consciousness Creates the Material World* (New York: Jeremy Tarcher/Putnam Books, 1993).

14   Warner Heisenberg, Quoted in Adam Becker, *What Is Real?: The Unfinished Quest for the Meaning of Quantum Physics* (Basic Books, 2018).

15   Warner Heisenberg, Quoted in Deepak Chopra, "Physics Must Evolve Beyond the Physical," *Activitas Nervosa Superior* post received: July 23, 2018/Accepted: March 27, 2019, https://35s3f14rw1s1sr3rc1nk656ib9-wpengine.netdna-ssl.com/wp-content/uploads/2019/04/2019-Chopra-Activitas_Nervosa_Superior.pdf.

16   John Wheeler, Quoted in Anil Ananthaswamy, What Does Quantum Theory Actually Tell Us about Reality? *Scientific American blogs*, September 3, 2018, https://blogs.scientificamerican.com/observations/what-does-quantum-theory-actually-tell-us-about-reality/.

17   Andrew Truscott, "Experiment Confirms Quantum Theory Weirdness," Press release from Australian National University in

ScienceDaily, May 27, 2015,
https://www.sciencedaily.com/releases/2015/05/150527103110.htm

18 Kenneth Ring and Sharon Cooper, *Mindsight* (Universe, 2008).

19 Larry Dossey, *Recovering the Soul: A Scientific and Spiritual Approach* (iUniverse, Incorporated, 2008), 18.

20 R. Craig Hogan, Video of Carole Describing Her Guided Afterlife Connection with Kate, January 5, 2015.

21 Journal of a participant in the Self-Guided Afterlife Connections procedure. July 1, 2015.

22 Images from Hal Puthoff, "CIA-Initiated Remote Viewing at Stanford Research Institute." *Institute for Advanced Studies at Austin* (1996), http://www.bioMindsuperpowers.com/Pages/CIA-InitiatedRV.html.

23 Hogan, *Your Eternal Self.*

24 Olivia Goldhill, "The Idea that Everything from Spoons to Stones Are Conscious Is Gaining Academic Credibility," *Quartz Daily Brief*, January 27, 2018. Cited in Yvonne Owens, "The Knower and the Known Are One," Blog January 29, 2018, https://medium.com/@yewtree2/the-knower-and-the-known-are-one-6c943edc9ab5.

25 Max Planck, Interview in *The Observer*, January 25, 1931, 17.

26 Deepak Chopra, Menas Kafatos, Bernardo Kastrup, and Rudolph Tanzi, "Why a Mental Universe Is the 'Real' Reality," *SFGATE*, February 15, 2017, https://www.sfgate.com/opinion/chopra/article/Why-a-Mental-Universe-Is-the-Real-Reality-7465416.php.

27 Bruce Rosenblum and Fred Kuttner, *The Quantum Enigma* (Oxford University Press, 2011), 81.

28 Richard Henry (2005). Cited in Arjun Walia, "'Consciousness Creates Reality'—Physicists Admit the Universe Is Immaterial, Mental, &

Spiritual." *Collective Evolution,* November 11, 2014, https://www.collective-evolution.com/2014/11/11/consciousness-creates-reality-physicists-admit-the-universe-is-immaterial-mental-spiritual/.

[29] Cosmic Scientist, "Physicists Conclude that the Universe Is 'Spiritual, Immaterial & Mental,'" April 28, 2016, https://cosmicscientist.com/physicists-conclude-that-the-universe-is-spiritual-immaterial-mental/

[30] John Wheeler, Cited in Amanda Gefter, "The Evolutionary Argument Against Reality," *QuantaMagazine.org,* April 21, 2016, https://www.quantamagazine.org/the-evolutionary-argument-against-reality-20160421.

[31] Peter Russell, "Is Reality All in the Mind?" *Peter Russell: Spirit of Now,* (n.d.), https://www.peterrussell.com/SCG/ideal.php.

[32] Richard Conn Henry, "The Mental Universe," *Nature,* 436, 29 (2005).

[33] Amit Goswami, "Quantum Politics: Part 1," March 31, 2015, https://www.amitgoswami.org/2015/03/31/quantum-politics-part-i/.

[34] Hogan, *Your Eternal Self.*

[35] Stuart Hameroff, "Fractal Brain Hierarchy, Consciousness and Orch OR." Paper presented at the 2012 Toward a Science of Consciousness conference, Tucson, Arizona, April 9-14, 2012.

[36] Julian Barbour, *The End of Time: The Next Revolution in Our Understanding of the Universe* (Oxford University Press, 2001).

[37] Sean Carroll, "What Is Time? Professor Sean Carroll explains the theories of Presentism and Eternalism," *The Great Courses Plus,* Video presentation, August 7, 2018, https://www.youtube.com/watch?v=MAScJvxCy2Y.

[38] R. Craig Hogan, *Earth School: Answers and Evidence* (Normal, IL: Greater Reality Publications, 2020).

39 Keith Rayner, "The Perceptual Span and Peripheral Cues in Reading." *Cognitive Psychology*, 7 (4) (1975) 65–81.

40 Bruce Lipton, *The Biology of Belief* (Hay House Inc., 2016).

41 Emerging Technology from the arXiv, "New Measure of Human Brain Processing Speed," *MIT Technology Review*, August 25, 2009, https://www.technologyreview.com/2009/08/25/210267/new-measure-of-human-brain-processing-speed/.

42 Mihaly Csikszentmihalyi and R. Lucky, cited in Daniel Levitin, *The Organized Mind: Thinking Straight in the Age of Information Overload* (Plume/Penguin Random House, 2015).

43 Daniel Levitin, *The Organized Mind: Thinking Straight in the Age of Information Overload* (Plume/Penguin Random House, 2015).

44 David DiSalvo, "Your Brain Sees Even When You Don't," *Forbes*, June 22, 2013, https://www.forbes.com/sites/daviddisalvo/2013/06/22/your-brain-sees-even-when-you-dont/#7d5eac2b116a.

45 Lipton, *The Biology of Belief.*

46 Lipton, *The Biology of Belief.*

47 Jennifer Milne, Craig Chapman, Jason Gallivan, et al. "Connecting the Dots: Object Connectedness Deceives Perception but Not Movement Planning," *Psychological Science*, June 13, 2013, https://doi.org/10.1177/0956797612473485

48 Rupert Hawksley, "The World's Fastest-Playing Pianist," *The Telegraph*, November 14, 2014, https://www.telegraph.co.uk/culture/music/classicalmusic/11230512/The-worlds-fastest-playing-pianist.html.

49 Elizabeth Loftus, "Powers of the Subconscious," *Closer to the Truth*. Interview by Robert Lawrence, December 9, 2015, https://www.youtube.com/watch?v=mAZbq7bV64c.

50 David Eagleman, "How the Subconscious Affects Us," *Closer to Truth*, Interview by Robert Lawrence, March 25, 2020, https://www.youtube.com/watch?v=KW_b-GGaHbU.

51 Thalia Wheatley, "What Is Self-Awareness?" *Closer to the Truth*, Interview by Robert Lawrence Kuhn, January 9, 2017, https://www.youtube.com/watch?v=znLmfY1VZzs.

52 Rupert Sheldrake, "Is Consciousness Fundamental?" *Closer to the Truth,* Interview by Robert Lawrence Kuhn, January 6, 2017, https://www.youtube.com/watch?v=46kgmgI9fPs.

53 David Eagleman, *Incognito: The Secret Lives of the Brain*. (Vintage, 2012).

54 Dean Radin, *The Conscious Universe: The Scientific Truth of Psychic Phenomena* (New York: HarperCollins Publishers, 1997), 118-124.

55 Dick Bierman and Dean Radin, "Anomalous Anticipatory Response on Randomized Future Conditions," *Perceptual and Motor Skills*, April 1, 1997, https://pdfs.semanticscholar.org/c577/a7b2f3bdd4ba2723d2b8065680 e98bf34576.pdf.

56 Danny Penman, "Have Scientists Really Proved that Man Can See into the Future?" *NewsMonster*, May 9, 2007, http://www.newsmonster.co.uk/content/view/186/72/on May 11, 2007.

57 Rupert Sheldrake and Pamela Smart, "Experiments for Telephone Telepathy," *Journal of the Society for Psychical Research*, 67 (July 2003): 184-199.

58 William Braud and Marilyn Schlitz, "A Methodology for the Objective Study of Transpersonal Imagery," *Journal of Scientific Exploration*, vol. 3, no. 1 (1989): 43-63.

59 William Braud, "Empirical Explorations of Prayer, Distant Healing, and Remote Mental Influence," Institute of Transpersonal Psychology, Unpublished paper (1990),

https://static.secure.website/wscfus/326656/uploads/EmpiricalExplor
ationsOfPrayer.pdf.

60 Marilyn Schlitz and William Braud, "Reiki-Plus Natural Healing: An
Ethnographic/Experimental Study," *Psi Research*, 4 (1985): 100-123.

61 Marilyn Schlitz and Stephen LaBerge, "Covert observation increases
skin conductance in subjects unaware of when they are being
observed: a replication," *The Journal of Parapsychology*,
http://findarticles.com/p/articles/mi_m2320/is_n3_v61/ai_20749204.

62 William Braud, "Empirical explorations."

63 Jean Achterberg and Karin Cooke, "Evidence for correlations
between distant intentionality and brain function in recipients: a
functional magnetic resonance imaging analysis," *Journal of
Alternative and Complementary Medicine*, 6 (2011): 965-71.

64 Nitamo Montecucco, Report by Cyber: Ricerche Olistiche (1992).
Retrieved December 17, 2007, from
http://www.goertzel.org/dynapsyc/ 1996/subtle.html.

65 William Braud, Donna Shafer, and Sperry Andrews, "Electrodermal
Correlates of Remote Attention: Autonomic Reactions to an Unseen
Gaze," *Proceedings of Presented Papers*, Parapsychology Association
33rd Annual Convention (1990): 14-28.

66 Rupert Sheldrake, "The Sense of Being Stared At," *Journal of the
Society for Psychical Research*, 62, (1998): 311-323.

67 Stephen LaBerge and Marilyn Schlitz, "Covert Observation Increases
Skin Conductance in Subjects Unaware of When They Are Being
Observed: A Replication," *The Journal of Parapsychology*, 61 (1997).

68 Study cited in Dean Radin, Colleen Rae, and Ray Hyman, "Is There a
Sixth Sense?" *Psychology Today*, July/August 2006,
http://www.psychologytoday.com/articles/index.php?term=pto-
20000701-000034&page=3.

69 Braud et al., "Electrodermal Correlates."

70 Paul McKenna and Giles O'Bryen, *The Paranormal World of Paul McKenna* (Faber & Faber, 1997).

71 Guy Playfair, *Twin Telepathy: The Psychic Connection* (Vega, 2003).

72 Radin et. al., "Is There a Sixth Sense?"

73 Playfair, *Twin Telepathy.*

74 Akiane Kramarik, Interview in the *Washington Times* newspaper, April 11, 2019, https://www.govmint.com/coin-authority/post/divine-inspiration-a-portrait-of-the-artist-akiane-kramarik-

75 Cited in Carol Corneliuson, "Spiritually Motivated Artists Who, Like Akiane Kramarik, Were Inspired by God," Art & SoulWorks blog, November 10, 2015, https://art-soulworks.com/blogs/posts/98899590-spiritually-motivated-artists-who-like-akiane-kramarik-were-inspired-by-god

76 Clemency Burton-Hill, "She Dreamt Up a Set of Piano Variations in E-flat While Asleep: Alma Deutscher Is Not Your Average 10-year-old. Clemency Burton-Hill Meets the Child Prodigy," BBC, May 18, 2015, http://www.bbc.com/culture/story/20150518-little-miss-mozart?OCID=AsiaOne

77 Burton-Hill, "She Dreamt Up."

78 Morley Safer, Savants and Genius: A Wonderful Mystery documentary. *Genius: Sponsored by Suzanne St. Pierre*, 1983, https://www.youtube.com/watch?v=rTrJjbfG4xg

79 Hogan, *Your Eternal Self.*

80 Nicolas Burra, Alexis Hervais-Adelman, Dirk Kerzel, Marco Tamietto, Beatrice de Gelder, and Alan J. Pegna, "Amygdala Activation for Eye Contact Despite Complete Cortical Blindness," *The Journal of Neuroscience.* 19, 33 (25), June 2013: 10483-10489.

81 "Study Suggests Brain May Have 'Blindsight.'" Associated Press, October 31, 2005, http://www.msnbc.msn.com/id/9879390/.

82 "When Blindsight is 20/20," ShowPsych, February 6, 2020, https://www.youtube.com/watch?v=p6GDNpylILE&t=18s.

83 Sharon Begley, "In Our Messy, Reptilian Brains," *Newsweek* online, 2007, http://www.msnbc.msn.com/id/ 17888475/site/newsweek/.

84 "Amazing blind teen uses echolocation to 'SEE,'" Familes.com, October 26, 2006, http://special-needs.families.com/blog/ amazing-blind-boy-uses-echolocation-to-see-watch-the-video-clip.

85 "Blind man's 'superpower' lets him bike, skate and navigate the world, *HUMAN Limits*, August 8, 2016. https://www.youtube.com/watch?v=EFvH7NF4MSw.

86 "Blind man's 'superpower'.

87 Rob StGeorge, "Ellen Bourdeaux — Super Savant —Superhuman 44," Sapien Plus, http://sapienplus.com/ellen-bourdeaux/.

88 "When Blindsight is 20/20."

89 Nicholas Humphrey, "Prof. Nicholas Humphrey on Blindsight and Consciousness," January 30, 2019, https://www.youtube.com/watch?v=tV5oby1blH8.

90 Henry Sidgwick, "On vision with sealed and bandaged eyes," *Journal of Society for Psychical Research,* Volume I, 1884-1885, June 1884: 84-86.

91 Dewey Webb, "The Flamboyant Clairvoyant," *Phoenix New Times*, September 11, 1911.

92 Dr. Richard Ireland website, "Dr. Richard Ireland: His Gifts," www.drrichardireland.com/gifts.html.

93 Vibravision®, https://mp-usa.org/vibravision/.

94 Rob Schwartz, *Your Soul's Plan: Discovering the Real Meaning of the Life You Planned Before You Were Born* (Frog Books, 2009), 51.

95 Leslie Flint, "Recording of a Séance in Which Madame Curie Spoke on November 30, 1984," Leslie Flint Foundation.

96 R. Craig Hogan, "Self-Guided Afterlife Connections: Development and Study," unpublished study, 2012, http://selfguided.spiritualunderstanding.org/Self-guidedAfterlifeConnections.pdf

97 "Blind man's 'superpower' lets him bike, skate and navigate the world, *HUMAN Limits*, August 8, 2016. https://www.youtube.com/watch?v=EFvH7NF4MSw.

98 Radin, 1997, pp. 118-124.

99 Andrew Truscott, "Experiment Confirms."

100 Russell Hurlburt, "Not Everyone Conducts Inner Speech: Inner speech Is Frequent but Not for Everyone," *Psychology Today* post, October 26, 2011, https://www.psychologytoday.com/us/blog/pristine-inner-experience/201110/not-everyone-conducts-inner-speech.

101 Chopra et. al., "Why a Mental Universe."

102 Guy Montgomery, Katherine DuHamel, and William Redd, "A meta-analysis of hypnotically induced analgesia: how effective is hypnosis?" *International Journal of Clinical and Experimental Hypnosis*, Vol. 48 (2000): 138-153.

103 Arthritis Foundation, "Hypnosis for Pain Relief," https://www.arthritis.org/health-wellness/treatment/complementary-therapies/natural-therapies/hypnosis-for-pain-relief.

104 CBS News, "Hypnosis, No Anesthetic, for Man's Surgery," April 22, 2008, https://www.cbsnews.com/news/hypnosis-no-anesthetic-for-mans-surgery/.

105 Anthony Peake, *The Daemon: A Guide to Your Extraordinary Secret Self* (Arcturus, 2010).

106 Donald Hoffman, *The Case Against Reality: why evolution hid the truth from our eyes* (W. W. Norton & Company, 2019).

107 Tom Campbell, *My Big Toe: A Trilogy Unifying Philosophy, Physics, and Metaphysics* (Lightning Strike Books, 2007).

108 Max Tegmark, quoted in Robert Lawrence Kuhn, "The Illusion of Time: What's Real?" Space.com, filmed July 6, 2015, https://www.space.com/29859-the-illusion-of-time.html.

109 Brian Greene, "Past, present and future coexist. 'Now time' explained easy," filmed April 4, 2017, https://www.youtube.com/watch?v=idsw99SSwKc.

110 Daniel Siegel, "What Is a Healthy Mind?," Science and Nonduality, video filmed February 21, 2019, https://www.youtube.com/watch?v=-A_aYHEac6I.

111 Schäfer, Lothar, *Infinite Potential: What Quantum Physics Reveals About How We Should Live*. (Deepak Chopra, April 2, 2013). From the introduction to the book.

112 Maharishi Mahesh Yogi, *Maharishi Vedic University Introduction*. (Holland: Maharishi Vedic University Press, 67-68.

113 Edgar Cayce, *Akashic Record Reader* (A.R.E. Press, 1998), Reading 1650-1.

114 Joseph Howard Tyson, *Madame Blavatsky Revisited* (Lincoln, NE: iUniverse, 2007).

115 Emanuel Swedenborg, *Heaven and Hell*. Originally written in 1743-1745. Translated by George F. Dole (New Century Edition, 2010), #463.

116 Darold Treffert, *Islands of Genius* (London: Jessica Kingsley Publishers, 2011).

117 Darold Treffert, "Kim Peek," SSMHealth, n.d., https://www.agnesian.com/page/kim-peek.

118 Tijn Touber, "Life goes on," *Ode*, 29 (2007, January).

119 "The Human Camera (Autistic Savant Documentary)," Real Stories, video filmed September 27, 2016, https://www.youtube.com/watch?v=phkNgC8Vxj4

120 Morley Safer, "Savants and Genius: A Wonderful Mystery documentary," *Manufacturing Intellect,* video filmed October 24, 2017, https://www.youtube.com/watch?v=rTrJjbfG4xg.

121 Safer, "Savants and Genius."

122 Allison Langdon, "People Who Remember Every Second of Their Life," *60 Minutes Australia,* filmed September 21, 2018, https://www.youtube.com/watch?v=hpTCZ-hO6iI.

123 Raziye Akkoc, "'A ski accident left me with advanced mental abilities': US woman tells her extraordinary story," *The Telegraph,* April 17, 2015, https://www.telegraph.co.uk/news/worldnews/northamerica/usa/11 544405/A-ski-accident-left-me-with-advanced-mental-abilities-US-woman-tells-her-extraordinary-story.html.

124 Michelle Whitedove, "America's Psychic Challenge Michelle Whitedove Winner," Lifetime TV, September 24, 2008, https://www.youtube.com/watch?v=RgbALQzZl-s.

125 Katherine Ramsland, "Psychic detectives," Court TV Crime Library, http://www.crimelibrary.com/criminal_mind/forensics/psychics/index.html.

126 Victor Zammit, "Australian psychics beat 'orthodox' science," n.d., http://victorzammit.com/articles/sensingmurder.html.

127 "Psychic Detectives," *Nancy Grace,* filmed December 30, 2005, http://transcripts.cnn.com/TRANSCRIPTS/0512/30/ng.01.html.

128 "Psychic Detectives."

129 Damian Bertrand, "Shelise & Julian," *Reincarnated: Past Lives on LMN®,* video aired March 22, 2014.

130 Robert Snow, *Looking for Carroll Beckwith: The True Stories of a Detective's Search for His Past Life* (Daybreak Books, 1999).

131 "Is This REALLY Proof that Man Can See into the Future?" DailyMail.com, May 4, 2007, https://www.dailymail.co.uk/sciencetech/article-452833/Is-REALLY-proof-man-future.html.

132 "Is This REALLY Proof."

133 Radin, *The Conscious Universe.*

134 Radin, *The Conscious Universe.*

135 Joe McMoneagle and Charles Tart, *Mind Trek: Exploring Consciousness, Time, and Space Through Remote Viewing* (Hampton Roads Publishing, 1993).

136 Radin, *The Conscious Universe,* 104.

137 Jeffrey Mishlove, "Archaeological Remote Viewing in Japan with Joseph McMoneagle," *New Thinking Aloud with Jeffrey Mishlove,* filmed August 11, 2016, https://www.youtube.com/watch?v=F-8puX-83o4.

138 Ingo Swann and Harold Sherman, "An Experimental Psychic Probe of the Planet Jupiter," April 27, 1973, paper released for public consumption April 1, 2008, https://www.cia.gov/library/readingroom/docs/NSA-RDP96X00790R000100040010-3.pdf.

139 Stephan Schwartz, Randall De Mattei, and Roger Smith, "The Caravel Project: The Location, Description, and Reconstruction of Marine Sites through Remote Viewing, Including a Comparison with Aerial Photography, Geologic Coring, and Electronic Remote Sensing," *Institute for Nautical Archaeology,* 19 (2019): 113-139.

140 Radin, *The Conscious Universe,* 101.

141 Jessica Utts, "An Assessment of the Evidence for Psychic Functioning," Division of Statistics, University of California, Davis, 1995.

142 Hogan, *Your Eternal Self.*

143 Oliver Lodge, *The Case For and Against Psychical Belief* (Bibliolife, 1927).

144 "Patience Worth," 2019, https://www.encyclopedia.com/science/encyclopedias-almanacs-transcripts-and-maps/patience-worth.

145 Walter Franklin Prince, *The Case of Patience Worth* (New Hyde Park, NY: University Books, 1964). Originally published by Boston Society for Psychic Research, 1927.

146 Leslie Flint, Recording of the voice of Alice Green in a direct-voice session, December 18, 1967, Leslie Flint Educational Trust, https://www.leslieflint.com/alice-green-december-1967

147 Ramesh Raskar, "Imaging at a Trillion Frames Per Second," TED, video filmed July 26, 2012, https://www.youtube.com/watch?v=Y_9vd4HWlVA

148 D. Shristi, "Process of Creative Thinking: 4 Stages." Psychology Discussion, n.d., http://www.psychologydiscussion.net/thinking/process-of-creative-thinking-4-stages-thinking-processes-psychology/3127

149 David Eagleman, "Incognito: What's Hiding in the Unconscious Mind?" Interview on *Fresh Air*, https://www.npr.org/2011/05/31/136495499/incognito-whats-hiding-in-the-unconscious-mind

150 Eagleman, "Incognito."

151 Eagleman, "Incognito."

152 Nadia-Elysse Harris, "Derek Amato Becomes Musical Genius After Brain Injury: What Is Acquired Savant Syndrome?" *Medical Daily*,

October 19, 2013, https://www.medicaldaily.com/derek-amato-becomes-musical-genius-after-brain-injury-what-acquired-savant-syndrome-video-260369.

153 "Derek Amato, Sudden Musical Genius," HUMAN Limits. UPROXX, video filmed August 29, 2016, https://www.youtube.com/watch?v=GTHDuZo7G3Y.

154 Darold Treffert, "Brain Gain: A Person Can Instantly Blossom into a Savant—and No One Knows Why," *Scientific American,* July 25, 2018, https://blogs.scientificamerican.com/observations/brain-gain-a-person-can-instantly-blossom-into-a-savant-and-no-one-knows-why/.

155 CBS Denver, "Teen Credits Concussion with Giving Him His Musical Talents." *CBS Denver Local* online, 2013. https://denver.cbslocal.com/2013/11/20/teen-credits-concussion-with-giving-him-his-musical-talents/

156 "Teen Credits Concussion.

157 James Joyce Encyclopedia. "Prodigious aspects of James Joyce Mind," n.d., http://www.jamesjoyceencyclopedia.com/data/Conclusion/Prodigious%20aspects%20of%20JJ%20Mind.htm.

158 Richard Lazarus, *The Case Against Death* (Time Warner Books UK, 1993), 83.

159 Ian Stevenson and Satwant Pasricha, "A Preliminary Report of an Unusual Case of the Reincarnation Type with Xenoglossy," *Journal of the American Society for Psychical Research,* 74 (1980): 331-348.

160 Walter Semkiw, *Born Again: Reincarnation Cases Involving Evidence of Past Lives, with Xenoglossy Cases Researched by Ian Stevenson, MD* (Pluto Project, 2011).

161 Lazarus, *The Case Against Death*, 85.

162 Tony Thomas, "Teen Woke Up from Coma Speaking Different Language," WSB-TV, video filmed October 19, 2016, https://www.youtube.com/watch?v=nttfgZKK2r4

163 "5 People Who Started Speaking Foreign Languages After Being in a Coma," video filmed June 18, 2019, https://www.youtube.com/watch?v=CkMufQ5QSh4&feature=youtube.

164 Joel Whitton and Joe Fisher, *Life Between Life: Scientific Explorations into the Void Separating One Incarnation from the Next* (Doubleday, 1986), 210.

165 Whitton and Fisher, *Life Between Life*.

166 Joe Fisher, *The Case for Reincarnation* (Bantam, 1985), 202.

167 Ian Stevenson, *Unlearned Language: New Studies in Xenoglossy* (Charlottesville, Virginia, USA: University Press of Virginia, 1984).

168 Lazarus, *The Case Against Death*, 84.

169 Peter Ramster, *The Search for Lives Past* (Somerset Film and Publishing Pty. Ltd., 1990): 227.

170 Lazarus, *The Case Against Death*, 121.

171 Lazarus, *The Case Against Death*, 121.

172 Peter Mariën, Jo Verhoeven, Peggy Wackenier, S. Engelborghs, and P. De Deyn, "Foreign accent syndrome as a developmental motor speech disorder," *Cortex*, 45 (7) (2009): 870–878.

173 Peter Mariën, Stefanie Keulen, and Jo Verhoeven, "Neurological Aspects of Foreign Accent Syndrome in Stroke Patients," *Journal of Communication Disorders*, 77 (January 2019): 94–113.

174 Jason Padgett, *Struck by Genius: How a Brain Injury Made Me a Mathematical Marvel* (Houghton Mifflin Harcourt, 2014).

175 Darold Treffert and Daniel Tammet, *Islands of Genius: The Bountiful Mind of the Autistic, Acquired, and Sudden Savant* (Jessa Kingsley Publishers, 2011).

176 Ken Walters, "My stroke made me an artist," *The Guardian,* September 12, 2008, https://www.theguardian.com/lifeandstyle/2008/sep/13/healthandwellbeing.

177 "My stroke made me an artist."

178 Jon Sarkin, "Jon Sarkin website," 2020, https://www.jsarkin.com/knowjon.

179 Monica Kinney, "An artist is born after car crash," *The Philadelphia Inquirer,* August 19, 2012, https://www.inquirer.com/philly/columnists/monica_yant_kinney/20120819_Monica_Yant_Kinney__An_artist_is_born_after_car_crash.html.

180 "Pip Taylor develops amazing ability to draw after suffering brain injury," News.com.au, March 20, 2014.

181 Darold Treffert, "Brain Gain."

182 Darold Treffert, "Brain Gain."

183 Franco Magnani website, http://www.francomagnani.com/about2.aspx.

184 Reid Hastie, "A computer simulation model of person memory," *Journal of Experimental Social Psychology,* 24 (1988): 423−147, cited in *Psychology Research and Reference,* https://psychology.iresearchnet.com/social-psychology/social-cognition/associative-networks/.

185 Alan Baddeley and Robert Logie, *Working memory: The multiple-component model,* cited in Akira Miyake and Priti Shah, eds., *Models of Working Memory* (Cambridge, UK: Cambridge University Press, 1999), 28-61.

[186] Alan Botkin and R. Craig Hogan, *Induced After-Death Communication: A New Therapy for Healing Grief and Trauma* (Hampton Roads, 2005).

[187] Gioia Diliberto, "Patience Worth: Author From the Great Beyond," *Smithsonian Magazine*, September 2010, https://www.smithsonianmag.com/arts-culture/patience-worth-author-from-the-great-beyond-54333749/

[188] William Tiller, Walter Dibble, and Michael Kohane, *Conscious Acts of Creation: The Emergence of a New Physics* (Pavior Publishing 2001).

[189] William Tiller, "Subtle Energies," *Science and Medicine*, vol. 6, no. 3 (May/June 1999).

[190] Dean Radin, Ryan Taft, and Garret Yount, "Effects of Healing Intention on Culture Cells and Truly Random Events," *The Journal of Alternative and Complementary Medicine*, vol. 10, no. 1 (2004): 103-112.

[191] Masaru Emoto, *The Secret Life of Water* (Atria, 2005).

[192] Dean Radin, Gail Hayssen, Masaru Emoto, and Takashige Kizu, "Double-Blind Test of the Effects of Distant Intention on Water Crystal Formation," *Explore*, September/October 2006, 408-11.

[193] "Study on the Maharishi Effect: Can group meditation lower crime rate and violence?" Transcendental Meditation News & More, March 10, 2016, https://tmhome.com/benefits/study-maharishi-effect-group-meditation-crime-rate/.

[194] John Hagelin, David Orme-Johnson, Maxwell Rainforth, Kenneth Cavanaugh, Charles Alexander, "Effects of group practice of the Transcendental Meditation Program on preventing violent crime in Washington, D.C.: Results of the National Demonstration Project to Reduce Crime and Improve Governmental Effectiveness in Washington, D.C.," *Social Indicators Research*, 47 (June-July, 1993): 153-201.

[195] Dillbeck, Michael, et al., "The Transcendental Meditation program and crime rate change in a sample of 48 cities, *Journal of Crime and Justice*, 4 (1981): 25-45.

[196] David Orme-Johnson, Kenneth Cavanaugh, Catherine Alexander, P. Gelderloos, Michael Dillbeck, A. G. Lanford, and Abou Nader, *T.M.* (In press, pp. 2532-2548), "The influence of the Maharishi Technology of the Unified Field on world events and global social indicators: The effects of the Taste of Utopia Assembly," cited in Robert Kenny, "What can science tell us about collective consciousness?" *Leaderful Teams Consulting*, November 10, 2007, http://www.collectivewisdominitiative.org/papers/kenny_science.htm#end63.

[197] Amanda Gefter, "Haunted by His Brother, He Revolutionized Physics," Nautilus. Video filmed January 16, 2014. http://nautil.us/issue/9/time/haunted-by-his-brother-he-revolutionized-physics

[198] Dean Radin, et al. "Consciousness and the Double-Slit Interference Pattern: Six Experiments," Physics Essays 25, 2 (2012).

[199] Helmut Schmidt, "Mental influence on random events," *New Scientist and Science Journal* (1971): 757-758.

[200] Helmut Schmidt, "Observation of a Psychokinetic Effect Under Highly Controlled Conditions," *Journal of Parapsychology*, vol. 57 (Dec. 1993).

[201] Montague Ullman, "Herpes Simplex and Second Degree Burn Induced Under Hypnosis," *The American Journal of Psychiatry*, v. 103, no. 6 (May 1947).

[202] Rachael Moeller, "Study Suggests Common Knee Surgery's Effect Is Purely Placebo," *Scientific American*, July 12, 2002, https://www.scientificamerican.com/article/study-suggests-common-kne/.

[203] Bruno Klopfer, "Psychological Variables in Human Cancer," *Journal of Prospective Techniques*, 31 (1957): 331-40.

[204] Pamela Maraldo, *Medicine: In Search of a Soul: The Healing Prescription* (Balboa Press, 2017).

205 Maraldo, *Medicine: In Search of a Soul.*

206 Michael Talbot, *The Holographic Universe* (Harper Perennial, 2011), 98-100.

207 Bennett Braun, *Treatment of Multiple Personality Disorder* (American Psychiatric Publishing, 1986).

208 Radin, *The Conscious Universe*, 118-124.

209 Playfair, *Twin Telepathy.*

210 William Braud and Marilyn Schlitz, "A methodology for the objective study of transpersonal imagery," *Journal of Scientific Exploration*, 3 (1983): 43-63.

Bibliography

"5 People Who Started Speaking Foreign Languages After Being in a Coma." Video filmed June 18, 2019, https://www.youtube.com/watch?v=CkMufQ5QSh4&feature=youtu.be

"Amazing blind teen uses echolocation to 'SEE.'" Familes.com, October 26, 2006, http://special-needs.families.com/blog/ amazing-blind-boy-uses-echolocation-to-see-watch-the-video-clip.

"Derek Amato, Sudden Musical Genius." HUMAN Limits. UPROXX, video filmed August 29, 2016, https://www.youtube.com/watch?v=GTHDuZo7G3Y.

"Is This REALLY Proof that Man Can See into the Future?" DailyMail.com, May 4, 2007, https://www.dailymail.co.uk/sciencetech/article-452833/Is-REALLY-proof-man-future.html.

"Patience Worth." 2019, https://www.encyclopedia.com/science/encyclopedias-almanacs-transcripts-and-maps/patience-worth.

"Pip Taylor develops amazing ability to draw after suffering brain injury." News.com.au, March 20, 2014.

"Psychic Detectives." *Nancy Grace*, filmed December 30, 2005, http://transcripts.cnn.com/TRANSCRIPTS/0512/30/ng.01.html.

"Study on the Maharishi Effect: Can group meditation lower crime rate and violence?" Transcendental Meditation News & More, March 10, 2016, https://tmhome.com/benefits/study-maharishi-effect-group-meditation-crime-rate/.

"Study Suggests Brain May Have 'Blindsight.'" Associated Press, October 31, 2005, http://www.msnbc.msn.com/id/9879390/.

"The Human Camera (Autistic Savant Documentary)." Real Stories Video filmed September 27, 2016, https://www.youtube.com/watch?v=phkNgC8Vxj4

"When Blindsight is 20/20." ShowPsych, February 6, 2020, https://www.youtube.com/watch?v=p6GDNpyIlLE&t=18s.

Achterberg, Jean and Karin Cooke. "Evidence for correlations between distant intentionality and brain function in recipients: a functional magnetic resonance imaging analysis." *Journal of Alternative and Complementary Medicine*, 6 (2011): 965-71.

Akkoc, Raziye. "'A ski accident left me with advanced mental abilities': US woman tells her extraordinary story." *The Telegraph*, April 17, 2015, https://www.telegraph.co.uk/news/worldnews/northamerica/usa/11 544405/A-ski-accident-left-me-with-advanced-mental-abilities-US-woman-tells-her-extraordinary-story.html.

Arthritis Foundation. "Hypnosis for Pain Relief." https://www.arthritis.org/health-wellness/treatment/complementary-therapies/natural-therapies/hypnosis-for-pain-relief

Baddeley, Alan, and Robert Logie. *Working memory: The multiple-component model*, cited in Akira Miyake and Priti Shah, eds., *Models of Working Memory* (Cambridge, UK: Cambridge University Press, 1999), 28-61.

Barbour, Julian. *The End of Time: The Next Revolution in Our Understanding of the Universe* (Oxford University Press, 2001).

Bertrand, Damien. "Shelise & Julian." *Reincarnated: Past Lives on LMN®*, video aired March 22, 2014.

Begley, Sharon. "In Our Messy, Reptilian Brains." *Newsweek* online.http://www.msnbc.msn.com/id/ 17888475/site/newsweek/, 2007.

Bierman, Dick, and Dean Radin. "Anomalous Anticipatory Response on Randomized Future Conditions. Perceptual and Motor Skills." April

1, 1997,
https://pdfs.semanticscholar.org/c577/a7b2f3bdd4ba2723d2b8065680
e98bf34576.pdf.

Botkin, Alan, and R. Craig Hogan. *Induced After-Death Communication: A New Therapy for Healing Grief and Trauma* (Hampton Roads, 2005).

Braud, William, and Marilyn Schlitz. "A Methodology for the Objective Study of Transpersonal Imagery." *Journal of Scientific Exploration*, vol. 3, no. 1 (1989): 43-63.

Braud, William, and Marilyn Schlitz. "A Methodology for the Objective Study of Transpersonal Imagery." *Journal of Scientific Exploration*, 3 (1983): 43-63.

Braud, William, Donna Shafer, and Sperry Andrews. "Electrodermal Correlates of Remote Attention: Autonomic Reactions to an Unseen Gaze." *Proceedings of Presented Papers*, Parapsychology Association 33rd Annual Convention, (1990): 14-28.

Braud, William. "Empirical Explorations of Prayer, Distant Healing, and Remote Mental Influence." Institute of Transpersonal Psychology. Unpublished paper (1990), https://static.secure.website/wscfus/326656/uploads/EmpiricalExplo rationsOfPrayer.pdf.

Braun, Bennett. *Treatment of Multiple Personality Disorder* (American Psychiatric Publishing, 1986).

Browne, Sylvia. *End of Days: Predictions and Prophecies about the End of the World* (Penguin Group, 2012), 12.

Burra, Nicolas, Alexis Hervais-Adelman, Dirk Kerzel, Marco Tamietto, Beatrice de Gelder, and Alan J. Pegna. "Amygdala Activation for Eye Contact Despite Complete Cortical Blindness." *The Journal of Neuroscience.* 19, 33 (25) (June 2013): 10483-10489.

Burton-Hill, Clemency. "She Dreamt Up a Set of Piano Variations in E-flat While Asleep: Alma Deutscher Is Not Your Average 10-year-old. Clemency Burton-Hill Meets the Child Prodigy." BBC, May 18,

2015, http://www.bbc.com/culture/story/20150518-little-miss-mozart?OCID=AsiaOne.

Business Insider. "Here's What the Internet Will Look Like in 5, 10, and 15 Years." https://www.businessinsider.com/sc/future-of-the-internet-in-5-years-2015-2.

Campbell, Tom. *My Big Toe: A Trilogy Unifying Philosophy, Physics, and Metaphysics* (Lightning Strike Books, 2007).

Carroll, Sean. "What Is Time? Professor Sean Carroll explains the theories of Presentism and Eternalism." *The Great Courses Plus*, Video presentation, August 7, 2018, https://www.youtube.com/watch?v=MAScJvxCy2Y.

Cayce, Edgar. *Akashic Record Reader* (A.R.E. Press, 1998), Reading 1650-1.

CBS Denver. "Teen Credits Concussion with Giving Him His Musical Talents." *CBS Denver Local* online, 2013. https://denver.cbslocal.com/2013/11/20/teen-credits-concussion-with-giving-him-his-musical-talents/

CBS News. "Hypnosis, No Anesthetic, for Man's Surgery." April 22, 2008, https://www.cbsnews.com/news/hypnosis-no-anesthetic-for-mans-surgery/.

Chopra, Deepak, Menas Kafatos, Bernardo Kastrup, and Rudolph Tanzi. "Why a Mental Universe Is the "Real" Reality." *SFGATE*, February 15, 2017, https://www.sfgate.com/opinion/chopra/article/Why-a-Mental-Universe-Is-the-Real-Reality-7465416.php.

Chopra, Deepak. "Is Consciousness Ultimate Reality?" An interview by Robert Lawrence Kuhn. Closer To Truth, May 2, 2020. Video at https://www.youtube.com/watch?v=ske-PYBCq54.

Corneliuson, Carol. "Spiritually Motivated Artists Who, Like Akiane Kramarik, Were Inspired by God." Art & SoulWorks blog, November 10, 2015, https://art-soulworks.com/blogs/posts/98899590-spiritually-motivated-artists-who-like-akiane-kramarik-were-inspired-by-god

Cosmic Scientist. "Physicists Conclude that the Universe Is 'Spiritual, Immaterial & Mental,'" April 28, 2016, https://cosmicscientist.com/physicists-conclude-that-the-universe-is-spiritual-immaterial-mental/

Crick, Francis. "Taking an Inward Look: A Scientific Search for the Soul." *Telicom*, October 1994.

Csikszentmihalyi, Mihaly and R. Lucky. Cited in Daniel Levitin, *The Organized Mind: Thinking Straight in the Age of Information Overload* (Plume/Penguin Random House, 2015).

Dennett, Daniel. Quoted in Reuben Westmaas, "There's No Such Thing as Consciousness, According to Philosopher Daniel Dennett." *Curiosity makes you smarter*, https://curiosity.com/topics/theres-no-such-thing-as-consciousness-according-to-philosopher-daniel-dennett-curiosity/.

Diliberto, Gioia. "Patience Worth: Author From the Great Beyond." *Smithsonian Magazine*, September 2010, https://www.smithsonianmag.com/arts-culture/patience-worth-author-from-the-great-beyond-54333749/

Dillbeck, Michael, et al. "The Transcendental Meditation program and crime rate change in a sample of 48 cities, *Journal of Crime and Justice*, 4 (1981): 25-45.

DiSalvo, David. "Your Brain Sees Even When You Don't." *Forbes* (June 22, 2013), https://www.forbes.com/sites/daviddisalvo/2013/06/22/your-brain-sees-even-when-you-dont/#7d5eac2b116a

Dossey, Larry. *Recovering the Soul: A Scientific and Spiritual Approach* (iUniverse, Incorporated, 2008), 18.

Dr. Richard Ireland website, "Dr. Richard Ireland: His Gifts." www.drrichardireland.com/gifts.html.

Duffy Marsan, Carolyn. "10 Fool-Proof Predictions for the Internet in 2020." *Network World*, January 4, 2019, https://www.networkworld.com/article/2238913/10-fool-proof-predictions-for-the-internet-in-2020.html.

Eagleman, David. *Incognito: The Secret Lives of the Brain*. (Vintage, 2012).

Eagleman, David. "Incognito: What's Hiding in the Unconscious Mind?" Interview on *Fresh Air*, https://www.npr.org/2011/05/31/136495499/incognito-whats-hiding-in-the-unconscious-mind

Eagleman, David. "How the Subconscious Affects Us." *Closer to Truth*. Interview by Robert Lawrence, March 25, 2020, https://www.youtube.com/watch?v=KW_b-GGaHbU.

Emerging Technology from the arXiv. "New Measure of Human Brain Processing Speed." *MIT Technology Review* (August 25, 2009), https://www.technologyreview.com/2009/08/25/210267/new-measure-of-human-brain-processing-speed/.

Emoto, Masaru. *The Secret Life of Water* (Atria, 2005).

Fisher, Joe. *The Case for Reincarnation* (Bantam, 1985), 202.

Flint, Leslie. "Recording of a Séance in Which Madame Curie Spoke on November 30, 1984." Leslie Flint Foundation.

Flint, Leslie. Recording of the voice of Alice Green in a direct-voice session, December 18, 1967. Leslie Flint Educational Trust. https://www.leslieflint.com/alice-green-december-1967.

Gefter, Amanda. "Haunted by His Brother, He Revolutionized Physics." Nautilus. Video filmed January 16, 2014. http://nautil.us/issue/9/time/haunted-by-his-brother-he-revolutionized-physics

Goldhill, Olivia. "The Idea that Everything from Spoons to Stones Are Conscious Is Gaining Academic Credibility." *Quartz Daily Brief*, January 27, 2018. Cited in Yvonne Owens, "The Knower and the Known Are One." Blog January 29, 2018, https://medium.com/@yewtree2/the-knower-and-the-known-are-one-6c943edc9ab5.

Goswami, Amit. "Quantum Politics: Part 1." March 31, 2015, https://www.amitgoswami.org/2015/03/31/quantum-politics-part-i/.

Goswami, Amit. *The Self-Aware Universe: How Consciousness Creates the Material World* (New York: Jeremy Tarcher/Putnam Books, 1993).

Greene, Brian. "Past, present and future coexist. 'Now time' explained easy." filmed April 4, 2017, https://www.youtube.com/watch?v=idsw99SSwKc.

Hagelin, John, David Orme-Johnson, Maxwell Rainforth, Kenneth Cavanaugh, and Charles Alexander. "Effects of group practice of the Transcendental Meditation Program on preventing violent crime in Washington, D.C.: Results of the National Demonstration Project to Reduce Crime and Improve Governmental Effectiveness in Washington, D.C." *Social Indicators Research*, 47 (June-July, 1993): 153-201.

Hameroff, Stuart. "Fractal Brain Hierarchy, Consciousness and Orch OR." Paper presented at the 2012 Toward a Science of Consciousness conference, Tucson Arizona, April 9-14, 2012.

Harris, Nadia-Elysse. "Derek Amato Becomes Musical Genius After Brain Injury: What Is Acquired Savant Syndrome?" *Medical Daily*, October 19, 2013, https://www.medicaldaily.com/derek-amato-becomes-musical-genius-after-brain-injury-what-acquired-savant-syndrome-video-260369.

Hastie, Reid. "A computer simulation model of person memory." *Journal of Experimental Social Psychology*, 24 (1988): 423–147, cited in *Psychology Research and Reference*, https://psychology.iresearchnet.com/social-psychology/social-cognition/associative-networks/.

Hawksley, Rupert. "The World's Fastest-Playing Pianist." *The Telegraph*, November 14, 2014, https://www.telegraph.co.uk/culture/music/classicalmusic/11230512/The-worlds-fastest-playing-pianist.html.

Heisenberg, Warner. Quoted in Adam Becker, *What Is Real?: The Unfinished Quest for the Meaning of Quantum Physics* (Basic Books, 2018).

Heisenberg, Warner. Quoted in Deepak Chopra, "Physics Must Evolve Beyond the Physical." *Activitas Nervosa Superior* post received: 23 July 2018/Accepted: March 27, 2019, https://35s3f14rw1s1sr3rc1nk656ib9-wpengine.netdna-ssl.com/wp-content/uploads/2019/04/2019-Chopra-Activitas_Nervosa_Superior.pdf.

Henry, Richard. Cited in Arjun Walia, "'Consciousness Creates Reality'—Physicists Admit the Universe Is Immaterial, Mental, & Spiritual." *Collective Evolution*, November 11, 2014, https://www.collective-evolution.com/2014/11/11/consciousness-creates-reality-physicists-admit-the-universe-is-immaterial-mental-spiritual/.

Henry, Richard. "The Mental Universe." *Nature*, 436, 29 (2005).

Hill, William Ely. "My Wife and My Mother-in-Law" *Puck*, November 6, 1915. Image adapted from a German postcard.

Hoffman, Donald. Cited in Amanda Gefter, "The Evolutionary Argument Against Reality." QuantaMagazine.org, https://www.quantamagazine.org/the-evolutionary-argument-against-reality-20160421.

Hoffman, Donald. *The Case Against Reality: why evolution hid the truth from our eyes* (W. W. Norton & Company, 2019).

Hogan, R. Craig. Video of Carole Describing Her Guided Afterlife Connection with Kate, January 5, 2015.

Hogan, R. Craig. "Self-Guided Afterlife Connections: Development and Study." Unpublished study, 2012, http://selfguided.spiritualunderstanding.org/Self-guidedAfterlifeConnections.pdf.

Hogan, R. Craig. *Earth School: Answers and Evidence* (Normal, IL: Greater Reality Publications, 2020).

Hogan, R. Craig. *Your Eternal Self* (Normal, IL: Greater Reality Publications, 2008).

Humphrey, Nicholas. "Prof. Nicholas Humphrey on Blindsight and Consciousness." January 30, 2019, https://www.youtube.com/watch?v=tV5oby1blH8.

Hurlburt, Russell. "Not Everyone Conducts Inner Speech: Inner Speech Is Frequent but Not for Everyone." *Psychology Today* post, October 26, 2011, https://www.psychologytoday.com/us/blog/pristine-inner-experience/201110/not-everyone-conducts-inner-speech.

Images from Hal Puthoff, "CIA-Initiated Remote Viewing at Stanford Research Institute." *Institute for Advanced Studies at Austin* (1996), http://www.bioMindsuperpowers.com/Pages/CIA-InitiatedRV.html.

James Joyce Encyclopedia. "Prodigious aspects of James Joyce Mind." n.d., http://www.jamesjoyceencyclopedia.com/data/Conclusion/Prodigious%20aspects%20of%20JJ%20Mind.htm.

Kinney, Monica. "An artist is born after car crash." *The Philadelphia Inquirer*, August 19, 2012, https://www.inquirer.com/philly/columnists/monica_yant_kinney/20120819_Monica_Yant_Kinney__An_artist_is_born_after_car_crash.html.

Klopfer, Bruno. "Psychological Variables in Human Cancer." *Journal of Prospective Techniques*. 31 (1957): 331-40.

Kramarik, Akiane. Interview in the *Washington Times* newspaper, April 11, 2019, https://www.govmint.com/coin-authority/post/divine-inspiration-a-portrait-of-the-artist-akiane-kramarik-.

LaBerge, Stephen, and Marilyn Schlitz. "Covert Observation Increases Skin Conductance in Subjects Unaware of When They Are Being Observed: A Replication." *The Journal of Parapsychology*, 61 (1997).

Langdon, Allison. "People Who Remember Every Second of Their Life." *60 Minutes Australia*, filmed September 21, 2018, https://www.youtube.com/watch?v=hpTCZ-hO6iI.

Lazarus, Richard. *The Case Against Death* (Time Warner Books UK, 1993), 83.

Levitin, Daniel. *The Organized Mind: Thinking Straight in the Age of Information Overload* (Plume/Penguin Random House, 2015).

Lipton, Bruce. *The Biology of Belief* (Hay House Inc., 2016).

Locke, John. In Roger Woolhouse (ed.), *An Essay Concerning Human Understanding* (New York: Penguin Books, 1998).

Lodge, Oliver. *The Case For and Against Psychical Belief* (Bibliolife, 1927).

Loftus, Elizabeth. "Powers of the Subconscious." *Closer to the Truth*. Interview by Robert Lawrence, December 9, 2015, https://www.youtube.com/watch?v=mAZbq7bV64c.

Magnani, Franco. Website, http://www.francomagnani.com/about2.aspx.

Maraldo, Pamela. *Medicine: In Search of a Soul: The Healing Prescription* (Balboa Press, 2017).

Mariën, Peter, Stefanie Keulen, and Jo Verhoeven. "Neurological Aspects of Foreign Accent Syndrome in Stroke Patients." *Journal of Communication Disorders*, 77 (January 2019): 94–113.

Mariën, Peter, Jo Verhoeven, Peggy Wackenier, S. Engelborghs, and P. De Deyn. "Foreign accent syndrome as a developmental motor speech disorder." *Cortex*, 45 (7) (2009): 870–878.

Max Planck. Interview in *The Observer*, January 25, 1931, 17.

McKenna, Paul, and Giles O'Bryen. *The Paranormal World of Paul McKenna* (Faber & Faber, 1997).

McMoneagle, Joe, and Charles Tart. *Mind Trek: Exploring Consciousness, Time, and Space Through Remote Viewing* (Hampton Roads Publishing, 1993).

Michelle Whitedove, "America's Psychic Challenge Michelle Whitedove Winner." Lifetime TV, September 24, 2008, https://www.youtube.com/watch?v=RgbALQzZl-s.

Milne, Jennifer, Craig Chapman , Jason Gallivan, et al. "Connecting the Dots: Object Connectedness Deceives Perception but Not Movement Planning." *Psychological Science*, June 13, 2013, https://doi.org/10.1177/0956797612473485.

Mishlove, Jeffrey. "Archaeological Remote Viewing in Japan with Joseph McMoneagle." *New Thinking Aloud with Jeffrey Mishlove*, filmed August 11, 2016, https://www.youtube.com/watch?v=F-8puX-83o4.

Moeller, Rachael. "Study Suggests Common Knee Surgery's Effect Is Purely Placebo." *Scientific American*, July 12, 2002, https://www.scientificamerican.com/article/study-suggests-common-kne/.

Montecucco, Nitamo. Report by Cyber: Ricerche Olistiche (1992). Retrieved December 17, 2007, from http://www.goertzel.org/dynapsyc/ 1996/subtle.html.

Montgomery, Guy, Katherine DuHamel, and William Redd. "A meta-analysis of hypnotically induced analgesia: how effective is hypnosis?" *International Journal of Clinical and Experimental Hypnosis*, 48 (2000): 138-153.

Orme-Johnson, David, Kenneth Cavanaugh, Catherine Alexander, P. Gelderloos, Michael Dillbeck, A. G. Lanford, and Abou Nader. *T.M.* In press, pp. 2532-2548, "The influence of the Maharishi Technology of the Unified Field on world events and global social indicators: The effects of the Taste of Utopia Assembly." Cited in Robert Kenny, "What can science tell us about collective consciousness?" *Leaderful Teams Consulting*, November 10, 2007, http://www.collectivewisdominitiative.org/ papers/kenny_science.htm#end63.

Padgett, Jason. *Struck by Genius: How a Brain Injury Made Me a Mathematical Marvel* (Houghton Mifflin Harcourt, 2014).

Peake, Anthony. *The Daemon: A Guide to Your Extraordinary Secret Self* (Arcturus, 2010).

Penman, Danny. "Have Scientists Really Proved that Man Can See into the Future?" *NewsMonster*, May 9, 2007, http://www.newsmonster.co.uk/content/view/186/72/.

Playfair, Guy. *Twin Telepathy: The Psychic Connection* (Vega, 2003).

Prince, Walter Franklin. *The Case of Patience Worth* (New Hyde Park, NY: University Books, 1964). Originally published by Boston Society for Psychic Research (1927).

Radim. Dean, et al. "Consciousness and the Double-Slit Interference Pattern: Six Experiments." *Physics Essays*, vol. 25, no. 2 (2012).

Radin, Dean, Gail Hayssen, Masaru Emoto, and Takashige Kizu. "Double-Blind Test of the Effects of Distant Intention on Water Crystal Formation." *Explore*, (September/October 2006): 408-11.

Radin, Dean, Colleen Rae, and Ray Hyman. "Is There a Sixth Sense?" *Psychology Today*. (July/August 2006), http://www.psychologytoday.com/articles/index.php?term=pto-20000701-000034&page=3.

Radin, Dean, Ryan Taft, and Garret Yount. "Effects of Healing Intention on Culture Cells and Truly Random Events." *The Journal of Alternative and Complementary Medicine*, vol. 10, no. 1 (2004): 103-112.

Radin, Dean. *The Conscious Universe: The Scientific Truth of Psychic Phenomena.* (New York: HarperCollins Publishers, 1997), 118-124.

Ramsland, Katherine. "Psychic detectives." Court TV Crime Library, http://www.crimelibrary.com/criminal_mind/forensics/psychics/index.html.

Ramstedt, Martin. *Hinduism in Modern Indonesia* (London: RoutledgeCurzon, 2004), 41.

Ramster, Peter. *The Search for Lives Past* (Somerset Film and Publishing Pty. Ltd., 1990): 227.

Raskar, Ramesh. "Imaging at a Trillion Frames Per Second." TED, video filmed July 26, 2012, https://www.youtube.com/watch?v=Y_9vd4HWlVA.

Rayner, Keith. "The Perceptual Span and Peripheral Cues in Reading." *Cognitive Psychology*, 7 (4) (1975) 65–81.

Ring, Kenneth, and Sharon Cooper. *Mindsight* (Universe, 2008).

Rosenblum, Bruce, and Fred Kuttner. *The Quantum Enigma* (Oxford University Press, 2011), 81.

Russell, Peter. "Is Reality All in the Mind?" *Peter Russell: Spirit of Now*. https://www.peterrussell.com/SCG/ideal.php.

Safer, Morley. "Savants and Genius: A Wonderful Mystery documentary." *Manufacturing Intellect*, filmed October 24, 2017, https://www.youtube.com/watch?v=rTrJjbfG4xg.

Safer, Morley. "Savants and Genius: A Wonderful mystery documentary." *Genius: Sponsored by Suzanne St. Pierre*, https://www.youtube.com/watch?v=rTrJjbfG4xg.

Sarkin, Jon. "Jon Sarkin website." 2020, https://www.jsarkin.com/knowjon.

Schilling, David. "Knowledge Doubling Every 12 Months, Soon to Be Every 12 Hours." Industry Tap Into News, April 19, 2013, http://www.industrytap.com/knowledge-doubling-every-12-months-soon-to-be-every-12-hours/3950.

Schlitz, Marilyn, and William Braud. "Reiki-Plus Natural Healing: An Ethnographic/Experimental Study." *Psi Research*, 4 (1985): 100-123.

Schlitz, Marilyn, and Stephen LaBerge. "Covert observation increases skin conductance in subjects unaware of when they are being observed: a replication." *The Journal of Parapsychology*, http://findarticles.com/p/articles/mi_m2320/is_n3_v61/ai_20749204.

Schmidt, Helmut. "Mental influence on random events." *New Scientist and Science Journal* (1971): 757-758.

Schmidt, Helmut. "Observation of a Psychokinetic Effect Under Highly Controlled Conditions." *Journal of Parapsychology*, vol. 57 (Dec. 1993).

Schwartz, Rob. *Your Soul's Plan: Discovering the Real Meaning of the Life You Planned Before You Were Born* (Frog Books, 2009), 51.

Schwartz, Stephan, Randall De Mattei, and Roger Smith. "The Caravel Project: The Location, Description, and Reconstruction of Marine Sites through Remote Viewing, Including a comparison with Aerial Photography, Geologic Coring, and Electronic Remote Sensing." *Institute for Nautical Archaeology*, 19 (2019): 113-139.

Semkiw, Walter. *Born Again: Reincarnation Cases Involving Evidence of Past Lives, with Xenoglossy Cases Researched by Ian Stevenson, MD* (Pluto Project, 2011).

Schäfer, Lothar, *Infinite Potential: What Quantum Physics Reveals About How We Should Live.* (Deepak Chopra, April 2, 2013).

Shakhnazarova, Nika. "Old or Young? Whether You See a Young or Old Woman in This Classic Optical Illusion May Depend on Your Age, Researchers Say." *The Sun*, https://www.thesun.co.uk/news/7307450/optical-illusion-young-or-old-woman-depends-on-age/.

Sheldrake, Rupert, and Pamela Smart. "Experiments for Telephone Telepathy." *Journal of the Society for Psychical Research*, 67 (July 2003): 184-199.

Sheldrake, Rupert. "The Sense of Being Stared At." *Journal of the Society for Psychical Research*, 62 (1998): 311-323.

Sheldrake, Rupert. "Is Consciousness Fundamental?" *Closer to the Truth.* Interview by Robert Lawrence Kuhn, January 6, 2017, https://www.youtube.com/watch?v=46kgmgI9fPs.

Shristi, D. "Process of Creative Thinking: 4 Stages." Psychology Discussion, n.d. http://www.psychologydiscussion.net/thinking/process-of-creative-thinking-4-stages-thinking-processes-psychology/3127.

Sidgwick, Henry. "On vision with sealed and bandaged eyes." *Journal of Society for Psychical Research,* Volume I, 1884-1885 (June 1884): 84-86.

Siegel, Daniel. "What Is a Healthy Mind?" Science and Nonduality, video filmed February 21, 2019, https://www.youtube.com/watch?v=-A_aYHEac6I.

Snow, Robert. *Looking for Carroll Beckwith: The True Stories of a Detective's Search for His Past Life* (Daybreak Books, 1999).

Stevenson, Ian, and Satwant Pasricha. "A Preliminary Report of an Unusual Case of the Reincarnation Type with Xenoglossy." *Journal of the American Society for Psychical Research,* 74 (1980): 331-348.

Stevenson, Ian. *Unlearned Language: New Studies in Xenoglossy* (Charlottesville, Virginia, USA: University Press of Virginia, 1984).

StGeorge, Rob. "Ellen Bourdeaux — Super Savant —Superhuman 44." Sapien Plus, http://sapienplus.com/ellen-bourdeaux/.

Swann, Ingo, and Harold Sherman. "An Experimental Psychic Probe of the Planet Jupiter." April 27, 1973, paper released for public consumption April 1, 2008. https://www.cia.gov/library/readingroom/docs/NSA-RDP96X00790R000100040010-3.pdf.

Swedenborg, Emanuel. *Heaven and Hell.* Originally written in 1743-1745. Translated by George F. Dole (New Century Edition, 2010), #463.

Talbot, Michael. *The Holographic Universe* (Harper Perennial, 2011), 98-100.

Taylor, Adam. "47 Percent of the World's Population Now Use the Internet, Study Says." *Washington Post,* November 22, 2016, https://www.washingtonpost.com/news/worldviews/wp/2016/11/22/47-percent-of-the-worlds-population-now-use-the-internet-users-study-says/?utm_term=.ff4a94128b32.

Tegmark, Max. Quoted in Robert Lawrence Kuhn, "The Illusion of time: What's Real?" Space.com, filmed July 6, 2015, https://www.space.com/29859-the-illusion-of-time.html.

Thomas, Tony. "Teen Woke Up from Coma Speaking Different
    Language." WSB-TV, video filmed October 19, 2016,
    https://www.youtube.com/watch?v=nttfgZKK2r4.

Tiller, William, Walter Dibble, and Michael Kohane. *Conscious Acts of
    Creation: The Emergence of a New Physics* (Pavior Publishing 2001).

Tiller, William. "Subtle Energies." *Science and Medicine,* vol. 6, no. 3
    (May/June 1999).

Touber, Tijn. "Life goes on." *Ode,* 29 (2007, January).

Townsend, Aubrey. Paper for the Monash University course "Origins
    of Modern Philosophy B."
    https://prevos.net/humanities/philosophy/external/.

Treffert, Darold, and Daniel Tammet. *Islands of Genius: The Bountiful
    Mind of the Autistic, Acquired, and Sudden Savant* (Jessa Kingsley
    Publishers, 2011).

Treffert, Darold. "Brain Gain: A Person Can Instantly Blossom into a
    Savant—and No One Knows Why." *Scientific American,* July 25,
    2018, https://blogs.scientificamerican.com/observations/brain-gain-
    a-person-can-instantly-blossom-into-a-savant-and-no-one-knows-
    why/.

Treffert, Darold. "Kim Peek." SSMHealth, n.d.,
    https://www.agnesian.com/page/kim-peek.

Treffert, Darold. *Islands of Genius* (London: Jessica Kingsley Publishers,
    2011).

Truscott, Andrew. "Experiment Confirms Quantum Theory
    Weirdness." ScienceDaily. Press release, 2015,
    https://www.sciencedaily.com/releases/2015/05/150527103110.htm.

Tyson, Joseph Howard. *Madame Blavatsky Revisited* (Lincoln, NE:
    iUniverse, 2007).

Ullman, Montague. "Herpes Simplex and Second Degree Burn Induced
    Under Hypnosis." *The American Journal of Psychiatry,* v. 103, no. 6
    (May 1947).

Utts, Jessica. "An Assessment of the Evidence for Psychic Functioning." Division of Statistics, University of California, Davis (1995).

Vibravision®, https://mp-usa.org/vibravision/.

Walters, Ken. "My stroke made me an artist." *The Guardian,* September 12, 2008, https://www.theguardian.com/lifeandstyle/2008/sep/13/healthandwellbeing.

Webb, Dewey. "The Flamboyant Clairvoyant." *Phoenix New Times,* September 11, 1911.

Wheatley, Thalia. "What Is Self-Awareness?" *Closer to the Truth.* Interview by Robert Lawrence Kuhn, January 9, 2017, https://www.youtube.com/watch?v=znLmfY1VZzs.

Wheeler, John. Cited in Amanda Gefter, "The Evolutionary Argument Against Reality." *QuantaMagazine.org,* April 21, 2016, https://www.quantamagazine.org/the-evolutionary-argument-against-reality-20160421.

Wheeler, John. Quoted in Anil Ananthaswamy, What Does Quantum Theory Actually Tell Us about Reality? *Scientific American blogs,* September 3, 2018, https://blogs.scientificamerican.com/observations/what-does-quantum-theory-actually-tell-us-about-reality/.

Whitton, Joel, and Joe Fisher. *Life Between Life: Scientific Explorations into the Void Separating One Incarnation from the Next* (Doubleday, 1986), 210.

Yogi, Maharishi Mahesh. *Maharishi Vedic University Introduction.* (Holland: Maharishi Vedic University Press, 67-68.

Zammit, Victor. "Australian psychics beat 'orthodox' science." n.d., http://victorzammit.com/articles/sensingmurder.html.